THE CLARK BROTHERS

Strategic Squatters
In The North East
Of Victoria

THE CLARK BROTHERS

Strategic Squatters In The North East Of Victoria

GARRY MOORE

Copyright © Garry Moore 2023
Cover design, Typesetting: Working Type Studio
(www.workingtype.com.au)

The right of Garry Moore to be identified as the Author of the Work has been asserted in accordance with the Copyright, Designs and Patents Act 1988.

All rights reserved. No part of this publication may be reproduced, stored in a retrieval system, or transmitted in any form or by any means without the prior written permission of the publisher, nor be otherwise circulated in any form of binding or cover other than that in which it is published and without a similar condition being imposed on the subsequent purchaser.

Garry Moore
Strategic Squatters: Strategic Squatters In The North East Of Victoria
ISBN: 978-0-6458855-2-1

CONTENTS

Introduction	1
The Clark Family	7
Origins	7
John Clark Senior and his Antecedents	9
Elizabeth Clark (née Jenkins) and her Antecedents.	10
The Clark Family's Life in Kent	11
Emigration	12
Early Years in New South Wales	14
John Clark Junior's Marriage to Martha Davis	16
Early Entrepreneurial Steps	18
John Clark Junior	27
Settling on the Goulburn River	27
Northwood	30
The Travellers Rest Inn	31
Relations With Aborigines	32
The Faithfull Massacre	33
A Licence for the Travellers Rest Inn	36
Surveying Mitchellstown	36
Lady Jane Franklin	37
James Dredge	38
John Clark Senior and Elizabeth Clark at the Goulburn River	39
The Move to Seymour	41
The First Robert Burns Inn	42
Further Relations With Local Aborigines	43
Mr. Clark's Brother	44
The Maidens	47
A Murray River Squatting Run	48
Warfare on the Murray River	49
Surveying Seymour	51
Freehold Land Purchases in Seymour	52
The Perricoota Punt	52

Legal Problems	53
The Robert Burns Inn – The Tolmie Lease	54
The Sale of Northwood	55
The Second Robert Burns Inn	56
The Robert Burns Inn – The McLaurin Lease	56
The Robert Burns Inn and Social Life in Early Seymour	58
John Clark's Flour Mill	59
Further Squatting Runs	60
Moving Away From Seymour	61
Mary Clark's Marriage to Edward Argyle	63
Planning Retirement	64
The Sale of Perricoota	65
Moranding Subdivided	65
The Sale of John Clark's Remaining Seymour Properties	67
The Robert Burns Inn Becomes the Royal George Inn	67
The Purchase of Gooparl	68
The Death of John Clark	69
John Clark's Will	70
Martha Clark's Marriage to William McIntosh	71
The Death of Martha McIntosh	72
Martha McIntosh's Will and Codicil	72
John and Martha Clark's Children: Mary Argyle	74
John and Martha Clark's Children: Elizabeth Smith, Thomas Clark, Jane Bull, Martha McGill, Rebecca Clark and Margaret Savage	77

William Henry Clark — **89**

William Clark's Marriage to Elizabeth Harris	89
Arriving on the Ovens River	91
Settling on the Ovens River	92
First Years at Wangaratta	94
Pastoral Contraction and Expansion	97
Thomas and George Clark's Arrival At, and Lives In, Wangaratta	98
William Clark and Land Law Changes	100
From Ovens Crossing Place to Wangaratta	101
Punt Operator	102
The Sale of Whitfield	104
A Short Stay at Eaglehawk Gully Near Bendigo?	104
Freehold Land Acquisitions and the Commercial Hotel	105
Children	108
Wangaratta Homes	110
Further Freehold Land Acquisitions	112
Flour Miller	113
Brewer	114

Gold Miner	114
A Rural Move	115
Churchman	116
Local Politics	118
Education	120
Other Community Activities	120
William Clark's Appearance and Character	121
The Death of William Clark	124
William Clark's Will	125
Estate Administration	128
The Death of Elizabeth Clark	130

Richard Clark — 141

Missing Years	141
Richard Clark's Move to the Port Phillip District	141
The Construction of the First Black Swan Inn	144
The Establishment, Naming and Growth of Benalla	145
Marriage to Mary Sparrow	146
Squatting at Hurdle Creek	147
Postmaster	147
The Black Swan Inn and the Early Benalla Community	148
Disposing of the Hurdle Creek Run	149
Crossing the Broken River	149
Squatting on the Junction Run	151
Property Purchases	152
A Suggested Fifth Child	153
The Trial of Thomas Kelly	153
The Construction of the Second Black Swan Inn	154
The Death of Mary Clark	155
Marriage to Sarah Maddock	155
The Decline of the Second Black Swan Inn	156
Richard Clark's Other Economic Pursuits	159
The Cancellation of Richard Clark's Junction Run Squatting Licence.	160
The Marriage of Sarah Jane Clark	161
Richard Clark's Financial Decline	161
The Death of Sarah Clark	163
The National Bank's First Legal Action	164
The Death of Richard Clark	164
The Purported Sale of Richard Clark's Lands to William Clark	165
The National Bank's Second Legal Action	168
The Fates of Richard Clark's Surviving Children	170

Conclusion — 177

Appendix 1	**181**
Extracts from the diary of John Conway Bourke	
Appendix 2	**185**
Extracts from John Conway Bourke's Autobiographical Notes for Mr. Edward Wilson	
Appendix 3	**187**
Estate of the late William Henry Clark	
Genealogical Charts	**191**
Maps And Plans	**195**
Bibliography	**209**
Books	209
Articles	211
Genealogical Materials	215
Legislation	217
Government Gazettes	218
Court Reports	218
Other Government Records	219
Newspapers and Journals	220
Miscellaneous Unpublished Documents	221

INTRODUCTION

In the late 1830s, three young brothers – John, William and Richard Clark – separately settled in the Port Phillip District of the Colony of New South Wales. John and William Clark made their ways south with stock from the Yass Plains of the Colony, across the Murray River and into the fabled Port Phillip District in the footsteps of Major Mitchell. Richard Clark may have followed the same trajectory. However, it seems more likely that he entered the District from the south via Van Diemen's Land.[1]

John Clark initially settled on the left bank of the Goulburn River at what is now known as Mitchelton. William Clark took up land at the junction of the Ovens and King Rivers where Wangaratta is now to be found. Richard Clark, the youngest of the three brothers, established himself between his two older brothers; settling on the Broken River at the site of present-day Benalla.

Although early European entrants into the Port Phillip District, John and William Clark (and perhaps Richard Clark) were assuredly not the first to follow "The Major's Line" into what was to become Victoria.[2] Governor Bourke of New South Wales sanctioned the opening of the District to settlement in September 1836, and the years 1838 to 1840 seemingly constituted the major period of pastoral expansion.[3] Joseph Powell noted that in 1838 alone, the road from Yass was reported to have been "crowded with sheep and cattle" travelling south.[4]

---

1 In 1839, a total of 172 ships arrived in Port Phillip Bay from Van Diemen's Land. In contrast, only 28 sailed into the Bay in that year from Sydney: see A. G. L. Shaw, "Vandemonian Influences on Port Phillip Settlement" in (1989-90) 2(2) *Bulletin Of The Centre For Tasmanian Historical Studies* 15 at p. 20.

2 "The Major's Line" refers to the wagon wheel tracks left by the exploring party led by the New South Wales Surveyor General, Major Thomas Mitchell, on their return journey to the Murray River from Victoria's Western District in 1836. The line extended in a north-easterly direction from Portland to Howlong: see the Pastoral Expansion Map below.

It has been suggested that there has been an over-emphasis on The Major's Line in relation to early European settlement of the North East of Victoria. Joseph Powell, for one, has asserted that:

"It is usual to regard Mitchell's returning route as the controlling axis for pastoral expansion, but although this was a major highway during the early rush of squatters from New South Wales, and in some areas remained the common base from which boundaries and homestead sites were located, the view is superficial and to a degree misleading. Station holders in the northeast of Victoria encountered the expedition before it re-crossed the Murray, and since the mountain barrier had discouraged further southerly movement for them, the obvious direction to take was along the route which Mitchell had pioneered."

See Joseph Powell, *The Making of Rural Australia* (1974), p. 25. See also Shaw, *op. cit.*, p. 20.

3 See Powell, *op. cit.*, pp. 26-27.

4 See Powell, *op. cit.*, p. 35. The road south from Yass may have been crowded in 1838, but the European population in the Port Phillip District during this period was small overall. The first census conducted in the District on 12 September 1838 recorded a total population of 3,511 whites – 3,080 males and 431 females. The livestock return listed 310,946 sheep, 13,272 head of cattle and 524 horses: see *Statistical Register of the State of Victoria for the Year 1914: Part V – Population; 1836 – 1911*, p. 29 (https://tinyurl.com/ybhqdqtl) (at 25 February 2023). See also Robert Boyes, *First Years At Port*

Europeans, including the Clark brothers, lost no time in occupying the available pasture land of the Port Phillip District. In the words of Richard Broome:

> "The speed of pastoral settlement in Port Phillip's interior was startling, making it one of the fastest land occupations in the history of empires, as sheep and their European keepers spread across the central third of Victoria in less than a decade to 1845. The movement stretched northwards from the harbours along the coast from Portland to Port Albert, and south-west along Major Mitchell's 1836 line of march between present-day Howlong (west of Albury) and Portland, which was rutted and easily visible with his wagon tracks for decades."[5]

For well over a century and a half, historical accounts of the pastoral settlement of the Port Phillip District tended to extol in unalloyed terms the efforts and impact of the pioneer settlers. By way of example, in 1932, Hugh Strachan, a noted Geelong wool broker, observed in his Foreword to Ralph Billis and Alfred Kenyons' *Pastoral Pioneers Of Port Phillip*:

> "Frequently we read of the gold fields days as the principal period of Australian development. It is well to reflect, however, that long before gold mining became a factor in the affairs of this country, nearly all the land south of the Murray fit for grazing had been explored and occupied. Those colonists who explored and occupied the country laid as well the foundations of national stability. Without assistance or encouragement, often in the face of opposing forces, they subdued the wilderness. They established flocks and herds of unrivalled excellence, and from the primeval bush they fashioned some of the most noted properties of the Empire."[6]

Yet the grazing lands on which the European pastoralists settled was not, of course, devoid of prior occupants. For millennia, Strachan's "wilderness" had been home to Aboriginal clans and tribes for whom the "primeval bush", and all on it, were intrinsic to their being. The wishes and the interests of the blacks on the one hand and the whites on the other were in large measure irreconcilable. As Richard Broome has eloquently put it:

> "We must try to imagine the depth of feeling of this contest between original owners, who saw the land as life, as their cultural essence and identity, and newcomers, who saw it as an arcadia, the reward for their uprooting from distant homes and hearths.

Phillip (1935), pp. 88-89. Over the course of the year 1839, 1,036 European immigrants arrived from Great Britain and Ireland, 1,664 from Van Diemen's Land, 35 from South Australia, 4 from New Zealand and 517 from New South Wales north of the Murray River: see Boyes, *op. cit.*, p. 99. As at 31 December 1839, the estimated European population of the Port Phillip District was 5,822 persons – 4,104 males and 1,718 females: see Boyes, *op. cit.*, p. 100.

5   See Richard Broome, *Aboriginal Victorians: A History Since 1800* (2005), p. 54.
6   See Hugh Strachan's Foreword to Ralph Billis and Alfred Kenyon, *Pastoral Pioneers of Port Phillip* ("*Pastoral Pioneers*") (1974, 2nd ed.), p. ix.

The subsequent interactions of these groups were diverse, complex and deadly serious – sometimes literally so."7

Richard Broome has also observed that:

"...the intensity of the struggle over land in Port Phillip meant that the Aboriginal to European loss of life ratio, through violence on the Port Phillip frontier, was high at about twelve Aboriginal deaths to every European death."8

Whether any of the Clark brothers was personally involved in the frontier warfare between the blacks and the whites in the earliest years of the Port Phillip District is not now known. However, it would not be in the least bit surprising if one or more of them actively participated in the violence; much of which almost certainly went unreported. As will be seen below, each of the brothers had first hand contacts from time to time with local Aborigines.9 All three no doubt regarded the local blacks as savages; and the contempt in which they held the Aborigines was no doubt tinged in the late 1830s and early 1840s with a significant measure of fear. In this, they were probably little different from the majority of their European compatriots.

Each of the Clark brothers was initially a squatter on land legally belonging to the Crown. Of "squatters", Ralph Billis and Alfred Kenyon noted:

"In Australia, the word 'squatter' was first applied by the Government officials to the stockholder depasturing his herds and flocks on lands of the Crown, and it certainly had at first a derogatory meaning; but in the continuous conflicts with the authorities, the term was adopted by the graziers themselves as a sign of honour...."10

---

7   See Broome, *op. cit.*, p. xi. The plight of the rapidly dispossessed Aborigines did, however, excite the indignation and sympathy of a number of whites of a humanitarian disposition. One such man, a former Assistant Protector of Aborigines in the Port Phillip District, James Dredge, wrote in 1845:
    "What an anomalous aspect, then, does the present position of the Australian aborigines in New South Wales exhibit? Their lands are taken from them at the mere will of the British Government, and sold or let to strangers without any reference to their approbation, convenience, or necessities – they are forced off to make way for others, and no suitable provision is elsewhere made for them as an equivalent....[T]hey cannot perambulate the land without coming in contact with the flocks and herds which are spread over the country...; while at the stations generally, they are an unsupportable annoyance, and are driven off to prevent depredations; so that, in their own country, they have no rest for the soles of their feet, but like aliens they are despised and oppressed....Where, it may be asked, throughout the wide spread dominions of Britain, does there exist a people so helplessly situated, so degraded, so neglected, so oppressed?"
    See James Dredge, *Brief notes of the aborigines of New South Wales* (Printed in 1845 by James Harrison in Geelong and included in a microfiche with *The Aborigines of Australia* by Joseph Orton, State Library of Victoria, LTMF 161). More from James Dredge will be found below.
8   See Broome, *op. cit.*, p. xxiv.
9   What is certain is that John Clark's wife, Martha, two of their children and a visitor to John's newly-established Inn on the Goulburn River at Mitchelton, were besieged for a time in early February 1838 in the Inn by a band of local Aborigines. John Clark was away in Melbourne at the time. Fortunately, it would seem that no firearms were discharged during the siege, and the Aborigines ultimately departed with no one sustaining injuries: see footnotes 111 and 112, and their accompanying texts, below. See also **Appendix 1** below.
10 See Ralph Billis and Alfred Kenyon, *Pastures New: An Account Of The Pastoral Occupation Of Port Phillip* ("*Pastures New*") (1930), p. 20.

Billis and Kenyon went on to state:

> "The ordinary squatter of colloquial parlance, who personally took up his run, stocked it, built his hut and lived in it, was the settler. The more lordly landowners, stockholders and graziers usually lived in the town and kept superintendents to look after their stations."[11]

Of humble English stock, the Clark brothers initially answered Billis and Kenyons' characterisation of "settlers". However, they were each far from "ordinary". In the first place, they were survivors. The early 1840s were years of depression in the Australian Colonies. The pastoral economy faltered. Of the 481 people who held pastoral licences in the Port Phillip District in 1840, fewer than half remained by 1845. Most of those who left their runs were broken by the depression.[12] The three Clark brothers were among those who were able to hold on and afterwards prosper.

In the second place, each of the Clark brothers turned his hand to other commercial pursuits alongside his pastoral interests. All three successfully established and ran hotels.[13] All three had interests in flour mills. Notably, John and William Clark each made a lot of money in operating punts over the Goulburn and Ovens Rivers respectively. All three of the brothers also speculated in non-pastoral freehold land.

Both John and Richard Clark went on to engage in the provision of postal services. For his part, William Clark also acquired interests in brewing and gold mining. And in addition to milling grain, Richard Clark also grew it. Further, Richard for a time acted as an insurance agent.

Each of the three Clark brothers was community-minded. William Clark, in particular, was active in the Anglican Church, in local Wangaratta politics, in the governance of the Wangaratta National and Common Schools and in organised horse racing in Wangaratta.

It is not now known to what, if any, extent John, William and Richard Clark jointly planned their moves to the Port Phillip District. After establishing their respective squatting

---

11 See Billis and Kenyon, *Pastures New*, p. 21.
12 See Terry Dingle, *The Victorians: Settling* (1984), p. 27. It might be noted that Michael Cannon has argued that:
   "Men of all classes and conditions took eagerly to squatting, dazzled by the promise of rich rewards and freedom from the constrictions of town life. With an infinite variety of backgrounds and resources, they faced up boldly to the job which confronted them – and very soon fell into two new types. There were the men who sooner or later yielded to adversity, fading back rapidly into the anonymous multitudes of the towns. And there were those who refused to submit to the worst that nature and man could do to them – the iron-hard survivors who form the legendary first generation of successful squatters. The survivors and the defeated: former social distinctions seemed trivial in the face of such an elemental test of a man's worth."
   See Michael Cannon, *Life in the Country* (1973), p. 19.
13 In 1893, an anonymous columnist, who published a series of articles in Benalla's *North Eastern Ensign* under the headline "Recollections of Benalla", wrote:
   "A stranger travelling from Albury to Melbourne at that time [1853] would conclude that Clarke and Clark (without the 'e') owned all the hotels along the road. There was Clark at Wangaratta, Clark at Benalla, Clarke at Honeysuckle Creek (now Violet Town) and Clarke at Longwood. And about this time, Mr John Clark had let his Seymour hotel to Mr A McLaren, but the name Clark was to be seen on the premises."
   See the *North Eastern Ensign*, Friday, 4 August 1893, p. 3. It might be noted, however, that the Clarkes of Violet Town and Longwood are not known to have been related to John, William and Richard Clark.

runs in the District, they are in any event known to have maintained at least some level of contact with each other. However, the frequency and depth of that contact is lost to history.

Each of the three Clark brothers was a pioneering and significant figure in the North East of Victoria. In one of the series of articles published under the headline "Recollections of Benalla" in the *North Eastern Ensign* in 1893, the anonymous author wrote of John, William and Richard Clark:

> "This trio of brothers, whose names are almost unknown to the present generation, are deserving of a monument to their memory in each of the respective towns in which they resided, and so liberally assisted to establish as centres in the north-eastern part of Victoria."[14]

---

14   See the *North Eastern Ensign*. Friday, 30 June, 1893, p. 3.

THE CLARK FAMILY

Origins

John, William and Richard Clarks' origins lay in the Medway River valley in the English County of Kent.[15] John and William were born in, or in close proximity to, the village of Snodland; John on 15 June 1806, and William on 23 November 1809.[16] Richard Clark was likely born in late July or early August 1816 in, or near to, the village of Halling.[17] Halling lies approximately 1.5 km to the north of Snodland.

The brothers were three of the seven children born to John Clark Snr and the latter's wife, Elizabeth Clark (née Jenkins). John Snr married Elizabeth on 2 March 1806 in St. John the Baptist's Church, Wateringbury. Wateringbury is a village lying about 10.5 km to the south of Snodland.[18]

John Clark Jnr was the firstborn of his parents' children. Next came Elizabeth Mary Clark; born on 1 April 1808 and baptised in Snodland's All Saints' Church on 8 May 1808. She died when only nine months old shortly prior to 17 October 1808. William Clark was the next born. Then came Mary Ann Clark; born in 1814 and christened on 16 October 1814. Like her two younger siblings, Mary Ann was baptised in St John the Baptist's Church,

---

15   See the West Kent Parishes Map below.
16   John Clark was baptised on 13 July 1806 in St. James the Great's Church in nearby East Malling: see FamilySearch: *England Births and Christenings, 1538 – 1975: John Clark* (1806) (https://tinyurl.com/yd2nsh8k)
     (at 2 February 2023). See also "Clark, John (1806-1857)" online in the *Moore Considine Family Website* (https://tinyurl.com/58ntx5sc) (at 2 February 2023); the letter dated 1 December 1865 from Richard Clark to Martha Clark, John Clark's widow ("*Richard Clark's 1865 letter*"); (2008) 12(1) *Snodland Historical Society Newsletter*, pp.3-4 (https://tinyurl.com/j26229j) (at 2 February 2023); and photo 1 below. John was his parents' first child, and East Malling was his mother's home village. She likely returned to the village to seek family help with the birth. East Malling lies about 6 km to the south of Snodland. In turn, Snodland is situated some 10.5 km from the City of Rochester and around 14.5 km from the Kent County Town of Maidstone. In contrast, William was christened as William Henry Clark in Snodland's All Saints' Church on 28 January 1810: see *New South Wales Deaths Register: William Clark* (1871) (No. 2828/1872); "Clark, John (1809 – 1872)" online in the *Moore Considine Family Website* (https://tinyurl.com/58ntx5sc) (at 2 February 2023); and photo 2 below.
17   See "Clark, Richard (1816 – 1869)" online in the *Moore Considine Family Website* (https://tinyurl.com/58ntx5sc) (at 2 February 2023). Richard was baptised on 11 August 1816, almost certainly in Halling's St. John the Baptist's Church: see *WikiTree – Richard Clark* (https://tinyurl.com/2ybkgmtj) (at 2 February 2023); and photo 3 below.
18   See Family Search:*England Marriages, 1538 – 1973: John Clark and Elizabeth Jenkins* (FHL microfilm 992,538 and 992,639); and photo 4 below.

Halling. She died in infancy on 6 January 1816. Next came Richard Clark. He was followed by George Clark; born in 1818.[19]

The circumstances surrounding the birth of John and Elizabeth Clark's remaining child, Thomas Kent Clark, are presently clouded by a measure of mystery. Thomas has been variously said to have been born in 1814, 1812, 1810 and 1809. However, the precise date of his birth remains unclear. No baptismal record for him has as yet been discovered. It may be that Thomas was simply not christened. Thomas Clark's obituary, published in the *Ovens and Murray Advertiser* on 25 January 1879, had him dying on 24 January 1879 at the age of "about 65".[20] If accurate, this would have him born in about 1814. Given that his younger sister, Mary Clark, was born in 1814, it appears possible but unlikely that Thomas was also born in that year.

Two websites have Thomas born in or about 1812. The *Moore Considine Family Website* has him born in Kent in 1812; dying in Wangaratta in 1879 at 67 years of age. The *WikiTree – Thomas Clark (abt. 1812-1879) Website* asserts that Thomas was born "about 1812" in Halling, Kent.[21] However, neither of these websites provides a source for the birth date advanced in each.

Turning to Thomas' British Army records, his Attestation page states that he joined the Royal Artillery Regiment on 1 May 1826 at the age of 17 years. The page further states that he was discharged on 1 November 1842 at the age of 33 years and 215 days.[22] This would imply that Thomas was born on 31 March 1809. Given that his brother, William Clark, was born on 23 November 1809, this birth date is almost certainly incorrect.

Finally, Thomas' Death Certificate, for which his nephew, William J. Clark, was the informant, states that Thomas was 69 years old when he died on 24 January 1879.[23] If correct, this would suggest that he was born either early in January 1810 or, given William Clark's birth date, very early in 1809. However, there is reason to believe that Thomas was born after, and not before, William.

According to the Description page in Thomas' British Army records, Thomas was born in "Holling", Kent.[24] "Holling" is clearly a mistaken rendering of "Halling". Of Thomas' siblings, John Clark Jnr was christened in East Malling (his mother's home parish), and Elizabeth and William Clark in Snodland. On the other hand, Mary, Richard and George Clark were all baptised in Halling – seemingly the parish of Thomas' birth.[25]

---

19 See the *Moore Considine Family Website* (https://tinyurl.com/58ntx5sc) (at 2 February 2023); and *Richard Clark's 1865 letter*.

20 See the *Ovens and Murray Advertiser*, Saturday, 25 January 1879, p. 4.

21 See *WikiTree – Thomas Clark (abt. 1812-1879)* (https://tinyurl.com/y59u4tov) (at 2 February 2023).

22 See UK National Archives, *Service Records for Thomas Clark – Attestation Page* (RC3368989-6729f21-4eda-49ac-b739-3b95b1c69435/WO 69_8_001.jpg).

23 See *Victoria Deaths Register: Thomas Clark* (1879) (No. 3289/1879).

24 See UK National Archives, *Service Records for Thomas Clark – Description Page* (RC 3368989-6729f21-4eda-49ac-b739-3b95b1c69435/WO 69_8_002.jpg). Interestingly, this page went on to describe Thomas as being 5' 2" tall, of ruddy complexion and with brown hair and eyes. It also asserted that he had been a labourer prior to his enlistment in the British Army.

25 It is possible that Thomas' birth coincided with his family moving from Snodland to Halling, and that given with

Weighing all of the above, it seems likely that Thomas Clark was born in late 1810 or perhaps in 1811. If so, he would clearly have had to overstate his age when he enlisted in the Royal Artillery Regiment. In the end, it may well be that he was himself unclear as to the precise date of his birth.

John Clark Senior and his Antecedents

John Clark Snr was born to William Clark and the latter's wife, Sarah Clark (née How), shortly prior to 19 March 1786. He was baptised on the latter date in All Saints' Church, Snodland.[26] Not a great deal is presently known of his antecedents and life. Like him, his immediate ancestors appear to have been from the Medway River valley.

John Clark Snr's father, William Clark, was probably born in 1758 to John and Mary Clark. He was baptised in Maidstone on 5 March 1758.[27] William Clark most likely worked throughout his life as an agricultural labourer. Petty Sessional Records for the Malling Division of Kent (PS/Ma 3) indicate that he was working as a "servant" in Snodland in 1773. A summary of these Records produced by the Snodland Historical Society note with respect to William Clark that:

> "In Nov. 1773 hired himself as servant to Mr Fletcher of Snodland for 3s 6d a week; lived with him until Michaelmas 1775; the day after hired himself as servant to George Featherstone of Halling for 9 Guineas – 1 year; then hired himself to John Fletcher again for 'something more than two years' at 4s a week."[28]

Like his father, John Clark Snr's mother, Sarah Clark, was probably born in 1758. Her parents were apparently Francis How and his wife, Sarah How (née Proctor). Sarah Clark was christened in Maidstone on 29 October 1758. She grew up with her parents and siblings in Lenham, a village some 16 km to the east of Maidstone.[29]

William and Sarah Clark were married on 6 June 1779 in Snodland.[30] John Clark Snr was the fifth of their eight children.[31] As at 4 April 1791, William and Sarah, together with their

---

the stresses which might have been associated with the move, his baptism was simply overlooked: see footnote 8 in *WikiTree – John Clark (abt. 1786-1848)* (https://tinyurl.com/y4atp97g) (at 3 February 2023).

26 See the *Moore Considine Family Website* (https://tinyurl.com/58ntx5sc) (at 3 February 2023).

27 See *WikiTree – William Clark (abt. 1758-aft.1791)* (https://tinyurl.com/ybdw4434) (at 3 February 2023).

28 See Snodland Historical Society, *Genealogy, Snodland Parishioners, 1700 -1799(c)* (https://tinyurl.com/yc3xemd7) (at 3 February 2023).

29 See FamilySearch: *England Births and Christenings, 1538 – 1975: Sarah How (1758)* (https://tinyurl.com/2p83k3t3) (at 3 February 2023); and *WikiTree – Sarah (How) Clark (1758)* (https://tinyurl.com/y8we8hny) (at 3 February 2023).

30 *Ibid.* See also FamilySearch: *England Marriages, 1538 – 1975: William Clark and Sarah How (1779)* (https://tinyurl.com/3cvzz2c5a) (at 3 February 2023).

31 John Clark Snr's siblings, all born in Snodland, were Mary Clark (born in 1779), Frances Clark (born in 1782), James Clark (also born in 1782), William Clark (born in 1783), Thomas Clark (born in 1788), Sarah Clark (born in 1790) and Ann Clark (also born in 1790): see *WikiTree – Sarah (How) Clark (1758)* (https://tinyurl.com/y8we8hny) (at 3 February 2023); and the *Moore Considine Family Website* (https://tinyurl.com/58ntx5sc) (at 3 February 2023).

surviving children, were living in Halling.³² The dates of William's and Sarah's deaths are presently unascertained.

Elizabeth Clark (née Jenkins) and her Antecedents.

Elizabeth Jenkins was born in East Malling and christened in that village's St James the Great's Church on 22 April 1787.³³ She was the third of 12 children born in East Malling to Henry Jenkins and his wife, Mary Jenkins (née King).³⁴ Henry Jenkins was born in about 1758 in East Malling and died there in 1844. Mary Jenkins was probably born in late 1762 or very early in 1763. She was baptised on 10 January 1763 in St. James the Great's Church, East Malling.³⁵ She likely died at East Malling in 1823, being buried in the churchyard of St. James the Great's Church on 17 November of that year.³⁶

It is likely that Henry Jenkins worked as an agricultural labourer, rather than owning and farming land at East Malling. However, one of John Clark Snr's and Elizabeth Jenkins' great-great-granddaughters, Ellen Clark, is on record as asserting that her ancestors had been yeomen, with a known family tree extending back to the Sixteenth Century.³⁷

As it turns out, it would seem that Ellen Clark's assertions were at least partly correct. Elizabeth Jenkins' family can seemingly be traced at least as far back on her mother, Mary King's, side to Mary's great- (x 10)-grandfather, John Kemsley. He was born in about 1425 in Bredhurst, a hamlet located between Chatham and Maidstone in Kent. In 1450, Jack Cade led an insurrection of men from Kent, among them yeomen and other men of substance, listing grievances which they attributed to corruption and abuses of power on the part of the government of King Henry VI. The rebels forced their way into London and only agreed to withdraw on a promise of amnesty. Amongst those pardoned for their part in the uprising was a John Kemsley of Bredhurst. He appears likely to have been Mary King's ancestor.³⁸

---

32 See Snodland Historical Society, *Genealogy, Snodland Parishioners, 1790 -1799(c)* (https://tinyurl.com/yc3xemd7) (at 3 February 2023).

33 See the *Moore Considine Family Website* (https://tinyurl.com/58ntx5sc) (at 3 February 2023).

34 Elizabeth Jenkins' siblings were Samuel Jenkins (born in 1784), Sarah Jenkins (born in 1786), Henry Jenkins (born in 1788), Ann Jenkins (born in 1790), John Jenkins (born in 1791), Ridley Jenkins (born in 1793), Thomas Jenkins (born in 1794), Jane Jenkins (born in 1796), Charlotte Jenkins (born in 1797), William Jenkins (born in 1798) and Margaret Jenkins (born in 1800): see the *Moore Considine Family Website* (https://tinyurl.com/58ntx5sc) (at 4 February 2023); and the *Willett Website* https://tinyurl.com/366jvy6f) (at 4 February 2023).

35 See the *Willett Website* (https://tinyurl.com/366jvy6f) (at 4 February 2023).

36 See East Malling Burials, 1570-1924: *Mary Jenkins 1823* (https://tinyurl.com/y3jb63ql).

37 Ellen Clark's assertion is to be found in a biographical note read out at her funeral in 2002: see Pat Morgan, "[AVNE] Clark Family – Wangaratta" in *AUS – VIC – NE – L Archives* (http://tinyurl.com/hn537qa) (at 10 January 2021).

38 As to the Jack Cade Rebellion, see *Wikipedia – Jack Cade's Rebellion* (https://tinyurl.com/yyc46onf) (at 4 February 2023); and the *Marr, Aitken, Watts Family Page – John Kemsley* (https://tinyurl.com/ycm5amxx) (at 4 February 2023). See also Colin Thornton-Kemsley, *Kentish Kemsleys and Their Descendants* (1980), pp.4-8 and 43.
   Mary Jenkins (née King)'s mother was Ann Elizabeth King (née Kemsley), born in about 1723. Ann's father was a Stephen Kemsley; born in about 1690. Stephen's father was a Stephanus Kemsley, born in about 1656. Stephanus' father was an Elias Kemsley, born in about 1630: see, with respect to each of Ann, Stephen, Stephanus and Elias, the *Willett Website* (https://tinyurl.com/366jvy6f) (at 5 February 2023). Elias Kemsley's father was an Adam Kemsley, born in about 1600: see the *Marr, Aitken, Watts Family Page* (https://tinyurl.com/bdf729w7) (at 5 February 2023). Adam's father was a Robert Kemsley, born in about 1568: see the *Marr, Aitken, Watts Family Page* (https://tinyurl.com/5497h578) (at 5 February 2023); and the *King Family Tree*; (https://tinyurl.com/4knww5ep) (at 5 February 2023). Robert's father was a Thomas Kemsley, born in about 1547: see the *Marr, Aitken, Watts Family Page* (https://tinyurl.com/yckts6yz) (at 5 February 2023); and the *King Family Tree* (https://tinyurl.com/bdcn2npu) (at 5 February 2023).

The Kemsleys apparently once owned considerable lands in Kent in the vicinity of Maidstone.[39] However, there is nothing to suggest that that Elizabeth Clark or her parents inherited any of it.

The Clark Family's Life in Kent

In the years immediately following their marriage, John Clark Snr and Elizabeth Clark lived with their growing family in, or in close proximity to, Snodland before moving to nearby Halling. Like his father, William Clark, John likely worked as an agricultural labourer for a number of successive employers. Elizabeth was no doubt occupied with child rearing and home duties.

The Clark family were in all likelihood surrounded in the Medway River valley by family and friends. In *Richard Clark's 1865 letter*, Richard wrote in part to his sister-in-law, Martha Clark:

> "The nearest direction I can give you to find Snodland where my brother John was born is to go to Stroud or Rochester Kent and then enquire for the parish of Halling which is 4 or 5 miles from there; that is the parish that we were all reared in although John was in the parish of Snodland which is a mile from Halling but [in] either of these parishes you will find some one that will recollect us. There was a family of the name Jupp which you would be likely to find some of them in Halling. There was a school-mate of mine, in Snodland that had a coal wharf about 12 or 13 years ago by name of Thomas Peters. There was also a cousin of ours in Snodland which if living

---

Thomas' father was a Robert Kemsley, born in about 1521: see the *Marr, Aitken, Watts Family Page* (https://tinyurl.com/2tp97yaj) (at 5 February 2023); and the *King Family Tree* (https://tinyurl.com/2p83uvtj) (at 5 February 2023). Robert's father was a William Gregory Kemsley, born in about 1495: see the *Marr, Aitken, Watts Family Page* (https://tinyurl.com/ydtjr3yp) (at 3 February 2023); and the *King Family Tree* (https://tinyurl.com/6tem99x3) (at 5 February 2023). William's father was a Robert Kemsley, born in about 1470: see the *Marr, Aitken, Watts Family Page* (https://tinyurl.com/2s4d24yy) (at 5 February 2023); and the *King Family Tree* (https://tinyurl.com/bdz2n5h5) (at 5 February 2023). Robert's father was a John Kemsley, born in about 1449: see the *Marr, Aitken, Watts Family Page* (https://tinyurl.com/mu4xyctt) (at 5 February 2023); and the *King Family Tree* (https://tinyurl.com/ycyu7r6u) (at 5 February 2023). Finally, John's father was also a John Kemsley, born in about 1425: see the *Marr, Aitken, Watts Family Page* (https://tinyurl.com/ycm5amxx) (at 5 February 2023).

39 John Kemsley Snr's great-great-great-grandson, Thomas Kemsley, was a yeoman farmer living at Bredhurst. In the 1560s, it seems that he acquired 91 acres of land formerly forming part of Bredhurst Manor. By his Will, Thomas devised his *Gyldrynes* farm at Bredhurst, together with further land at Boxley, to his eldest son, William Kemsley. He left his *Hempstead* farm near Bredhurst to his second son, Robert Kemsley. Further, he left lands at Lidsing and Lighe near Chatham to his youngest son (and Elizabeth Clark's direct ancestor), Adam Kemsley. Finally, he left other lands in the Parishes of Bredhurst, Stockbury and Hartlip to his widow, Joan Kemsley. His will went on to specify that:
"mye bodye to be buried within the chancel of the Parish church of Bredhurst aforesaid on the north syde of the tombe of one Norwood there lying."
See Thornton-Kemsley, *op. cit.*, p. 7; Roger Crockett, *The Early History of Bredhurst Manor* (https://tinyurl.com/jtgzunk) (at 5 February 2023); and the *Marr, Aitken, Watts Family Page – Thomas Kemsley* (https://tinyurl.com/yck-ts6yz) (at 5 February 2023). John Kemsley Snr's daughter-in-law, Isabella Kemsley, by her Will, left two pieces of Bredhurst woodland to her son, John Kemsley, on condition that he should hold "a drinking" for the local inhabitants each year on the night of All Saints Day. Apparently, this tradition continued in Bredhurst until the Nineteenth Century: see Thornton-Kemsley, *op. cit.*, p. 6; William Ireland, *England's Topography: Or A New And Complete History Of The County Of Kent* (1829), Vol. 3, p. 151 (https://tinyurl.com/zmx5vuh) (at 5 February 2023); and *Wikipedia – Bredhurst* (https://tinyurl.com/hwqzuck) (at 5 February 2023). It is interesting to note that there is a Kemsley Street Road still extant in Bredhurst: see photo 5 below – and "Kemsley Street Road" is the road's proper name, not a typographical error.

I dare say is there yet by name of William Kempt. There is another family by name of Hawks that used to live in Snodland. There are sure to be some of them left."[40]

It is not known now whether any of the Clarks' surviving children received much in the way of formal education in England. However, it seems clear that John Jnr, William and Richard Clark were all able to read and write as adults in Australia. Accordingly, Thomas and George Clark probably also learned to read and write. However, whatever formal education each of the brothers did receive was likely of short duration. It also seems very likely that each of the Clark boys initially commenced work as an agricultural labourer in the Medway River valley at an early age.

Emigration

On 10 September 1826, John Clark Jnr departed England on the *Cumberland* bound for New South Wales. He was 20 years old at the time of his departure. He arrived at Port Jackson on 24 January 1827.[41]

It is now not known precisely why John decided to immigrate to Australia. However, two sets of circumstances almost certainly constituted important causal considerations. In the first place, he faced a depressed rural economy and poor prospects in England prior to his departure. The English population doubled between 1800 and 1850. In rural areas following the final enclosures of common lands, millions of poorer people became wholly dependent on badly-paid, and frequently scarce, seasonal labouring jobs to survive. Many of the landless were forced to become itinerants, often resorting to petty crime to survive.[42] John, like numerous others, probably felt that he had little or no future in England.

In the second place, John's decision to immigrate was very likely influenced by the almost simultaneous departure of his aunt, Charlotte Jenkins, and her children from England to New South Wales. Charlotte Jenkins was the wife of John Jenkins. John Jenkins, in turn, was a younger brother of Elizabeth Clark.

On 31 July 1820, John Jenkins and three accomplices were convicted of burglary at the Kent Summer Assizes in Maidstone and sentenced to death by hanging. The death sentences of all four men were subsequently commuted to transportation for life.[43] After

---

40 See *Richard Clark's 1865 letter*, pp. 3-4. This letter was seemingly written in answer to a query from Martha Clark, whose daughter, Mary Argyle, was apparently about to visit England. Richard and Martha remained close, even after John Clark Jnr's death and Martha's subsequent remarriage. By her Will executed on 6 January 1868, Martha appointed Richard to be one of her executors and a trustee of her estate: see *Martha McIntyre's Will* in *Public Records Office of Victoria* ("PROV"), *VPRS* 7591/P0001, Unit 28B.

41 See *New South Wales – 1828 Census: Householders' Returns* (AONSW: Series 1273, Reels 2506-2507 and 2551-2552). John was one of nine steerage passengers on the *Cumberland*: see the *Sydney Gazette and New South Wales Advertiser*, Thursday, 25 January 1827, p. 3.

42 See James Boyce, *1835: The Founding of Melbourne and the Conquest of Australia* (2011), pp. 33-34. See also Christine Bean, *From Tradesman to the Poor House (Gransden Family Website)* (https://tinyurl.com/y7z2xkx4) (at 7 February 2023); and Carl J. Griffin, "Parish Farms and the poor law: a response to unemployment in southern England" in (2011) 59 *Agricultural History Review* 176 at p.177.

43 John Jenkins and his accomplices (Thomas Wood, John Hollands and Thomas Webster), all four described as labourers,

a period of incarceration in a prison hulk anchored off Sheerness in the Thames estuary, John Jenkins sailed for New South Wales on board the convict transport ship *Speke 1*, leaving his wife and children in Kent destitute and dependent on poor law relief.[44] He disembarked in Sydney on about 10 May 1821, and was subsequently assigned to work as a labourer for James Atkinson on the latter's *Oldbury* property at Sutton Forest in the Southern Highlands of New South Wales.[45]

John Jenkins must have impressed the man to whom he was assigned, James Atkinson. In England on business in 1825, Atkinson assisted his assigned servant's wife, Charlotte Jenkins, to successfully petition the Home Secretary, Robert Peel, to send her and her children as free immigrants to join her husband and their father in New South Wales.[46] On 8 September 1826, Charlotte and her children set sail from England on the *Granada*, arriving in Sydney on 23 January 1827.[47] Later in 1827, she received a Crown Grant of 60 acres of land at Sutton Forest. Her husband, John Jenkins, was then assigned to her by the New South Wales Government to work the land.[48]

---

were convicted of breaking into the house of Elizabeth King, a widow of East Malling (and quite likely a relative of Elizabeth Clark's mother), and stealing from it four beds, blankets, counterpanes, pillows, bolsters, a pair of snuffers and a pincushion, all to the value of £43. 2s. 6d. On hearing that consideration was being given to further commutation of the sentences of John Jenkins and John Hollands from transportation for life to transportation for seven years, Sir Henry Hawley, of *Laybourne Grange* near Maidstone, apparently wrote to the Home Office to oppose such a course, arguing that:

"They [Jenkins and Hollands] are, and have long been known to have been, such desperate bad men, that the neighbourhood has been for some two or three years in a constant alarm for themselves and their property."

See Ian McNeill, *In Search of our Colonial Heritage: A Story of John Jenkins and His Family*, p. 3 (an undated manuscript in the possession of the Berrima and District Historical and Family History Society).

44 *Ibid.*

45 See McNeill, *op. cit.*, pp. 3-4. James Atkinson lived between 1795 and 1834. He was born at Oldbury near Ightham in Kent and immigrated to New South Wales in 1820. He was initially employed in Sydney as Principal Clerk in the Colonial Secretary's Office. However, in 1822, he resigned from that position to take up two Crown land grants at Sutton Forest in the County of Argyle: *Oldbury* and *Mereworth*. These two properties totalled 1,500 acres in area. Atkinson was regarded both as a progressive farmer and as a humane master of his assigned transportee servants: see T. M. Perry, "Atkinson, James (1795-1835)" in *Australian Dictionary of Biography* (https://tinyurl.com/5n78rk27) (at 7 February 2023).

46 In supporting letters to the Home Office, Atkinson stated that John Jenkins had been in his service for four years and, in contrast to Sir Henry Hawley (see footnote 43 above), observed that during that period John had conducted himself "in a very regular and industrious manner". It further appears that Governor Brisbane of New South Wales also supported the proposed family reunion: see McNeill, *op. cit.*, p. 4.

It is striking to note that Atkinson sailed back from England in the *Cumberland* on the same voyage as bought John Clark Jnr to New South Wales in 1827. However, Atkinson sailed as a cabin passenger, rather than in steerage like John. He was returning to New South Wales after spending around two years in England. With so few passengers and such a long passage, it seems highly likely that John and Atkinson became well-acquainted, particularly as both were ultimately bound for the same property at Sutton Forest: see the *Sydney Gazette and New South Wales Advertiser*, Thursday, 25 January 1827, p. 3.

47 *Ibid.* See also the *Sydney Gazette and New South Wales Advertiser*, Wednesday, 24 January 1827, p. 2.

48 See McNeill, *op. cit.*, p. 6. John Jenkins received a ticket of leave on 5 August 1829, a conditional pardon on 8 September 1836 and an absolute pardon on 1 December 1838: see McNeill, *op. cit.*, p. 7. See also Bill Gammage, *Narrandera Shire* (1986), p. 38.

In his *An Account of the State of Agriculture and Grazing in New South Wales*, Atkinson described the country in the vicinity of his Sutton Forest properties thus:

"In the country westward of the Blue Mountains, and also in the counties of Argyle and Antrim, are large tracts of open forest, where the basis of the soil is granite; this country is thinly covered with trees, of the white and blue gum kinds, and large blocks of granite, of a course texture, and grey colour, are seen lying about the surface. This country, though pleasing to the eye, having a beautiful park-like appearance, is poor and seldom adapted for cultivation; but the soil is light, dry, and extremely well suited for sheep grazing, the surface being covered with thin but very nutritive herbage. In the County of Argyle are some small tracts, where whinstone predominates; this is the finest description of forest land in the country, equally well adapted for grazing or for cultivation; the soil is firm and rich, and the herbage of the most nutritive description."

See James Atkinson, *An Account of the State of Agriculture and Grazing in New South Wales* (1826), pp. 5-6.

Landing in Sydney a day after his aunt and cousins, John Clark Jnr almost certainly moved with, or immediately after, them (and perhaps James Atkinson) to Sutton Forest. He probably worked initially as an agricultural labourer on Atkinson's property before moving to work on his aunt's land after it was granted to her. In the 1828 New South Wales Census, he was recorded as living with the Jenkins family at Sutton Forest.[49]

In about 1833, John Clark Snr and Elizabeth Clark followed the example of their eldest son and emigrated from England to New South Wales.[50] In so doing, they were very probably influenced by favourable reports of life in the young colony posted home by John Clark Jnr. However, worsening economic circumstances in England might also have influenced their decision to emigrate.[51] John and Elizabeth Clark were almost certainly accompanied on their voyage to Australia by three of their younger sons: William, Richard and George Clark.

The Clarks' remaining son, Thomas Clark, remained in England by reason of having enlisted in the British Army on 1 May 1826.[52]

After disembarking in Sydney, John and Elizabeth Clark, together with at least William and George Clark, and likely also with Richard Clark, probably moved quickly to join John Clark Jnr and the Jenkins family at Sutton Forest.

Early Years in New South Wales

Little has as yet come to light regarding Richard's movements between his likely arrival in Australia in around 1833 and his next recorded appearance, in the Port Phillip District, in around 1839. What few particulars are presently known of those movements are derived from two brief sources: Richard's Death Certificate and a newspaper obituary for his only son to survive him, John Robert Clark. Richard's 1869 Death Certificate recorded that after emigrating from England, he had lived in "Tasmania, New South Wales and Victoria".[53] John Robert Clark's obituary asserted, in part:

> "Mr. and Mrs. Richard Clark were natives of England, but the husband was a sailor, and arrived in Victoria from Tasmania with a number of shipmates."[54]

---

49   See *New South Wales – 1828 Census Householders' Returns* (AONSW: Series 1273, Reels 2551-2552 and 2506-2507).

50   The precise timing and other details surrounding the Clark family members' voyage to New South Wales have not yet been ascertained. In *Richard Clark's 1865 letter*, he wrote:
"It is now 32 years since I left old England."

51   See footnote 42 and its accompanying text above.

52   UK National Archives, *Service Records for Thomas Clark – Attestation Page* (RC3368989-67293f21-4eda-49ac-b739-3b95b1c69435/WO 69_8_001.jpg). In an unpublished manuscript (*"Lorraine Key's manuscript"*), Lorraine Key, the wife of one of John Clark Snr's great-great-great-grandsons, refers to an undated letter, which must have been written prior to the end of 1842, by John Clark Snr to his son, Thomas Clark, whilst the latter was stationed with the Royal Horse Artillery at Newcastle-upon-Tyne in England. At the time that he wrote the letter, John Clark Snr appears to have been living with his eldest son, John Clark Jnr, at the latter's establishment on the Goulburn River: see *Lorraine Key's manuscript*, p. 2.

53   See *Victoria Deaths Register: Richard Clark* (1869) (No. 514/1869). The named informant for the information contained in the Death Certificate was Michael Farrell, Richard's son-in-law.

54   See the *Benalla Standard*, Tuesday, 31 July 1934, p. 3.

Although it is possible that Richard Clark could have found employment as a sailor immediately after arriving in Sydney, it seems more likely that he would have initially accompanied his parents and brothers on their journey to Sutton Forest. Once there, and with the memories of his voyage from England to Australia in mind, he may have decided that a life at sea was more attractive than living on the rural frontier in New South Wales. Returning to Sydney, he could well have secured a berth on a coastal trading vessel servicing the small British settlements along the coasts of New South Wales and Van Diemen's Land. Equally, Richard might have found employment on a fishing vessel. If that fishing vessel had been a whaler, it might have seen him whaling in the waters surrounding Van Diemen's Land, including Bass Strait. From Van Diemen's Land, it would have been but a short journey for Richard and some of his shipmates to the shores of the Port Phillip District.

It is not now known what John Clark Snr and his sons, William and George Clark, did for a living in their earliest years in New South Wales. Most likely they, like John Clark Jnr, all worked as agricultural labourers. Perhaps they initially worked on the Jenkins' property or for other Sutton Forest landowners. However, the Clark family probably did not remain long in Sutton Forest before moving south-west towards Goulburn and the Yass Plains.[55]

The Yass Plains, to the west of Goulburn, were first discovered by Europeans when a party which included the explorer Hamilton Hume arrived in 1821. European settlers arrived in the district later in the 1820s. By the early 1830s, the makings of a village had been established on the Yass River (a tributary of the Murrumbidgee River), with a post office being erected in 1835. Sheep grazing and breeding were the early economic mainstays of the area.[56]

It seems likely that all the Clark men in New South Wales continued to work as agricultural labourers during the first years following their move towards the Yass Plains. Who they may have worked for after they left Sutton Forest will probably never be known.

---

55 A short biographical newspaper article in 1993 dealing with William Clark observed that the latter "was 23 years old when his family settled in Yass": see the *Wangaratta Chronicle*, Monday, 4 January 1993, p. 21. If accurate, this would mean that the family likely arrived in the Yass district less than a year after John and Elizabeth and their sons first landed in New South Wales.

56 See *Wikipedia – Yass, New South Wales* (https://tinyurl.com/yxg4qoka) (at 8 February 2023). James Atkinson described the plains of New South Wales immediately to the west of the Great Dividing Range in the following terms: "Extensive plains are a distinguishing feature of the interior of New South Wales. These tracts, although termed plains in the Colony, are very seldom level, but generally a gently undulating surface, destitute of timber, and covered with grass; they extend, with many interruptions, but still forming one great chain, from Liverpool Plain, in the county of Cambridge, to Maniroom [Monaro] Plains, to the southward of Lake George, approaching nearer to the sea coast as they extend to the southward; many large portions of this immense tract are occupied in grazing by persons holding tickets of occupation, for which purpose, especially for sheep grazing, it is extremely well adapted, being covered with fine grass and herbage, and generally well watered; very little of this immense tract of open country has as yet been granted, or in the Colonial phrase, *located*, to individuals...."
See Atkinson, *op. cit.*, p. 6.

John Clark Junior's Marriage to Martha Davis

On 17 February 1835, John Clark Jnr married Martha Davis in an Anglican chapel on the Yass Plains.[57]

Martha was probably born in 1813 in or near to the small town of Bandon in County Cork, Ireland.[58] A daughter of George Davis and his wife, Mary Davis (née Norris), she had at least one sister, Jane Davis, and almost certainly other presently unascertained siblings.[59]

Martha Davis emigrated from Cork on 10 April 1832 with 201 other young Irish women bound for Sydney on the *Red Rover*.[60] She clearly did so in order to better herself. Life for her in Ireland would almost certainly have been difficult. As Elizabeth Rushen and Perry McIntyre have put it:

> "The beginning of the nineteenth century was a time of rapid population growth in Ireland, rising from five million in 1800 to seven million in 1821, and reaching over eight and a half million by the time the Great Famine struck in 1845. The rapid increase in population, combined with periodic food shortages, was exacerbated by a reliance on the potato as the main crop. Poor harvests – one productive year in every two or three – put extra stresses on the already marginal and impoverished population. Partial potato scarcities regularly occurred on a regional basis, but the years 1800-01, 1816-18, 1822 and 1831 were particularly cruel times of food shortages and consequent subsistence crises. These shortages were evident in the Irish Poor Inquiry of 1835, when hundreds of people were interviewed and their evidence portrayed heartbreaking stories of their fights for survival. During this period there was also a severe downturn in economic activity and increased unemployment. A regular series of epidemics, infections and fevers, such as the savage outbreak of cholera in 1832, combined with frequent outbreaks of typhus and dysentery to increase the misery of the population. Additional

---

57   See *New South Wales Marriages Register: John Clark and Martha Davis* (1835) (Vol. 19, No. 1392). It is of interest to note that the official witnesses to the marriage were the groom's cousin, Elizabeth Williams (née Jenkins), and her husband, Henry Williams. In early 1835, John Jenkins Snr, his wife Charlotte Jenkins and other members of their immediate family were still living in or close to Sutton Forest (although John and Charlotte Jenkins were to move to nearby Berrima at some time in the latter part of 1835): see McNeill, *op. cit.*, pp. 7-8. It would appear that John Clark Jnr was to maintain a measure of contact with his Jenkins kin over the balance of his life.

58   See *New South Wales, Australia, Assisted Immigrant Passenger Lists, 1826-1896 – Martha Davis* (https://tinyurl.com/ybga5zob) (at 9 February 2023); Elizabeth Rushen and Perry McIntyre, *Fair Game: Australia's First Immigrant Women* (2010), pp. 170-171. Bandon was originally settled by Protestants drawn from England in the Seventeenth Century. Many of its inhabitants in later years were engaged in the flax industry: see *Wikipedia – Bandon, County Cork* (https://tinyurl.com/buk5jfb) (at 9 February 2023). It would seem that prior to leaving Ireland, Martha Davis, a Protestant, had been employed as a flax worker, as well as a servant who had been in charge of children: see Rushen and McIntyre, *op. cit.*, pp 170-171.

59   See Susan Priestley, *Echuca: A History* (2009), p. 15. Martha's sister, Jane Davis, emigrated from Cork to Sydney in February 1836 on the *James Pattison*. Martha and Jane's father, George Davis immigrated to Australia in 1851 (presumably after the death of his wife, Mary Davis. On his death, he was buried in the Moama Cemetery on 30 January 1858. The headstone on his grave notes that he was from Bandon, and that the monument had been erected by his daughter, Martha: see Rushen and McIntyre, *op. cit.*, pp. 170-171.

60   *Ibid.* See also the *Sydney Monitor*, Saturday, 11 August 1832, p. 2.

stresses were placed on rural society by shifts in land usage from small holdings to larger pastoral properties."[61]

In response to the plight of the poor, the British Government established a Commission for Emigration in 1831, chaired by the Duke of Richmond. In turn, the Commission chartered the *Red Rover* and another vessel to convey young, unmarried women between the ages of 15 and 30 years to Australia. In so acting, the Commission was in part motivated by a perceived need to supply the Australian colonies with domestic servants and potential wives. The Commission paid £8 towards the costs of passage of each young woman, with the woman concerned or her family paying a further £8.[62]

Martha Davis and the other free emigrants disembarked from the *Red Rover* in Sydney on 10 August 1832.[63] Martha had been provided with pre-arranged employment as a plainworker working for William Bradbury and the latter's family at a wage of £10 per annum.[64] Following her arrival in Sydney, she almost certainly proceeded directly to the 400 acre Bradbury property, *Spring Ponds*, on the Goulburn Plains to the east of the Yass Plains.[65] It was no doubt whilst Martha was living with the Bradbury family on the Goulburn Plains that she first met John Clark Jnr. At the time of their marriage, he was also said to be living (and presumably working) on the Goulburn Plains.[66]

Following their marriage, John and Martha Clark moved into a house in on the Yass Plains located on or near to the main track taken by those moving between the Sydney region and the inland southern parts of New South Wales. The house would likely have been constructed by John, using split logs for the walls and with sheets of bark for the roof.

The first two of John and Martha Clark's seven children were born while John and Martha were living on the Yass Plains. Mary Clark was born on 24 April 1836. Her sister, Elizabeth Clark, was born on 27 April 1837. Both girls were christened on the same day, 30 November 1838, in All Saints' Anglican Church, Sutton Forest.[67]

---

61 See Rushen and McIntyre, *op. cit.*, p. 15. See also Elizabeth Rushen, *Colonial Duchesses: The Migration of Irish Women to New South Wales Before the Great Famine* (2014), p. 209.

62 See Rushen and McIntyre, *op. cit.*, pp. 12-19

63 See *The Australian*, Friday, 17 August 1832, p. 3. In an article which traced the arrival of the emigrants from the *Red Rover*, the *Sydney Monitor* observed that the young women were:
"all well dressed, and although we saw none affecting finery, the bonnets lined with silk, the comfortable hood-cloaks, the gloves, and the general neatness of attire proclaimed that a great many were most respectable young women. They are generally young, none appearing to exceed the age of four-and-twenty. Two or three have pretensions to beauty, of whom one, a girl, seemed to us, to be somewhat too conscious. However, we saw nothing forward, rude or immodest in any of them. We consider the arrival in such a Colony as this of these fine women one of the most beneficial events which has occurred since our arrival in it. They are worth a thousand male convicts, and ten thousand female convicts."
See the *Sydney Monitor*, Wednesday, 15 August 1832, p. 2.

64 See *New South Wales, Australia, Assisted Immigrant Passenger List, 1826-1896 – Martha Davis* (https://tinyurl.com/ybga5zob) (at 9 February 2023). A plainworker was a needleworker performing simple needlework.

65 A report prepared in Sydney in 1834 by a James Walker and forwarded to Peter Besnard, the Commission for Emigration's Agent in Cork, confirmed that Martha Davis was then in service with the Bradburys "up the country at £10 per annum": see James Walker, *Account of the present situation of the female emigrants from Cork to Sydney, New South Wales per the ship Red Rover in the year 1832* (CO 384/35). See also Rushen and McIntyre, *op. cit.*, p. 170.

66 See *New South Wales Marriages Register: John Clark and Martha Davis* (1835) (Vol. 19, No. 1392).

67 An unsigned note at the side of the relevant entry in the Register of All Saints' Church reads:

Early Entrepreneurial Steps

In evidence given on behalf of his brother, William Clark, in the New South Wales Supreme Court in June 1837, John Clark Jnr described himself as "a labourer on the Murrumbidgee".[68] In all likelihood, he was probably also working on his own behalf as a grazier; grazing, and perhaps breeding, his own cattle and horses in the vicinity of his house.[69]

By the second half of the 1830s, John and William Clark were both exhibiting signs of the entrepreneurial spirit that they shared with their younger brother, Richard Clark, and which was to become more evident as time passed.

At some point shortly after their marriage in 1835, John and Martha Clark almost certainly opened up their home for reward to provide accommodation and food for passing travellers. As will be seen below, it is likely that they so accommodated and fed one of the first of the overlanders, Joseph Hawdon, during one or more of the latter's trips between the Sydney area and the Port Phillip District in 1836 and 1837.[70]

For his part, William Clark, by early 1837, was probably selling liquor in the Yass Plains without a liquor licence. In that year, Constable Edward Roach, the Chief Constable stationed at Yass, seized a quantity of rum, wine and brandy from William's home under the direction of "local magistrates".[71] Although the liquor had apparently been purchased by William from a Yass Plains innkeeper, William was seemingly (and perhaps correctly) suspected of intending to use it for "sly grog selling". Again under the direction of "the local magistrates", one Patrick Fennell proceeded to sell the seized liquor. Undaunted, William successfully sued Fennell in trover in the New South Wales Supreme Court in Sydney to recover the value of the liquor so sold. On 5 June 1837, Mr Justice Dowling and two assessors awarded William damages of £114.[72]

It appears that William was not the only Clark on the Yass Plains who was confronted

---

"Martha proved to be a lady of great personal strength, endurance and ability. She did follow her husband down to the new land, being accommodated with her little ones in a bullock wagon. She was accompanied by a party of men who were previously unknown to her."
See Susan Clarke and Ian Argyle, *The Argyle Heritage* (2011), pp 177-178.

68 See the *Sydney Monitor*, Wednesday, 7 June 1837, p. 2; and *The Sydney Herald*, Thursday, 8 June 1837, p. 2.

69 See Brian Packard, *Joseph Hawdon: The First Overlander* (1997), p. 76; and Harry Speechly Parris, "Early Mitchellstown and Nagambie" ("*Early Mitchellstown*") in (1950) 23(3) *The Victorian Historical Magazine* 126 at p. 127. See also footnotes 73 and 75, and their accompanying texts, below.

70 Joseph Hawdon was born at Wackerfield in Durham in 1813. He emigrated from England to New South Wales in 1834. In 1836, and together with John Gardiner and John Hepburn, Hawdon led the first party to overland cattle from what later became southern New South Wales to Melbourne in the Port Phillip District. He died in 1871: see Alan Gross, "Hawdon, Joseph (1813-1871) in *Australian Dictionary of Biography* (https://tinyurl.com/22rn658a) (at 20 February 2023). See also footnotes 74, 75 and 82, and their accompanying texts, below.

71 The "local magistrates" were probably the brothers Henry and Cornelius O'Brien. In the 1820s, Henry O'Brien had taken up the *Douro* run on the Yass Plains, and had later established the first sheep station on the Murrumbidgee River at Jugiong. By the 1830s, he had grown to be the largest stakeholder in the district and a squatter of considerable influence. His brother, Cornelius O'Brien, held a run adjacent to *Douro* together with other properties. Both O'Briens were active Justices of the Peace in the area. In addition, Henry O'Brien served as a Commissioner of the Supreme Court of New South Wales: see Peter Scott, "O'Brien, Henry (1793-1866)" in *Australian Dictionary of Biography* (https://tinyurl.com/2xy39tse) (at 20 February 2023). The O'Briens will be referred to further in the text below.

72 See the *Sydney Monitor*, Wednesday 7 June 1837, p. 2; and *The Sydney Herald*, Thursday, 8 June 1837, p. 2. "Trover" was the original name for modern tort of conversion. It was a legal action to recover damages against a person for any wrongful interference with, conversion or detention of the goods of the plaintiff in a manner inconsistent with the plaintiff's possessory rights to the goods: see *Penfolds Wines Pty. Ltd. v Elliott* (1946) 74 CLR 204. £114 in 1837 on one measure would be equivalent to around $83,780 in 2023: see The Measuring Worth Foundation, *Measuring Worth* (https://tinyurl.com/bp9z77rt) (at 21 February 2023).

and affronted by the enforcement of the New South Wales liquor laws. In his book *New Crossing Place: The Story of Seymour and its Shire*, Harold Martindale asserted with respect to William's brother, John Clark Jnr, that:

> "He had combined the occupations of grazing and selling liquor on the Murrumbidgee, where, having been refused a licence for the latter activity, he was fined for his pains."[73]

Moving to the Port Phillip District

Martindale failed to provide any indication as to when John Clark Jnr's brushes with the New South Wales liquor laws occurred. Nor did he give any authority for his assertions. However, there are other authors who have not only replicated the essence of Martindale's contentions, but have also suggested that it was John's difficulties with the local legal officials on the Yass Plains which led him to move across the Murray River into the Port Phillip District of New South Wales, then in the very earliest stages of European occupation.

Brian Packard, for one, has noted in his biography, *Joseph Hawdon: The First Overlander*, with respect to a horseback ride made by Hawdon from his property at Elderslie, near Sydney, to Melbourne in November and December 1837:

> "At Yass, Hawdon stayed at an inn conducted by a John Clark. Clark was a settler in a small way in that district and as his homestead was situated by the main southern road, he supplemented his income by operating as a house of accommodation which included meals. He applied for a liquor licence, but was refused by the local bench which was dominated by the so-called "Kings of the Murrumbidgee", Cornelius and Henry O'Brien. Clark sold liquor anyway and this led to a longstanding feud with the O'Briens and persecution by them. He was therefore receptive to a suggestion by Joseph Hawdon that he should move his establishment to the crossing place on the Goulburn River, later to become Mitchellstown, where hopefully, he would be beyond the reach of his oppressors."[74]

Earlier, in an article entitled "Early Mitchellstown and Nagambie", Harry Parris observed:

> "John Clarke was settled on the Murrumbidgee and had about 500 head of cattle and a dozen horses. To increase his income, he wished to open a hotel, and applied to Commissioner O'Brien of Yass for a licence, but was refused. At this time, December, 1837, Joseph Hawdon was returning from Sydney and stayed at Clarke's house. Hawdon suggested to Clarke that he should shift to the Major Mitchell crossing at the

---

73 See Harold George Martindale, *New Crossing Place: The Story of Seymour and its Shire* (1958), p. 15. It is possible that the two brothers were at about the period in question illegally selling liquor in partnership with one another. It's also possible that William was employed by his older brother in the latter's illicit liquor sales business.

74 See Packard, *op. cit.*, p. 76.

Goulburn River. This Clarke did, without delay, and arrived at the Goulburn early in January, 1838, with his stock and men. Mrs. Clarke and two children, one and three years old, were left behind. But soon Mrs. Clarke arranged her husband's affairs and joined the first overland party that came along on their way to Port Phillip, and, in this way, arrived at her husband's place on the Goulburn. These overlanders were strangers to Mrs. Clarke, but they gave Mrs. Clarke and the children their best, and she slept in the dray, the men sleeping in the open."[75]

Both Packard and Parris cited documents handwritten by John Conway Bourke in support of their respective statements above.[76]

John Conway Bourke arrived in Sydney from England as a young transportee on 7 February 1836. Soon afterwards, it appears that he was assigned as a servant to Joseph Hawdon's brother, John Hawdon.[77] In late July and August 1837, he assisted the Hawdon brothers in driving a herd of cattle overland from the Hawdons' run at Howlong on the Murray River to Melbourne.[78] He was subsequently left in the Port Phillip District to assist in managing Joseph Hawdon's newly established run at Dandenong. Meanwhile, the two Hawdons rode back to their respective properties north of the Murray River, parting company at Yass.[79] It is possible that Joseph Hawdon and/or John Hawdon stayed with John Clark Jnr on the Yass Plains during this return journey.

In early November 1837, Joseph Hawdon entered into a contract with the New South Wales Governor, Sir Richard Bourke, to carry mail overland between Melbourne and Yass as part of a wider scheme for an overland mail service between Melbourne and Sydney.[80] In late November 1837, and having secured a mailman to carry the mail on horseback between Yass and Howlong, Hawdon set off from his property at Elderslie for Melbourne. He reached the latter settlement on 24 December 1837 and immediately secured John Conway Bourke to carry the mail between Melbourne and Howlong.[81] It would seem that whilst engaged

---

75 See Parris, *Early Mitchellstown*, p. 127. Some commentators in the past, such as Parris, have incorrectly referred to the Clark family name as "Clarke" rather than "Clark".

76 Packard cited Bourke's copy of a letter apparently written by Bourke to Edmund Finn (otherwise known as "Garryowen") on 8 December 1881 and held in the files of the Royal Historical Society of Victoria: see Packard, *op. cit.*, p. 289. This document appears to be now missing from the John Conway Bourke papers currently held by the Society. For his part, Parris cited a manuscript by Bourke also held by the Society and bearing the catalogue reference "4116C": see Parris, *Early Mitchellstown*, p. 121. Among the Bourke papers held by the Society and bearing the catalogue reference "Box 38-c, MS 4116" are manuscripts by Bourke described by the Society as being "Accounts of the beginning of the overland mail service from Melbourne to the Murray (1838) and the Burke and Wills expedition (1860)". However, there would seem to be no mention of the events referred to by Parris in these manuscripts, nor, indeed, in any of the other manuscripts and copy letters presently in the Society's possession. It might be noted that the Society held another Bourke manuscript which bore the catalogue reference "Box 38-e, MS 4116" and was said by the Society to be his "Account of the first Overland Mailing from Melbourne to the Murray". It is conceivable that this manuscript contained Parris' source material. Unfortunately, the document is now also missing from the Society's collection, and has been missing according to the Society since April 2013. Notwithstanding that the source materials separately relied on by Packard and Parris are now missing, there seems to be no reason to doubt that they at least once existed, that they were sighted by the two authors and that they were written by Bourke.

77 See Packard, *op. cit.*, p. 60..

78 See Packard, *op. cit.*, pp. 61-66.

79 See Packard, *op. cit.*, p. 67.

80 See Packard, *op. cit.*, pp. 71-72.

81 See Packard, *op. cit.*, pp. 75-76. See also Joseph Hawdon, *The Journal of a Journey from New South Wales to Adelaide*

in riding from Elderslie to Melbourne, Hawdon, having probably first met John Clark Jnr on the Yass Plains during or after one of Hawdon's two earlier overland cattle drives to Melbourne, stayed overnight with John and encouraged him to move to the Goulburn River.

The John Conway Bourke papers held by the Royal Historical Society of Victoria include at least one intriguing document which seemingly confirms Bourke's likely version of the events leading to John Clark Jnr's move to the Goulburn River. The document is a cutting from a newspaper article forming part of a series of articles jointly entitled *The Perils of a Pioneer: The Biography of John Bourke*. The article purports to recount the following conversation between Bourke and Joseph Hawdon, which was said to have occurred after Bourke had completed his first mail run from Melbourne to Howlong and back:

> " 'By the way,' said Mr. Hawdon, 'I have been expecting John Clarke to make his appearance every day. You don't know Clarke, but he is a decent fellow whom I met on the Murrumbidgee about a year ago. He was a settler there, and owned about 500 head of cattle and a dozen horses, but he has been persecuted by the O'Briens –
>
> 'Oh, the Kings of the Riverina' said Bourke, laughing.
>
> 'Yes. Of course. Clarke has been doing what a good many small squatters are guilty of. He kept a house at which you could always get a meal or a bed, but although he was refused a licence at Yass, he served his customers with brandy as well as beef, with the result that things have been made rather uncomfortable for him on the Murrumbidgee. Well, I have persuaded him to shift down to the Port Phillip country, and he is to squat on the Major's Crossing on the Goulburn. You need not be surprised if you find Clarke there on your next trip'."[82]

John Conway Bourke was clearly a self-important braggart – prone to exaggeration and, at times, to sloppy historical recollection.[83] Nevertheless, it seems highly likely that at least the core of his account of the dealings between Joseph Hawdon and John Clark Jnr was correct. As his diaries demonstrate, he knew both Hawdon and John well. He would have had no known motive for fabricating the account. Moreover, Bourke's version of events fits in with what is known of Hawdon's movements at relevant times.

(1952) (https://tinyurl.com/yde72jtb) (at 21 February 2023); and Arthur Andrews, "The First Overland Mail and the Howlong Station on the Murray) in (1917) 5(19) *The Victorian Historical Magazine* 107.

82 See "Max", *The Perils of a Pioneer: The Biography of John Bourke*, (1902) Vol. 3 (Royal Historical Society of Victoria, Box 38-k, MS 000106). There is more than a little mystery surrounding this series of articles. Although they are marked as having been published in *The Times* newspaper in 1902, they are not in fact to be found in that paper published in London, and the newspaper which did publish them is as yet unascertained. Moreover, the articles purport to have been authored by a "Max". The latter's true identity is also presently unascertained. Whoever "Max" was, he appears to have been intimately familiar with the story of Bourke's life. It seems quite possible, and perhaps likely, that "Max" was John Bourke himself, writing under a nom de plume. Interestingly, Bourke died on 5 August 1902: see the *Catholic Press*, Thursday, 23 August 1928, p, 10.

83 See Andrews, *op. cit.*, p. 108; and *The Argus*, Saturday, 1 January 1938, p. 8.

In any event, in about mid December 1837, John Clark Jnr left the Yass Plains with stock, horses and stockmen and moved south into the Port Phillip District. Following in Major Mitchell's "homewards" tracks, he settled on the left bank of the Goulburn River at present day Mitchelton in January 1838.[84] Although it appears highly likely that he was influenced in so moving by John Hawdon's suggestion and encouragement, it is clear that in the aftermath of both the Hume and Hovell expedition, and that of Major Mitchell, he would have already been well aware of the good lands to be had in the Port Phillip District.[85] Accordingly, it is probable that he made his move not simply to escape the apparent enmity of the O'Briens but also to better himself and his family in life.

In the last years of the 1830s, William Clark also left the Yass Plains for the Port Phillip District. He may well have been influenced by his elder brother's example. It is also quite possible that he had received some form of written communication from John after the latter's arrival on the Goulburn River in which his brother had extolled the qualities and virtues of the new Country. William might also have been motivated to move south by virtue of the effects of the severe drought which was then afflicting New South Wales, and which may had adversely impacted on his earnings around Yass.[86] Whatever was the case, William, like his brother John, would have been well aware that there was fine land to be had south of the Murray River.

In the next section of this book, I propose to deal with the lives of John Clark Jnr and his family after their arrival in the Port Phillip District. I will then seek to trace the lives of William Clark and Richard Clark, in turn, in what was to become Victoria.

---

84 See Hawdon, *op. cit.*, p. 14.

85 See J. H. L. Cumpston, *Thomas Mitchell: Surveyor General and Explorer* (1954), pp. 31-32. It is of interest to note that in early 1824, Hume and Hovell had breakfasted with James Atkinson on the latter's *Oldbury* property soon after the commencement of their expedition. John Clark's uncle, John Jenkins Jnr, had subsequently been assigned as a transported convict to work for Atkinson on *Oldbury*: see footnote 45 and its accompanying text above. Perhaps more significantly, Hume and Hovell again visited *Oldbury* during their return journey in January 1825: see Robert Macklin, *Hamilton Hume: Our Greatest Explorer* (2016), pp. 89 and 123.

86 In a letter to Lieutenant Governor Latrobe of Victoria dated 8 September 1853, the Wangaratta squatter, George Faithfull, wrote:

"It was in February 1838, that I first determined to remove my stock from the Colony of New South Wales to the famed land of Port Phillip. It was known for years prior to this time that much fine land lay in this neighbourhood, and extended from the Murrumbidgee to the Bay of Port Phillip. Hume and Hovell were the first discoverers of this fine country, but Sir Thomas Mitchell, some years afterwards in tracing down the Darling, opened up the great country to the westwards, which gave the stimulus to the proprietors of stock in New South Wales to migrate with their flocks and herds from a land at that time suffering from severe drought 'unto a land which is the glory of all lands'."

See Thomas Bride (ed.), *Letters from Victorian Pioneers* (1983), p. 218. See also James Gormly, *Exploration and Settlement of Australia* (1921), p. 379; and Kenneth Cox, *Angus McMillan: Pathfinder* (1973), p. 35.

1. St. James the Great's Church, East Malling, Kent, England.

2. All Saints Church, Snodland, Kent, England.

3. St. John the Baptist's Church, Halling, Kent, England.

4. St. John the Baptist's Church, Wateringbury, Kent, England.

5. Kemsley Street Road, Bredhurst, Kent, England.

JOHN CLARK JUNIOR

Settling on the Goulburn River

John Clark and his party reached the Goulburn River at the point at which it had been crossed by Major Mitchell's north-bound party in 1836. On their arrival at the River, they were met by a large party of men with stock encamped at the crossing. This party was led by Joseph Hawdon and Charles Bonney.[87]

Bonney and his men had arrived at the Goulburn River with some 1,200 head of sheep belonging to Joseph and John Hawdon a little prior to 17 January 1838 to await the arrival of Joseph Hawdon from his Howlong station with more men, drays and cattle. After meeting up, the combined parties were to drive the cattle down the Goulburn River, and the Murray and then on to Adelaide – thus becoming the first overlanders to do so. Joseph Hawdon arrived at the Goulburn River on 17 January 1838, slightly in advance of his men and cattle. The latter reached the River on 19 January 1838.

On the morning of 22 January 1838, Hawdon dispatched the sheep with three of his men to Melbourne, where the sheep were to be sold. Led by Bonney, the balance of the men then set off down the Goulburn River with the cattle. Before he rejoined Bonney and his party, Hawdon remained behind at the crossing for an hour to converse with John Clark. The likelihood is that John arrived at the River at some time between 17 and 22 January 1838. In his Journal, Hawdon referred to this meeting with John thus:

> "After remaining about an hour to arrange some business connected with the Mail with Mr. Clarke, who had just arrived at the River with the intention of residing here, I galloped forward and overtook the party."[88]

According to John Conway Bourke, the "business connected with the Mail" referred to by Hawdon related in fact to a sub-contract concluded between Hawdon and John Clark

---

87 Born at Sandon near Stafford in England, Charles Bonney lived from 1813 until 1897. He immigrated to New South Wales in 1834. After unsuccessfully endeavouring to form a squatting run near present day Kilmore, he was finally able to establish a run at Mount Macedon in late 1837: see H. G. Gibbney, "Bonney, Charles (1813-1897)" in *Australian Dictionary of Biography* (https://tinyurl.com/mr2yrv32) (at 24 February 2023).

88 See Hawdon, *op. cit.*, pp. 12-14.

whereby John agreed for an undisclosed reward to carry mail between the Goulburn River and Melbourne for Hawdon.[89]

Whether Hawdon and John Clark concluded their mail sub-contract on the Yass Plains before John's move to the Port Phillip District or on the bank of the Goulburn River is presently unknown. However, it seems that in any event the sub-contract was short-lived. Brian Packard had this to say about it:

> "Although John Clark was supposed to be the subcontractor for that part of the overland mail between the Goulburn River and Melbourne, he seemed to have had great difficulty in finding suitable men for the job, and John Conway Bourke conducted the whole mail largely on his own. About half way through the year Clark hired George Streatfield to take over the Goulburn River to Melbourne section, but Streatfield turned out to be an unfortunate choice as he was a hopeless drunkard. On 2 August 1838 he was found drunk when he should have been on the road with the mail and was sentenced to four hours in the stocks. His drinking was so bad that Clark was forced to remove him from the mail delivery and presumably the unfortunate Bourke had to again take over the entire run himself."[90]

Notwithstanding the departure of Hawdon and his party on 22 January 1838, John Clark and his men were not left on their own at the Goulburn River crossing for long. The following day, 23 January 1838, they were briefly visited by one of Australia's greatest European explorers, Edward John Eyre.[91]

In late 1837 and early 1838, Eyre and Hawdon were friendly competitors in a race to be the first to take cattle overland from New South Wales to Adelaide – a race which Hawdon, with Bonney, ultimately won. Whereas Hawdon and Bonney took their cattle down the Goulburn River to the Murray River and then down the latter and on to Adelaide, Eyre's party, having first crossed the Murray and then the Goulburn, unsuccessfully tried to take a more direct, westerly path across Victoria before being forced to move north from the Wimmera to return to the Murray and then, like Hawdon and Bonney, follow that River into South Australia. Having left the bulk of his party with his cattle near where they first struck the Murray with orders to follow him, Eyre was travelling south with three men and an empty cart to secure supplies in Melbourne when he met John Clark at the Goulburn River on 23 January 1838.[92]

---

89 See *John Conway Bourke's Diary*; entry for Friday, 7 May 1858 (Royal Historical Society of Victoria, Box 38-l, MS 4652). See also the *Port Phillip Gazette*, Saturday, 24 November 1838, p. 3.

90 See Packard, *op. cit.*, pp. 141-142. Unfortunately, Packard did not cite his source or sources for these assertions.

91 Edward John Eyre was born in 1815 at Whipsnade in Bedfordshire. He travelled to Sydney in 1833 and took up the *Woodlands* squatting run on the Molonglo Plains near Queanbeyan with Robert Campbell in 1834. Disposing of his interest in that run in 1837, he became another of Australia's first overlanders. He died in 1901: see Geoffrey Dutton, "Eyre, Edward John (1815-1901)" in *Australian Dictionary of Biography* (https://tinyurl.com/y7wmntsn) (at 25 February 2023).

92 See Edward John Eyre, *Autobiographical Narrative of Residence and Exploration in Australia 1832 – 1839* (ed. Jill Waterhouse, 1984), pp. 123-124

Eyre described his meeting with John Clark in the following terms:

> "On the south bank of the river we found a person by the name of Clark recently located (whose wife and children were with my drays) chiefly for the purpose of selling bad rum mixed with half water, for which he charged the market price of ten shillings per quart. From Mr. Clark were learnt that Mr. Hawdon had left his place only yesterday on his route to South Australia and that his party, consisting of eight men (besides himself and Mr. Bonney), two teams and 300 head of cattle, were following up [sic] the Goulburn intending to keep the course of the river all the way, instead of taking a shorter and more southerly course, as when I last saw him I understood he meant to do."[93]

Even if John Clark was selling, in Eyre's eyes, bad rum, it is, perhaps, pleasing to note that at least John was not "price-gouging". It seems likely that he had brought a quantity of rum from Yass down to the Goulburn River with him in anticipation of establishing an inn at the crossing. It is interesting to observe that John apparently sold some of the rum to Eyre prior to constructing an inn.

As noted above, Harry Parris, relying on a missing manuscript apparently written by John Conway Bourke, observed in 1950 that after arranging her husband's affairs on the Yass Plains, Martha Clark, together with her two infant daughters, "joined the first overland party that came along on their way to Port Phillip, and, in this way, arrived at her husband's place on the Goulburn".[94] For his part, Bourke, who knew John and Martha Clark well, was very fond of Martha – perhaps even enamoured of her.[95] She appears to have told him of her journey with the overlanders. In his anonymous biography of Bourke, "Max", seemingly recounting Bourke's version of her tale, wrote:

> "Mrs. Clark was loud in her praise of the party of strangers with whom she travelled from the Murrumbidgee. These men, she said, showed her the greatest respect and attention during the trip, at night giving her and the two little ones the entire shelter of the waggon, while they, irrespective of the nature of the weather, slept by their bush fires."[96]

As Eyre made clear in his *Autobiographical Narrative*, the party of overlanders with whom Martha Clark and her daughters were travelling was Eyre's party.[97] They reunited Martha

---

93 See Eyre, *op. cit.*, p. 124.
94 See footnote 75 and its accompanying text above.
95 Clearly at the least inspired by Bourke, "Max", in his anonymous biography of Bourke, asserted that:
"Mrs. Clark proved to be an estimable native of the Emerald Isle, fond of her husband and children. She was a fair sample of the courageous women who risked the terrors of life in the Australian bush in those early days, and did so much to assist the pioneering work that had to be faced."
See "Max", *op. cit.*
96 *Ibid.*
97 See footnote 93 and its accompanying text above.

and the children with John Clark at the Goulburn River towards the end of January or in early February 1838. They then continued on in Major Mitchell's tracks and rejoined Eyre himself at the Coliban River on 8 February 1838.[98]

According to John Conway Bourke, John Clark and his family were the first white people to settle on the Goulburn River.[99] Peter Snodgrass, who overlanded with cattle from the Sydney area to the Port Phillip District in May 1838 and then took up a run on the Goulburn River, provided confirmation. In a letter to Lieutenant Governor Latrobe dated 15 September 1853, Snodgrass observed that at the time he took up his run:

> "the only person living on the river was Mr. Clarke, who was resident at that part known as 'the old crossing place'; he had arrived there in the previous February. There were no residents to the north of the Goulburn, with the exception of two houses of accommodation at the Murray and Ovens river."[100]

It might be recalled that as of 12 September 1838, the first local census revealed that there were then 3,080 non-aboriginal men in the Port Phillip District and 431 non-aboriginal women.[101]

Northwood

Soon after arriving at the Goulburn River, John Clark and his stockmen set about establishing a squatting run on the river flats upstream of the crossing place. It appears likely that John constructed a hut and ancillary structures on the left bank of the River, some 10 km to the south of the crossing, as the nucleus for his run.[102] This run, known variously as *Clarke's Old Station* or *Northwood*, came to cover 30,720 acres.[103] Part of the run is now the site of the *Northwood Park* horse stud. *Northwood Park* was acquired in 2006 by Darley

---

98   See Ivan Rudolph, *Eyre – Timeline and Data* (https://tinyurl.com/ybbxtrar) (at 25 February 2023).

99   See *John Conway Bourke's Diary*; entry for Friday, 7 May 1858 (Royal Historical Society of Victoria, Box 38-l, MS 4652).

100 See Bride, *op. cit.*, p. 215. As will be seen in the next section of this book, the "house of accommodation" on the Ovens River referred to by Snodgrass was almost certainly a shanty constructed by Thomas Rattray on the site of what would later become Wangaratta. Rattray operated his shanty in conjunction with a punt he established to ferry passengers across the River. In October 1839, John Clark's younger brother, William Clark, purchased Rattray's premises and punt: see D. M. Whittaker, *Wangaratta* (1963), p. 28; and Anon., *Worthy of Mention* ("*Worthy of Mention*") (1992), pp.4-5 and 14.

101 See footnote 4 above.

102 On 12 August 1839, James Dredge, the Assistant Protector of Aborigines referred to in footnote 7 above, described in his diary a journey he made up the Goulburn River from Major Mitchell's crossing place. He noted that:
"My way along the bank of the Goulburn – sometimes on its very brink, and at other times, according to the sweep of this tortuous stream, at a considerable distance from it. At seven miles distance [from the crossing] I came to the cattle station of Mr. Clarke. This spot seems well sited – affording good runs of excellent pasturage."
See James Dredge, *Diaries, Notebook and Letterbook?, 1817 to 1845* ("*Dredge's Diaries*"); entry for Saturday, 12 August 1839 (State Library of Victoria, MS 11625). See also John Conway Bourke, *Autobiographical Notes for Mr. Wilson* (Royal Historical Society of Victoria, Box 38-f, MS 4117); **Appendix 2;** and the Mitchelton Map below.

103 See Billis and Kenyon, *Pastoral Pioneers*, p. 191; and Robert Spreadborough and Hugh Anderson, *Victorian Squatters* (1983), p. 178. See also Squatting Runs Map 1 below.

Australia Pty Ltd, a company owned by Sheikh Mohammed bin Rashid Al Maktoum, the Emir of Dubai.[104]

The Travellers Rest Inn

Following his arrival on the Goulburn River, John Clark also commenced building an inn to house himself, his family and paying guests. The site he chose to build his inn on was situated on the high ground above the left bank of the River in the immediate vicinity of Major Mitchell's crossing place. The site is now occupied by Mitchelton Winery's *Muse Restaurant*. John chose to call his Inn the *Travellers Rest Inn*.[105]

In his capacity as Joseph Hawdon's mailman, John Conway Bourke was a regular visitor to John Clark's establishment on the Goulburn River during 1838. It is likely that John Clark's mail sub-contract with Hawdon required him to provide accommodation and some other measures of material comfort or comforts to Bourke as the latter passed through the area.

During a stop-over in early February 1838, very soon after the arrival at the Goulburn River of Martha Clark and her two children, Bourke remarked that John Clark:

> "had not time to erect his necessary improvements. In fact, there was only the frame of a hut without the roof for the convenience of himself & family. I and the other two men slept under a tarpaulin tent about a furlong from his place close to the River bank."[106]

Clearly using information derived from Bourke, "Max", the latter's anonymous biographer, amplified this description of John Clark's inn when under construction at this time by stating:

> "Clark's homestead consisted of a three-roomed slab hut, which at the time referred to had not been roofed over permanently."[107]

Presumably, the part-built building was temporarily covered with a tarpaulin.

---

104 See *Darley* (https://tinyurl.com/bdf5bzsu) (at 25 February 2023). See also photo 6 below.
105 See Anon., *Mitchelton: An Adventure in History* (1974), p. 4. In a previous incarnation, the *Muse Restaurant* was known as the *Travellers Rest Riverbank Grill*: *ibid*. In 1959, prior to the development of the Mitchelton Winery and its restaurants, Harry Parris recorded that the site of John Clark's *Travellers Rest Inn* was then in a cultivated field and that:
"All that can be seen are a few loose stones that probably were part of Clark's chimney."
See Parris, *Early Mitchellstown*, p. 126. See also the Mitchelton Map and photos 7 and 8 below.
106 See *John Conway Bourke's Diary*; entry for Friday, 7 May 1858 (Royal Historical Society of Victoria, Box, 38-1, MS 4652).
107 See "Max", *op. cit*.

Relations With Aborigines

In the late 1830s and early 1840s, during the first years of European occupation of squatting runs along and in the vicinity of the Goulburn River, relations between the new settlers and local Aborigines were fraught. It was inevitable that those being dispossessed would resent and resist those displacing them. The impact of squatters and squatting generally on the traditional Aboriginal way of life was as immense as it was immediate. As James Ferguson has observed:

> "As vacant land was quickly taken up and the flocks and herds spread to compete with native wildlife, the local people were increasingly alienated from their traditional lands and their accustomed way of life disrupted. Hunting grounds were turned into sheep runs, yam fields were overrun, their elaborate fishing traps were destroyed and their previously clean and abundant rivers became muddied and polluted by stock. Out of ignorance, sacred sites were despoiled. As the pressure on the land increased, so did the opposition."[108]

Throughout the central portion of the Port Phillip District, Aboriginal clans carried on an extensive campaign against the intruders. This involved disruption of stock routes, harassment of pastoral workers and the dispersal and slaughter of cattle and sheep. To the squatters at the time, the attacks appeared to be well led and carefully coordinated.[109]

In the late 1830s and early 1840s, the area surrounding the crossing place on the Goulburn River where the Clarks had settled was within the territory of the Yarran-illum clan.

---

108   See James Ferguson, *Squatting: Romance and Reality* (2017), pp. 133-134.

109   See M. F. Christie, *Aborigines in Colonial Victoria 1835 – 86* (1979), pp. 63-65; and Ian Clark, *Goulburn River Aboriginal Protectorate* (2013), p. 19.

   In the early 1840s, Edward John Eyre wrote that European settlers, attempting to expel indigenous Australians from their ancestral lands, saw the Aborigines as "intruders in their own country…, vermin that infests the land": see Edward John Eyre, *Journals of Expeditions of Discovery into Central Australia, and Overland from Adelaide to King George's Sound, in the Years 1840-1* (1845), Vol. 2, p. 171.

   In contrast to the general settler perceptions regarding the lack of attachment of Aborigines to their country, James Dredge, the Assistant Protector of Aborigines, noted in a letter to Jabez Bunting the cruelty of "the original lords of the soil" being reduced to abject poverty while Europeans profited from their lands: see Wesleyan Methodist Missionary Society, Australasia 1812-1889 in *Letter from James Dredge to Jabez Bunting dated Saturday, 20 April 1839*" (National Library of Australia, Box 2, AJCP M125). Some three years later, Dredge described the Aboriginal peoples' attachment to their lands as historical, material and personal:

   "Within these boundaries of their own country, as they proudly speak, they feel a degree of security and pleasure which they can find nowhere else – here their forefathers lived and roamed and hunted, and here also their ashes rest. And this is the scene of their fondest and earliest recollections….With every nook they are familiar, they know just where their favourite roots are abundant, the haunts of the Kangaroo, Emu and Opossum – in short, it is their home."

   See *Dredge's Diaries*; entry for Monday, 6 June 1842. See also Jessie Mitchell, *'Country Belonging to Me': Land and Labour on Aboriginal Missions and Protectorate Stations, 1830-1850* (https://tinyurl.com/pxv69bz7) (at 26 February 2023).

   In an interesting ruling delivered during the trial in *R. v Bonjon* in 1841, Mr Justice Willis, the Melbourne-based judge of the Supreme Court of New South Wales, acknowledged the position Victorian Aborigines found themselves in by observing:

   "[T]he colonists and not the aborigines were foreigners; the former are exotics, the latter indigenous, the latter are native sovereigns of the soil, the former uninvited intruders."

   See the *Port Phillip Patriot and Melbourne Advertiser*, Monday, 20 September 1841, p. 5. Willis made this observation 151 years prior to the decision of the High Court in *Mabo v Queensland (No. 2)* (1992) 175 CLR 1. See also Ferguson, *op. cit.*, p. 136.

Members of the Kulin nation, they spoke the Daungwurrung (or Taungurung) language and were led by a clan head known a Berrut or Beer-ret.[110] Relations between the Yarran-illum Aborigines and the Clarks were tense for some time, having seemingly started badly.

In rather lurid terms, John Conway Bourke described an incident which occurred in early February 1838, soon after Martha Clark's arrival at the Goulburn River. According to Max, Bourke's anonymous biographer, John Clark had ridden to Melbourne to secure stores and to speak with Joseph Hawdon (no doubt about the mail sub-contract). He took with him the mail which Bourke had brought from Howlong, leaving the latter and two other men to look after Martha and the two Clark children.[111]

According to Bourke, some unstated number of days after John Clark had departed for Melbourne, Bourke, Martha Clark and the children were suddenly besieged in the unfinished *Travellers Rest Inn* at about 11.00 am by around 100 Aborigines bearing "tomahawks". One of the Aborigines entered the building brandishing his weapon. Another sought to enter Martha's bedroom. Martha and Bourke had loaded firearms ready for use but were not required to discharge them. The Aborigines ultimately retreated after the noisy arrival of one of John Clark's stockmen on horseback. However, they remained nearby for over 24 hours, and only finally departed after John Clark returned from Melbourne with two new employees to assist in finishing the construction of the Inn.[112]

Between 1838 and 1841, a number of more serious incidents occurred in the central and north-eastern parts of the Port Phillip District as Aboriginal bands actively sought to resist the European invasion of their lands. By way of example, on 21 April 1838, Aborigines attacked shepherds on runs occupied respectively by William Bowman and Alexander Mollison on the Coliban River and did considerable damage to property belonging to the two squatters. Again, on 19 May 1838, one of Bowman's shepherds was killed by Aborigines.[113]

The Faithfull Massacre

One of the most prominent of the attacks by Aborigines on Europeans in the early days of British settlement of the Port Phillip District was the so-called *Faithfull Massacre*.

In February 1838, the brothers George and William Pitt Faithfull set out from their

---

110 The clan name Yarran-illum apparently meant "river dwellers". The Daungwurrung clans and their downstream neighbours, the Ngurai-illam-wurrun were loosely labelled "the Goulburn tribe" by the squatters: see Clark, *op. cit.*, pp. 9 and 19.

111 See "Max", *op. cit.*

112 See *John Conway Bourke's Diary*; entry for 7 May 1858 (Royal Historical Society of Victoria, Box 38-1, MS 4652). A full transcript of Bourke's account of this incident is to be found in **Appendix 1** below. News of the siege ultimately reached the Sydney newspapers of the day. The *Sydney Monitor* reported it in the following, somewhat garbled, manner:
    "The premises of Mr. John Clarke, a publican, have been several times attempted to be taken by storm by a tribe of the Ovens River Blacks; it appears that their wish was to obtain the person of Mrs. Clarke, and they would no doubt on one occasion have succeeded had not Mr. C. happened to have an extra number of lodgers in his house that night, and they very gallantly assisted to repel the enemy, a few of whom were 'peppered' with small shot...."
    See the *Sydney Monitor*, Monday, 25 June 1938, p. 3.

113 See Henry Labouchere, "Australian Aborigines: Copies of Extracts of Despatches Relative to the Massacre of Various Aborigines in Australia in the Year 1838" in *Australian Aborigines: Return to an Address of the Honourable The House of Commons* (1839), p. 31 (https://tinyurl.com/4r4ru4du) (at 26 February 2023).

Springfield squatting run near Goulburn with servants, horses, cattle and sheep to find new pastures south of the Murray River.[114] George Faithfull reached the Ovens River with most of the men and stock in early April. His brother apparently lagged a little behind. George was aware from Hamilton Hume's account of his expedition that good grazing lands, the Oxley Plains, lay downstream between the Ovens and King Rivers. George decided to take his cattle to the Oxley Plains, but first sent a party of men with his brother's sheep on southward.[115]

The Faithfull's advance party reached the Broken River near present-day Benalla on 6 and 7 April 1838. There, on 11 April 1838, they were attacked by a party of Daungwarrung and local Waveroo Aborigines. Eight of the Faithfull men and one Aboriginal man were killed in the attack. The remaining Europeans scattered.[116]

On 14 April 1838, three of the surviving Faithfull stockmen (including the overseer, James Crossley) managed to reach John Clark's *Travellers Rest Inn* on the Goulburn River. It would appear from John Conway Bourke's account of their arrival that John Clark first took the survivors to be criminal escapees or bushrangers from north of the Murray River. However, after the men had convinced him of their story, he provided a horse for Crossley and dispatched him to Melbourne to alert Captain William Lonsdale, then the Police Magistrate and Commandant for the Port Phillip District.[117]

In immediate response to the *Faithfull Massacre*, a series of reprisal raids against Aborigines in the Broken River area were led by squatters who included Colonel Henry White of the *Mount Piper* run, Peter Snodgrass and George Faithfull. Large numbers of Aborigines were apparently killed in these raids.[118] In general, Aboriginal attacks on squatters, their stockmen and their stock were countered by punitive expeditions which resulted in the deaths of many Aborigines. There is, however, no record of John Clark participating in any of these punitive measures.

Notwithstanding squatter reprisals, Aboriginal attacks in the Goulburn River area continued for a number of years. On 12 November 1838, one such attack resulted in the death of George Mould, a shepherd employed on William Rutledge's run by the River.[119]

---

114   See George Faithfull's letter to Lieutenant Governor Latrobe of Victoria dated 8 September 1853 in Bride, *op. cit.*, p. 218.

115   See Bride, *op. cit.*, p. 219.

116   *Ibid*. See also Labouchere, *op. cit.*, p. 31; Judith Bassett, "The Faithfull Massacre at the Broken River, 1838" in (2009) 13:24 *Journal of Australian Studies*, pp. 18-34; and Packard, *op. cit.*, pp. 138-140. See also photos 9 and 10 below.

117   Bourke's account of the arrival and reception of the *Faithfull Massacre*'s survivors at John Clark's Inn is to be found in his *Autobiographical Notes for Mr. Edward Wilson* (Royal Historical Society of Victoria, Box 38-f, MS 4117). A transcript of this account is to be found in **Appendix 2** below. See also *John Conway Bourke's Diary*; entries for 13, 14 and 15 April 1838 (Royal Historical Society of Victoria, Box 38-h, MS 4651). It is interesting to note that in 1893, the *North Eastern Ensign*, in dealing with the *Faithfull Massacre*, stated:
  "[T]he innate treachery peculiar to the blacks developed itself in such a horrible manner that the tragedy takes a very prominent position in the earliest records of Victoria. Some of the party miraculously escaped. One or two succeeded in finding the Goulburn River, where a settlement had been formed in the early part of 1838 by one John Clark, and which is now known as Seymour."
  See the *North Eastern Ensign*, Tuesday, 20 June 1893, p. 3.

118   See Diane Barwick, "Mapping the Past: An Atlas of Victorian Clans 1835-1904" in *Aboriginal History* (1984); Vol. 8, Pt. 2, p. 121; and Clark, *op. cit.*, p. 19..

119   See the *Murrindindi Shire Heritage Study*; Vol. 1 – *Thematic History Final* (2011), pp. 17-18 (https://tinyurl.com/ydxfts9p) (at 26 February 2023).

John Clark's response to this and related incidents was recorded in the *Port Phillip Gazette* as follows:

> "Information has reached the Magistrates of Melbourne of the murder of another shepherd by the blacks, at the river Goulburn. The unfortunate man was in the employ of Mr. Rutledge, a gentleman arrived within these few months from the Sydney side, with a large quantity of stock. This circumstance connected with previous atrocities, has caused a great sensation; the general security of the settlers' possessions, and even lives, is to be doubted; the danger from their unconquerable malice and treachery grows every day more fearful, and unless some example is made, or some measures entered into for our safety, the province must be abandoned. We were told by Mr. Clark, the sub-contractor for the mail, resident on the Goulburn, that the natives who have always caused him much annoyance, had lately shewn so daring a front in their endeavour to perpetrate robbery that he trembles for the consequence."[120]

Particulars relating to the thwarted robbery or robberies referred to by John Clark are not presently known.

In due course, and with their numbers decimated by European violence and diseases, the attacks by Aborigines along and around the Goulburn River gradually tapered off and then finally ceased. In his letter of 15 September 1853 to Lieutenant Governor Latrobe, and entirely glossing over the impact of squatter retaliatory raids in which he notably participated, Peter Snodgrass described the course of relations between Aborigines and settlers in the Goulburn River area thus:

> "The number of aborigines on the Goulburn and its tributaries at the time of my first settling there, was probably about five or six hundred. They were generally scattered about in small tribes in various parts on the rivers and creeks, but occasionally collected in large numbers. At first they killed several of the men in the employment of the settlers, and some of their sheep and cattle; but, by using conciliatory measures, they gradually became well disposed towards the white inhabitants."[121]

In 1845, it was estimated that there were only 302 Aborigines surviving along the Goulburn River.[122]

---

[120] See the *Port Phillip Gazette*, Saturday, 24 November 1838, p. 3. The level of anxiety and antipathy engendered in the settler community by Aboriginal attacks is vividly demonstrated in the following judgment in the *Sydney Monitor* following the *Faithfull Massacre*:
"Every Colonist and servant is therefore obliged in self-defence to carry fire-arms, and they are resolved that, should the different tribes again unite to attack the stations, they (the settlers) will use their best exertions to shoot every black they meet in open warfare."
See the *Sydney Monitor*, Monday, 25 June 1838, p. 3.
[121] See Bride, *op, cit.*. p. 215.
[122] See Clark, *op. cit.*, p. 19.

A Licence for the Travellers Rest Inn

Notwithstanding the troubled state of squatter relations with local Aborigines, John Clark's Inn at the Goulburn River crossing place appears to have prospered to a modest extent over the course of 1838. Increasing numbers of settlers and others were both travelling across the River at the crossing place and, in some cases, settling in the area. In April 1838, John approached Captain Lonsdale in Melbourne seeking a licence for the *Travellers Rest Inn*. Lonsdale duly referred the licence application to the Governor of New South Wales, Sir George Gipps. By a letter dated 4 June 1838, the New South Wales Colonial Secretary, Edward Deas Thomson, advised Lonsdale that the Governor had provisionally approved the application.[123] In due course, the *Travellers Rest Inn* became the first licenced inn in the Port Phillip District outside of Melbourne.[124]

It seems clear that during the course of 1838, John Clark and his employees planted a wheat crop near to his Inn. He further planted potatoes, and likely other vegetables as well. In addition to completing the Inn, a number of huts and ancillary structures were constructed in close proximity to the latter.

Surveying Mitchellstown

Following the *Faithfull Massacre*, the New South Wales Government moved in June 1838 to have a sergeant and five mounted troopers establish a police post at the Goulburn River crossing place. The police established their post soon afterwards on the right bank of the river, on the opposite side and a little downstream of the *Travellers Rest Inn*. A little further downstream, the police fenced off a river bend to serve as a large paddock for their horses.[125] No doubt the troopers soon saw fit to make regular purchases of alcoholic beverages from John Clark at his Inn.

In August 1838, and at the direction of the New South Wales Government, the Surveyor-in-Charge of the Port Phillip District, Robert Hoddle, instructed Assistant Surveyor Henry Smythe to conduct a survey on the banks of the Goulburn River for a new township. Smythe was required to survey for five miles above and below the crossing place and the *Travellers*

---

[123] See letter dated 4 June 1838 from Edward Deas Thomson to William Lonsdale (PROV, *VPRS* 4/P0000, Unit 4, Folder 122). Deas Thomson's letter materially stated that:
"His Excellency approves a licence being issued to John Clark to enable him to keep a Public House on the Goulburn River at the reduced fee of twelve pounds ten shillings upon his obtaining the requisite Certificate under the 9 section of the Act of Council 3 Wm 4 No 8."
The Act of Council referred to in the letter, 3 Wm 4 No 8, was formally entitled *An Act for Licensing Public-houses, and for regulating the Retail of Fermented and Spirituous Liquors in New South Wales 1833*: see https://tinyurl.com/y9awn9hb (at 26 February 2023). The Certificate required by section 9 of the Act which was mentioned in the letter was one issued by Justices of the Peace to the Collector of Inland Revenue certifying that the applicant was of good character, and that he and two sureties had each entered into a recognisance of £50 to guarantee the applicant's compliance with the requirements of the licence. In John Clark's case, it is not presently known who his two sureties were, or which Justices of the Peace issued the required Certificate and precisely when they did so.

[124] See Martindale, *op. cit.*, p 27.

[125] See Martindale, *op. cit.*, pp. 27-28; Packard, *op. cit.*, p. 142; and Clark, *op. cit.*, p. 23. Other police posts were simultaneously established on the Murray and Ovens Rivers and on the Violet Creek: see Parris, *Early Mitchellstown*, p. 134.

Rest Inn. He completed his survey over the course of late August and early September 1838. John Clark assisted Smythe on 30 August 1838 to establish the likely high water mark on the river bank below the inn. Smythe went on to use this mark as a datum point for his survey.[126]

On 9 October 1838, Edward Deas Thomson gave notice that the site had been fixed and surveyed for a township on the Goulburn River. The name chosen for the proposed township was Mitchellstown, in honour of Major Mitchell.[127]

A short while prior to 23 January 1839, John and Martha's third child and only son, Thomas John Clark, was born at the crossing place on the Goulburn River.[128]

Lady Jane Franklin

On 10 April 1839, the Clarks received a distinguished visitor – Lady Jane Franklin, the wife of the Lieutenant Governor of Van Diemen's Land, Sir John Franklin. A highly intelligent and intrepid woman, Lady Franklin was also an indefatigable traveller. Between 6 April and 18 May 1839, she travelled overland with a large retinue from Melbourne to Sydney.[129] Throughout this journey, Lady Franklin kept a diary. Notwithstanding that the diary was composed in brief and more often than not ungrammatical notes, it provides a useful insight into the lives led by John and Martha Clark at the time of Lady Franklin's visit.

Lady Franklin's diary for 10 April 1839 reads in part as follows:

> "Arrived about 5 or earlier at Clark's station on l[eft] bank of Goulburn. 3 or 4 separate huts of plank and box bark and [a] stables building. Have been built 1 yr. Nearly 200 head of cattle with increases last year. [It] is a cattle station. Wife has 3 children – has never been well since her first child. When he first came last Jan'y twelve month[s], Clark's nearest neighbour was Dr. Hamlyn, now Green's station (Green had part of this station before) 37 miles off. The nearest is now Mr. Hume 9 m[iles] off on the other side of the river. He [Clark] keeps a public house, sells spirits, wines and salt meat – beef. He furnishes the police station with rations. Under Mr. Batman, he kills a bullock about once a month. [They] eat fresh what they can & salt the rest. In summer, [they are] obliged to do this immed'ly – in winter, keeps a week. 5 policemen here – 4 men & serg't. The latter is one of the most ridiculous dandies ever seen. Clark w[ould] not make his Inn answer if [it] did not join other things. [He said] in answer to question that on an average day only 1 person or not one person passed to or fro in a day. Till yesterday [he] had not seen any body for 4 or 5 weeks except the 2 postmen who meet here. [A] postman comes in Thursday evening. Another sets

---

126 See Parris, *Early Mitchellstown*, pp. 134-138; Martindale, *op. cit.*, p. 28; and Packard, *op. cit.*, p. 142.
127 See the *New South Wales Government Gazette* (No. 364), Wednesday, 17 October 1838, p. 852. See also Parris, *Early Mitchellstown*, pp. 139-140.
128 See *New South Wales Births Register: Thomas John Clark* (1839) (No. 2305/1839, V18392305 25A).
129 See Frances J. Woodward, "Franklin, Lady Jane (1791-1875)" in *Australian Dictionary of Biography* (https://tinyurl.com/4tz66t5p) (at 27 February 2023).

off Friday morning for Hume [Murray River]. Gets there in 3 or 4 days. [The] site of this place is laid out for [a] township, to be called Mitchell's town. A reserve is left on [the] other side of [the] river, & [a] 5 m. reserve back on this ford at Clark's is above the house a little way for carts. And a little way below is a punt and a dragging rope for passengers. [The] descent of [the] bank at both places is very bad. [The] banks are sand and steep. Water overflows seasonally leaving large depressions or water holes, & [the] embankment [is] pushed back. [We] weighed our provisions at Clark's as heard w'd perhaps not get more for 3 weeks till [we] arrived at [the] Murrumbidgee. [We] thought they w[oul]d suffice but bought 6 add[itional] bushels of oats which with [the] 3 [we have] already make 9. Clark sold his oats at 15 sh[illings] a bushel. [The] price at Melbourne is 8 or 9, at Launceston 4. Clark's are brought up by team. [He] thought of putting in maize but too little rain this season – maize requires rain while cobbing."[130]

Lady Franklin and her party slept under canvass at the crossing on the nights of 10 and 11 April 1839. On the morning of 12 April, their carts were forded across the Goulburn River, and the party and their personal luggage crossed in the punt which John Clark had almost certainly constructed on site. Lady Franklin described the passage over the River thus:

"[We] went a little way below Clark's to [his] punt – bad descent in [the] sand bank: a sq[uare] or oblong punt. One of our late orderlies dragged us over by [the] boat placed to the other side. [The river is] about 50 yds. wide here & appears deep. On top of [the] opposite bank [we] found the carts & at [the] bottom the luggage brought [over] in [the] punt. [The luggage was] dragged up [the] bank & [the] carts loaded."[131]

James Dredge

On 27 May 1839, John Clark was to greet another person newly arriving at the crossing place on the Goulburn River; a newcomer who was to remain on the banks of the River for considerably longer than Lady Franklin. The man so arriving was James Dredge. Dredge was one of four men who had been appointed by the New South Wales Government to be Assistant Protectors of Aborigines in the Port Phillip District. Aged 43 years at the time of his arrival, Dredge was charged with protecting Aborigines from "any encroachment on their property and from acts of cruelty, oppression or injustice".[132]

---

130   See *Diaries and Letters of Lady Jane Franklin* ("*Lady Franklin's Diaries*"); diary from 3 April to 20 April 1839, pp. 29 and 39 (National Library of Australia, MS 114 and Series A, File 2, Book 1).

131   See *Lady Franklin's Diaries*; diary from 3 April to 20 April 1839, p. 42. See also Penny Russell, *This Errant Lady: Jane Franklin's Overland Journey to Port Phillip and Sydney, 1839* (2002), pp. 43-45.

132   See Michael Cannon, *Historical Records of Victoria* (1983). Vol. 2B – Aborigines and Protectors, p. 378; and Rhonda Dredge, "An Awful Silence Reigns: James Dredge at the Goulburn River" in (1988) 61 *The Latrobe Journal* 18, pp. 18-19.

In his diary, Dredge described his arrival at the Goulburn River and his first meeting with John Clark in the following terms:

> "About 4 o'clock we came to the far-famed Goulburn River; here we met a Mr. Clark, the keeper of what is called here an Inn – affording, I suppose, accommodation for both man and horse. His residence, stores, stables, etc., are built of slabs and covered with bark, and are respectable specimens of that kind of architecture. The man was civil – as all men ought to be – and suggested a suitable place for our encampment. As the cart had not arrived, my boy and I looked around and, having made our selection, as soon as the cart came up we set up our tent in a snug nook formed by a bend in the river a little below Clark's."[133]

James Dredge and his family remained at the crossing place until 12 June 1840.[134] He constructed a bark-roofed slab hut on his bend of the Goulburn River and planted a vegetable garden nearby. He provided rice, flour, sugar and blankets to up to 400 local Aborigines. In consequence, many set up camp in close proximity to him.[135]

Dredge's diary provides a brief, albeit invaluable, guide to his Clark neighbours, and an insight into their still tense relations with the Aborigines in their area. His entry for 21 August 1839 is particularly interesting and informative. It states in part:

> "A fine cold morning. About half past seven, some blacks were seen on the opposite side of the river, near the Police Barracks. I hastened towards the river and observed five. I invited them to come over, and promised them flour, tea and sugar. They said they were 'plenty cold'. They asked for 'Korong' (boat). I advised them to go higher up towards Clark's. I then went to Clark's – he was [away?] from home – and asked the loan of a boat to help the blacks over. Mr. Clark's mother, with some earnestness, enquired if the blacks were going to remain over this side. I said I did not know. She said Mr. C. would not like them to come about his place as he had already suffered from them. I said I did not suppose they [the Aborigines] would annoy them and that whatever Mr. C. charged for the boat I would pay him."[136]

John Clark Senior and Elizabeth Clark at the Goulburn River

It would seem from James Dredge's diary entry that by 20 August 1839, John Clark Jnr's mother, Elizabeth Clark (and by inference his father, James Clark Snr) had left the Yass

---

133   See *Dredge's Diaries*; entry for Monday, 27 May 1839. See also Parris, *Early Mitchellstown*, pp. 142-143.
134   See Parris, *Early Mitchellstown*, p. 148.
135   See Rhonda Dredge, *op. cit.*, pp. 20-24.
136   See *Dredge's Diaries*; entry for Wednesday, 21 August 1839.

Plains and joined their eldest son and his family at their establishment on the Goulburn River. It might be noted that on 31 March 1839, the brig *Louisa* left Sydney bound for Melbourne. Two of its steerage passengers were said to be "John and Elizabeth Clarke".[137] The *Louisa* arrived at Melbourne on 15 April 1839.[138]

As mentioned above, *Lorraine Key's manuscript* refers to an undated letter written prior to 1842 by John Clark Snr to his third son, Thomas Clark, whilst the latter was stationed with the Royal Horse Artillery at Newcastle-upon-Tyne in England. At the time he wrote the letter, John Clark Snr (and no doubt his wife Elizabeth) appear to have been living with John Clark Jnr and his family on the Goulburn River.[139] In his *History of Violet Town and the Anglican Church of St. Dunstan*, the Reverend George Edwards, acknowledging that he was relying on his possibly faulty memory, wrote:

> "It's years since I saw these records in the Public Record Office, but if I recall aright, John Clark, then living with his son John at the Goulburn River, wrote to his son Thomas in England on May 7, 1839, saying that another son Richard was at the Black Swan Hotel, Benalla."[140]

It is quite possible that the letter referred to by George Edwards is the same letter as that mentioned by Lorraine Key in her manuscript. An arrival in Melbourne by sea on 15 April 1839 would have left ample time for John Clark Snr and Elizabeth Clark to have made their ways to the Goulburn River by 7 May 1839, let alone by 21 August 1839.

How John Clark Snr and Elizabeth Clark had occupied themselves on the Yass Plains after their two eldest sons had departed for the Port Phillip District is not now known. Likewise, it is not known how they spent their time on the Goulburn River. In all probability, they would have confined themselves to assisting their son and daughter-in-law in and around the *Travellers Rest Inn* and the *Northwood* run. In any event, they did not remain for long on the Goulburn; moving to William Clark's establishment on the Ovens River at some stage in the 1840s.

---

137 See the *Sydney Gazette and New South Wales Advertiser*, Saturday, 6 April 1839, p. 2.
138 See *Australian Shipping 1788-1968: Vessels Arriving By Year* (https://tinyurl.com/yawma5ks) (at 27 February 2023); and the *Port Phillip Gazette*, Wednesday. 17 April 1839, p. 2.
139 See *Lorraine Key's manuscript*, p. 2; and footnote 52 above.
140 See George Edwards, *History of Violet Town and the Anglican Church of St. Dunstan* (1984), p. 17 (https://tinyurl.com/y8jkf4tx) (at 27 February 2023). It would seem that the Victorian Public Records Office does not in fact hold the letter referred to by Edwards.

The Move to Seymour

On 4 September 1839, James Dredge noted in his diary that:

> "Most of the aborigines have been employed today in getting bark for Mr Clark. Three of them remaining unemployed, I sent then to get bark for me – my son Theo accompanying them."[141]

Dredge gave no indication as to what either he or John Clark wanted the bark for. However, it seems highly likely that both men sought to secure bark for roofing for one or more of their respective structures.

Bark gathering figured again in Dredge's diary a little over a month later when, on 7 October 1839, he wrote:

> "Mr. Clark this morning came to our place to get some of the natives to cut bark for him at the new crossing place twelve miles further up the river, whither he intends removing as soon as convenient, as it seems likely that the road will now be fixed in that direction. Thus, it appears likely that the site for a township – named 'Mitchell's Town' – will by this alteration be rendered ineligible, although surveyed by the government. War-ra-wulk, Billy-boop, Kor-po-look, Mer-re-ben, and Mi-a-long consented to go, and have gone accordingly. The girl, Boo-gul-mun-ning, went to Mrs. Clark, who seems anxious to get her services. Mrs. C. and her mother put her into a tub of water and washed her, and then clothed her in female attire. This I have learned from the other blacks."[142]

As early as October 1837, the squatters William and Stewart Ryrie had written a memorandum published in *The Australian* in Sydney in which they had noted that by crossing the Goulburn River higher up than Major Mitchell's crossing place, the track between Sydney and Melbourne which then followed The Major's Line could be shortened significantly. However, the Ryries also noted that a punt might be required at the suggested new crossing place.[143]

Whether motivated by the Ryries' memorandum or otherwise, increasing numbers of

---

141 See *Dredge's Diaries*; entry for Wednesday, 4 September 1839.
142 See *Dredge's Diaries*; entry for Monday, 7 October 1839. The reference in the diary entry to "Mrs. C. and her mother" washing Boo-gul-mun-ning probably refers to the girl's mother assisting Martha Clark in washing the former's daughter. It would seem that the Clarks' association with the local Aborigines ended badly on 7 October 1839. On the following day, Dredge noted in his diary that:
"This morning, Boo-gul-mun-ning came to our place in her new dress. She said she should not stop at Mrs. Clark's – that she [Mrs. Clark] had offered her rum – and that she ran away. 'No good rum'. This evening, War-ra-wulk returned saying that he should not cut more bark for Mr. C – 'No flour, no sugar, only milk and pickaninny bulgana [?]'."
See *Dredge's Diaries*; entry for Tuesday, 8 October 1839.
143 See *The Australian*, Friday, 6 October 1837, p. 2. The Ryries wrote their memorandum to promote a route outlined by them for an overland mail service between Melbourne and Yass; this some three months prior to Joseph Hawdon commencing his mail delivery service.

travellers began using the new crossing place identified by the Ryries. Travellers crossing at the old crossing place on the Goulburn River diminished in number. As may be inferred from John Clark's comments to Lady Franklin referred to above, this must have led to reduced patronage of John Clark's *Travellers Rest Inn*.[144] It was during 1839 that Major Mitchell's crossing place near the inn began to be referred to as "the Old Crossing Place", and the crossing upstream on the River as "the New Crossing Place".

As early as August 1839, a punt and puntman were assisting travellers to cross the Goulburn River at the New Crossing Place.[145] As John Clark's *Northwood* squatting run extended along the left bank of the River between the two crossing places, one can only agree with Harold Martindale that it seems quite likely that at an unknown earlier point in time, John had both constructed the punt and employed the puntman.[146]

The First Robert Burns Inn

During the latter part of 1839, John Clark built a new inn near the punt at the New Crossing Place. Like his *Travellers Rest Inn* at the Old Crossing Place, the new inn was almost certainly of slab construction. The bark cut by Aborigines for John on 7 October 1839 would clearly have been used in roofing the new structure.[147] Just as the *Travellers Rest Inn* had been the first European building erected at the Old Crossing Place, so the new inn was the first European building erected at the New Crossing Place. The new inn was located approximately 100 metres to the west of the current site of the *Royal Hotel*, and near to present day Manners Street.[148]

In the last week of December 1839, the Clarks moved from the *Travellers Rest Inn* at the Old Crossing Place to their new inn at the New Crossing Place.[149] John Clark named his new premises the *Robert Burns Inn*. According to Harold Martindale, this was:

> "a wisely chosen name in view of the [Scottish] names of many squatters in the vicinity...."[150]

---

144 See footnote 130 and its accompanying text above.

145 In his diary, James Dredge recorded crossing the Goulburn River at the New Crossing Place in August 1839. Dredge was accompanied to the New Crossing Place on this journey by an Aboriginal servant he called "Billy". Dredge described his River crossing in the following terms:
"I got I the punt and Billy swam across. For this conveyance, I paid [one shilling and six pence]."
See *Dredge's Diaries*; entry for Saturday, 12 August 1839. From this account, it might reasonably be inferred that the punt in question here was only a small conveyance, perhaps similar to the "boat" at the Old Crossing Place referred to be Dredge in his diary entry for 21 August 1839: see footnote 136 and its accompanying text above.

146 See Martindale, *op. cit.*, pp. 28-29. According to Martindale, this punt was constructed of "American deal": see Martindale, *op. cit.*, p. 42.

147 See footnote 142 and its accompanying text above.

148 See Martindale, *op. cit.*, p. 28. See also Seymour Village Plans (a) and (b) below. See also photos 11 and 12 below.

149 In his diary, James Dredge noted on 2 January 1840 that:
"Sent Jeffery (one of my men) to Clark's new Station, to which he removed last week and to which the mail is now conveyed."
See *Dredge's Diaries*; entry for Thursday, 2 January 1840.

150 See Martindale, *op. cit.*, p. 29. Although John Clark called his new establishment the *Robert Burns Inn*, it would

Undoubtedly, John would have moved quickly to erect ancillary structures in the vicinity of his new inn.

It is not clear whether John Clark continued to operate the *Travellers Rest Inn* at the Old Crossing Place for a time after me moved with his family to the New Crossing Place, and, if so, for how long. However, the *Travellers Rest Inn* ultimately closed and was either dismantled or, more likely, allowed to tumble down into ruin.[151]

Further Relations With Local Aborigines

In the months immediately following their move to the New Crossing Place, the Clarks' relations with local Aborigines did not improve. On 7 January 1840, James Dredge noted in his diary:

> "I have heard by my men that Clark suspects the blacks of stealing 'Potatoes'. Several of the children were detected in the morning near the garden, and they did not deny having taken some. I understand that Clark said he would shoot them if he found any of them on the premises. I endeavoured to convince them that I should afford them no protection if they did these things."[152]

It is not presently known where the Clarks' "garden" was in January 1840. While it could have been newly-planted at the New Crossing Place, the Clarks could then still have been resorting to a vegetable garden earlier planted at the Old Crossing Place.

By January 1840 at the latest, the overland mail between Melbourne and Sydney was being carried across the Goulburn River at the New Crossing Place rather than at the Old Crossing Place, and John Clark was still associated with the mail's delivery. James Dredge observed in his diary that on 22 January 1840:

---

seem that he never traded from it with a publican's licence issued to him under that name. Rather, he appears to have irregularly renewed his existing licence for the *Travellers Rest Inn* from year to year between1840 and 1844, relying on that licence to trade from his new inn: see the *Port Phillip Patriot and Melbourne Advertiser*, Thursday, 22 April 1841, p. 2; the *Port Phillip Patriot and Melbourne Advertiser*, Thursday, 21 April 1842, p. 2; the *Port Phillip Gazette*, Wednesday, 10 May 1843, p. 2; and the *Port Phillip Courier*, Saturday, 27 April 1844. P. 2

151 See footnote 105 above. It would appear that a punt service continued to operate across the Goulburn River at the Old Crossing Place for many decades. After John Clark left for the New Crossing Place, this punt was seemingly operated by a Donald McBean until 1872. Between 1872 and 1879, , George Ponting was the operator: see Joyce Hammond, *Bridging the Gap: Shire of Goulburn 1871 – 1971* (1971), p. 15; and *Strathbogie Shire Heritage Study: Stage 2* (2013), p. 115.

152 See *Dredge's Diaries*, entry for Tuesday, 7 January 1840. The destruction of native root vegetables, such as murnong or yam daisies (Microseris walteri), in the Port Phillip District by the depredations of settler stock deprived Aborigines of much of their customary food. Potatoes grown by the settlers for their own use were an obvious alternative. In April 1838, several Aboriginal men raided the potato patch of John Gardiner near the current location of the Melbourne Botanical Gardens. The Aborigines threatened Gardiner's man, William Underwood, with a gun, but at the same time pleaded hunger. Underwood and others were able to chase the would-be thieves away: see Broome ,*op. cit.*, p. 39.

Later, in early 1841, a landowner near the Bolin Swamp at Bulleen complained that Aborigines had stolen his potatoes. William Thomas, the local Assistant Protector of Aborigines, was forced to move the Aborigines away from the Swamp. In his Quarterly Report to Superintendent Latrobe, Thomas remarked:

"I could not but feel for the poor blacks. They had till this visit an undisturbed range among the lagoons and supplied themselves for a month or 5 weeks; now one side of the Yarra is forever closed to them."

See William Thomas, *Quarterly Report to Superintendent Latrobe ; March – May 1841* (PROV, VPRS 10, Unit 6, 1844/1761); and Broome, *op. cit.*, pp. 20-21.

"This morning early, the two N.P. [Native Policemen?] I sent to Clark's for papers, etc. returned bringing, very carefully, a Packet containing one official, one private Letter, and three newspapers. I rewarded them with a handkerchief and a fig of tobacco each...."[153]

Later in his diary entry for that day, 2 January 1840, Dredge again drew attention to the apparently poor relations between the Clarks and the local Aborigines:

"Some of [the Aborigines] returned towards evening complaining that a 'white fellow' at Mr. Clark's had been threatening them – and were very anxious that I should take the N.P. to frighten him. I, however, had learnt that one of the women had stolen a knife from the man which excited his ire. I deemed it therefore more desirable not to interfere unless applied to by him. Indeed, I am not sorry that the whites become offended with them so long as they do not come to a rupture with them."[154]

Mr. Clark's Brother

On 23 January 1840, James Dredge noted in his diary that:

"Mr. Clark's brother came this morning to complain that the blacks had been in their potato field during the night and carried off a considerable quantity of potatoes. I promised to do what I can to prevent a repetition of such practices, but that if they were detected, advised him to get them punished. When he was gone I informed 'Yab.bee' of the complaint, when he and the other men immediately laid the blame on the Lubras. This evening I heard much loud conversation going on amongst them. On enquiring the occasion of it, 'Yab.bee' informed me that the Lubras were again going off for potatoes, when he called them back. I told him to inform the men that I should hold <u>them</u> chargeable for the acts of the women, and that if they allowed any of them to steal potatoes I should withhold Flour etc. from them. He said that was right, and he would 'Yabber' (speak to them) about it. After a little more loud talk, they lay down."[155]

Dredge's diary entry for the following day, 24 January 1840, included the following passage:

"This morning Mr. Clark's brother and man came to complain that they had caught

---

153 See *Dredge's Diaries*; entry for Wednesday, 22 January 1840.
154 *Ibid.*
155 See *Dredge's Diaries*; entry for Thursday 23 January 1840.

one of the men, 'Lanare', who accompanied them, in the act of taking potatoes. Billy Hamilton – alias 'Yab.bee' – endeavoured to excuse him by saying that he was <u>only looking at them</u> and did not mean to take them away. This, however, is an unlikely story. I told them they had better prosecute, and punish the fellow for his offence, assuring them that I had no desire to come between him and the ends of Justice in such a matter. Beyond this I do not feel myself at liberty to proceed."[156]

The references to "Mr. Clark's brother" in these last two passages from James Dredge's diary are tantalising. Nowhere in his diary does Dredge provide any indication as to which of John Clark's four brothers – William, Thomas, Richard and George Clark – was likely to have been the brother referred to.

The brother mentioned by Dredge could not have been Thomas Clark. Thomas was not discharged from the British Army in Newcastle-upon-Tyne until 1 November 1842.[157]

Moreover, the brother could not have been George Clark. Not a great deal is currently known of the latter's life. However, it appears from George's Death Certificate that after immigrating to New South Wales with his parents and siblings, he had returned to live in the country of his birth, England, and that he had worked for some unknown period of time as a sailor. He seemingly only arrived in Victoria in about 1848; moving to live in Wangaratta.[158]

This leaves only William and Richard Clark who could have been the "brother" referred to by James Dredge; with Richard probably being the more likely of the two. In the early part of 1840, William would have been heavily involved in building up his own squatting run and businesses on the Ovens River some 140 km to the north-east of the New Crossing Place.[159] Moreover, William was newly married and unlikely to have travelled far from his young wife as she was settling in to life on the Ovens River.[160]

Although William Clark may have been the "brother' referred to by Dredge, it seems more likely that the person concerned was Richard Clark. During the course of 1840, it would appear that Richard was in the process of constructing an inn on the banks of the Broken River approximately 100 km to the north-east of the New Crossing Place at what was to become Benalla. However, that inn did not open until late in 1840.[161] Construction of it may not have commenced until sometime after January 1840. Richard is known to have had a material interest in the land surrounding the New Crossing Place, having purchased an

---

156 See *Dredge's Diaries*; entry for Friday 24 January 1840.
157 See UK National Archives, *Service Records for Thomas Clark – Attestation Page* (RC3368989-67293f21-4eda-49ac-b739-3b95b1c69435/WO 69_8_001.jpg).
158 See *Victoria Deaths Register: George Clark* (1854) (No. 3603/1854); *Inquest Deposition Files – George Clark* (PROV, VPRS 24/P0, Unit 20); and Jenny Coates, "George Clark and his unfortunate end" in *Conversations with Grandma* (https://tinyurl.com/y44gv9nd) (at 2 March 2023).
159 See Whittaker, *op. cit.*, p. 29.
160 The *Moore Considine Family Website* suggests that William Clark's wife, Elizabeth Clark, gave birth to the couple's first child, George Moore, in 1840. The child died in the same year: see the *Moore Considine Family Website* (https://tinyurl.com/58ntx5sc) (at 2March 2023). If Elizabeth Clark had been pregnant in early 1840, her pregnancy would have provided William Clark with another reason for not travelling to, or spending any time at, his brother's establishment at the New River Crossing.
161 See A. J. Dunlop, *Benalla Cavalcade: A History of Benalla and District* (1973), p. 31.

allotment in the first sale of Seymour township allotments on 20 March 1844.[162] Moreover, there is evidence to suggest that he kept in contact over the years with both John and Martha Clark.[163]

James Dredge's last recorded diary entry relating to the Clarks prior to Dredge's permanent departure from the Old Crossing Place on 12 June 1840 was made on 30 May 1840. In it, Dredge noted that:

> "This afternoon Mrs. Clark, mother of Mr. C., came running to our hut to complain that some black women had just been there, and had broken the padlock which fastened the barn door, and taken away some wheat. I went to the Miam Miams [Aboriginal huts], and enquired about it; there was evidence at every one that wheat had been there, the chaff having been dropped about. I advised the men – who said the women had got it – to compel them to take it back, or to go with it themselves. After a while, Koromable brought me some in a handkerchief. I advised him to take it back, but he said too much afraid. I afterwards found that Lanare had taken back that and another small quantity. I then went to Clark's and advised them to get their wheat into bags and store it:- a small quantity only remaining in the chaff."[164]

How relations between the Clarks and their Aboriginal neighbours progressed after Dredge's departure is presently unknown.[165]

Over the course of 1840, it may reasonably be assumed that John Clark devoted his energies to running his *Robert Burns Inn*, his punt across the Goulburn River at the New Crossing Place and his *Northwood* squatting run.[166] A little before 15 September 1840, John and Martha's fourth child, Jane Susanah Clark was born; probable at the New Crossing Place.[167]

---

162 See Martindale, *op. cit.*, p. 34; and footnotes 199 and 601, and their accompanying texts, below.

163 See *Richard Clark's 1865 letter*. It might be noted that Richard Clark's second wife, Sarah Clark (née Maddock), died in West Melbourne in June 1868, and was buried in John Clark's burial plot at the Melbourne General Cemetery: see *Victoria Deaths Register: Sarah Clark* (1868) (No. 6931/1868). In turn, Richard was one of two people appointed by Martha's Will to be her executors and trustees: see *Martha McIntyre's Will* (PROV, *VPRS* 7591/P0001, Unit 28B).

164 See *Dredge's Diaries*; entry for Saturday, 30 May 1840.

165 What is known is that the local Daungwurrung people did not like Dredge's successor, William Le Souef. On 27 November 1841, a delegation of Daungwurrung tribesmen called on Dredge in Melbourne and, according to Dredge:
"expressed an ardent wish that I would come and live with them; they said they would look out a good place and would all sit down there, build houses like the white fellows, and plant potatoes."
See *Dredge's Diaries*; entry for Saturday,, 27 November 1841. In the event, nothing came of this approach.

166 It seems clear that little, if any, of the *Northwood* run had been fenced by 1840. The lack of fencing gave rise to difficulties for John Clark. On 13 July 1840, he placed the following advertisement in the *Port Phillip Gazette*:
" **NOTICE**
The Undersigned hereby cautions Stockholders and others against removing from his Cattle Station, near the Travellers Rest, Goulburn River, stray Cattle or Stock of any description, without his knowledge, as on various occasions Cattle belonging to him have been driven away in this manner.
JOHN CLARK
Travellers Rest
Goulburn River, July 10."
See the *Port Phillip Gazette*, Wednesday, 15 July 1840, p. 4.

167 See *New South Wales Births Register: Jane S. Clark* (1840) (No. 2306/1840, V18402306 25A).

The Maidens

On 9 November 1840, Martha Clark's sister, Jane Davis, was married by the Reverend George Vidal in All Saints' Church, Sutton Forest to James Maiden.[168] It will be recalled that Jane emigrated from Ireland to New South Wales on the *James Pattison* in 1836.[169] Her movements as a free settler after her arrival in Sydney are presently obscure. However, at the time of her marriage to James Maiden, she was said to be living in the Parish of Sutton Forest, where she no doubt worked as a housemaid on a pastoral property.[170] In her early days at Sutton Forest, she would no doubt have been in contact of some form or other with her sister, Martha, who was then living on the Yass Plains following her marriage to John Clark.

For his part, James Maiden was born in Lancashire in 1809. On 8 March 1834, he was convicted of burglary at the Lancaster Assizes and sentenced to be transported to New South Wales for seven years.[171] He left England on 1 October 1834 on the *Bengal Merchant* and arrived at Port Jackson on 30 January 1835.[172] After landing in Sydney, Maiden was sent to the Goulburn district to work as an assigned farm servant.[173] Whilst in that district, he would almost certainly have met his future wife. It seems likely that he also came to know both John and Martha Clarke.

On 11 July 1839, James Maiden received a Ticket of Leave, which provided him with probationary freedom.[174] After securing his Ticket of Leave, it is possible that Maiden travelled overland to work for a short time for John Clark on the Goulburn River. However, the early part of 1840 probably saw him working as a stockman for two other squatters, William and Edward Postlethwaite, on their *Burnewang* squatting run. This was located on the Campaspe River, some 40 km to the south of its junction with the Murray River and near to present day Elmore. While working on *Burnewang*, Maiden probably met another stockman then working for the Postlethwaites, Edward Argyle. Argyle was later to become John and Martha Clark's son-in-law.[175]

It would appear that Maiden left *Burnewang* in late 1840 to travel to Sutton Forest and marry Jane Davis. Following their marriage, the two appear to have travelled south-west to the Edward River, where Maiden obtained work as a stockman on the *Morogo* run near the

---

168 See *New South Wales Marriages Register: James Maiden and Jane Davis* (1840) (Vol. 24B, No. 519). See also *New South Wales, Australia, Registers of Convicts' Applications to Marry, 1826-1851; 1840* (https://tinyurl.com/ydg5mrq2) (at 3 March 2023).

169 See footnote 59 above.

170 See *New South Wales Marriages Register: James Maiden and Jane Davis* (1840) *(Vol. 24B, No 519).*

171 See *New South Wales: Certificates of Freedom – James Maiden* (https://tinyurl.com/y79uck90) (at 5 March 2023).

172 See Charles Bateson, *The Convict Ships* (1959), pp. 301-303.

173 See *Museums of History New South Wales: State Archives Collection: Convicts Index 1791 – 1873; James Maiden* (https://tinyurl.com/z897nx3n) (at 5 March 2023).

174 *Ibid.* Maiden's period of probationary freedom ended when he was granted a full Certificate of Freedom on 11 November 1841: *ibid.*

175 See the *Sydney Morning Herald*, Thursday, 24 July 1856, p. 2; *Wikipedia – Moama* (https://tinyurl.com/y8acwqtq) (at 5 March 2023); and Clarke and Argyle, *op. cit.*, pp. 157 and 202-204.

Murray River. In early 1841, they left *Morogo* and moved down to the Clark establishment at the New Crossing Place on the Goulburn River.[176]

A Murray River Squatting Run

At some time later in 1841, James Maiden was asked by John Clark to assist in driving a herd of cattle from *Northwood* down the Goulburn River, and then a short way down and across the Murray River to the latter's right bank.[177] In so doing, he would almost certainly have been accompanied by John himself. Almost as surely, they would also have been accompanied by Jane Maiden. The object of this cattle drive was to enable John to lay claim to a new squatting run on the bank of the Murray River.

What inspired John Clark to form his run on the Murray River is unknown. It might have been that he was enticed by Maiden's account of the region arising out of the latter's time working on the *Morogo* run. Alternatively, Joseph Hawdon's 1838 cattle drive down the Goulburn River and on to Adelaide may have been John's stimulus. Again, John may have been appraised of the good riverine country along the Murray by one or more of those using his services on the Goulburn River.

The property claimed by John Clark on the Murray River lay roughly 20 km by land downstream from present day Moama. The run ultimately had an estimated area of 60,000 acres.[178] It was initially known as the *Long Swamp*, or alternatively the *Pig Face Plain*, run.[179] It later became known as the *Perricoota* run. The run had a frontage of around 20 km to the Murray River, stretching downstream to the region of Burrumbury Creek, and extending some eight km inland.[180]

James Maiden was left by John Clark in charge of John's newly acquired *Perricoota* run. Maiden and his wife, Jane, initially took up residence in a hut constructed on a bend in the Murray River towards the north-western end of the run.[181] Their lives were not easy. The area was afflicted by drought until 1842. A greater threat was posed by conflict with the local Yorta Yorta and Baraba Baraba Aborigines; a conflict which was seemingly much more significant than the conflict hitherto experienced by the Clarks on the Goulburn River.

---

176 See the *Sydney Morning Herald*, Thursday, 24 July 1856, p. 2.

177 *Ibid.* See also Susan Priestley, *Echuca: A History* (2009), p. 16; and Helen Coulson, *Echuca – Moama: Murray River Neighbours* (2009), p. 13.

178 See Judi Hearn, *Galleries of Pink Galahs: A History of the Shire of Murray 1838-1988*: (1990), p. 49.

179 The name "Long Swamp" was derived from a series of waterholes which ran inland through the middle of the run in a north-westerly direction, The waterholes are now known as the "Benarca Creek". "Pig face", or "inland pig face" (Carpobrotus modestus) is a succulent ground cover commonly found along the middle and lower reaches of the Murray River. Cattle apparently thrive on it: see Coulson, *op. cit.*, p. 118. See also *Victorian Resources Online: Statewide – Inland Pigface* (https://tinyurl.com/2zabmcbb) (at 5 March 2023)

180 See Coulson, *op. cit.*, p. 118. See also Squatting Runs Maps 2 (a) and (b) below. It is of interest to note that on 12 August 1977, the Geographical Names Board of New South Wales assigned the name "Clarke's Creek" to an anabranch of the Burrumbury Creek which lies within the original bounds of John Clark's *Perricoota* run: see *New South Wales Geographical Names Board Extract – Clarkes Creek* (https://tinyurl.com/3jt2trtu) (at 5 March 2023).

181 See Coulson, *op. cit.*, p.118.

Warfare on the Murray River

With respect to the racial conflict on the Murray River in the early 1840s, the *Sydney Morning Herald*, in an article almost certainly based at least in part on James Maiden's recollections, observed on 24 July 1856 that:

> "[The] natives of this part of the country were by no means desirous of fraternising with the whites; on the contrary, [they] were very troublesome in driving away and spearing the cattle, and it required a vigilant eye to protect men and cattle from the onslaught of the blacks. In all these disagreeables Maiden had more than his share; and, on one occasion, so hostile had the aboriginals become, that he and his wife (the latter, in order to deceive the blacks, wore male attire) had to stand a siege for many weeks, their hut being surrounded, attacked, and watched day and night, terror having driven away Maiden's mates."[182]

The area in the vicinity of the Maidens' first hut on John Clark's *Perricoota* run came to be known locally as "Slaughterhouse".[183] There are two different accounts of how the "Slaughterhouse" area acquired its name.

The first account is to be found in an article written by an otherwise anonymous "Special Correspondent" and published in *The Argus* on 25 January 1875. While travelling down the Murray River in the steamer *Hero*, he was advised that:

> "Thirty-six years ago or thereabouts, there resided in a hut erected at a bend in the river a settler and his wife and a friend. The Murray blacks, now dwindled down to a few wandering representatives, were then numerous and ferocious. A number of the blacks attacked these invaders on their domain, and attempted to destroy their hut. The settlers were well armed, and maintained a strong defence, and beat off their assailants from the front. The blacks then endeavoured to take them from the rear, but met with a fearful lesson. The settlers had a swivel gun, which they loaded to the muzzle. They fired into the thick of the blacks as they were crossing the river. The missiles did terrible execution, killing and wounding many, and driving the rest to seek safety in flight. Since then the spot has been known as "Slaughterhouse Point". I do not vouch for the truth of this legend; but tell the tale as it was told to me as an incident illustrative of the perils attaching to settlement in the early days."[184]

According to Helen Coulson, some seven or eight years after *The Argus*'s "Special

---

182 See the *Sydney Morning Herald*, Thursday, 24 July 1856, p. 2.
183 The words "Clarke" and "Slaughterhouse" jointly appear in the relevant area on a Survey Plan of the Murrumbidgee Squatting District drawn by Surveyor Thomas Townsend in 1849: see Coulson, *op. cit.*, pp. 91 and 119.
184 See *The Argus*, Tuesday, 25 January 1876, p. 6. See also Coulson, *op. cit.*, p. 119.

Correspondent, another anonymous correspondent, calling himself "The Bohemian", wrote in Deniliquin's *Pastoral Times* that James Maiden and others:

"sustained most serious losses from the depredations of the blacks and it was through these losses that *Perricoota* received its first name – the Slaughter House.."

"The Bohemian" confirmed that Maiden had "a small cannon", but that his knowledge of long range shooting was so defective that he could not hit his targets. According to "The Bohemian", the roar of the cannon was enough "to frighten the wits out of the natives, who took to the bush."[185]

The "range warfare" between local Aborigines and white settlers along the middle reaches of the Murray River apparently continued over most of the first half of the 1840s. It was contemporaneously documented during 1842 and 1843 by Henry Sayer Lewes, a squatter occupying the *Moira* run just upstream of *Perricoota*. On 21 September 1843, Lewes recorded in his journal that:

"Mr. John Clark's people driven out by the natives from his station down the Murray."[186]

The flight of "Mr. John Clark's people" from the *Perricoota* run was only temporary. However, it was seemingly the catalyst for John Clark and James Maiden to move the station homestead from the Slaughterhouse area to a site on the Murray river at the eastern end of the Long Swamp waterholes, near to where the present *Perricoota* homestead is situated.[187]

Following this rocky start, the *Perricoota* run prospered. In 1843, the New South Wales Commissioner of Crown Lands for the Murray District, Henry Bingham, recorded that there were five persons living on the station under Maiden's supervision; in "good huts" and managing some 300 head of sheep and an unspecified number of sheep.[188] It would seem that

---

185 See Coulson, *op. cit.*, p. 119. See also Hearn, *op. cit.*, p. 20. Although "The Bohemian" wrote a number of historically-based articles in the *Pastoral Times* in 1883, the one referred to here by Helen Coulson has not thus far been located. Coulson went on to note that:

"Maiden's swivel gun was mentioned by Capt. Wm. Randell as being part of the firearms welcome he received on reaching Moama in his steamer in 1854."

See Coulson, *op. cit.*, p. 119. See also the *South Australian Register*, Friday, 14 October 1853, p. 3; and Engineering Heritage SA, *Nomination for Engineering Heritage Recognition – PS Mary Ann, Mannum Dock Museum*, p. 29 (https://tinyurl.com/yb7xgpza) (at 5 March 2023).

James Maiden's swivel gun was by no means the only cannon in the possession of squatters along the Murray River. In 1853, William Randell raced his paddle steamer, the *Mary Ann*, up the Murray from its mouth in competition with the *Lady Augusta*, a like vessel captained by Francis Cadell. The two boats were the first to navigate up the River under mechanical power. On 7 September 1853, an unnamed "Special Correspondent" on board the *Lady Augusta* wrote:

"We were off again before daylight, and soon after breakfast reached Mr. William's cattle-station on the New South Wales side of the river. He was absent at the time, and his wife endeavoured to welcome us by the discharge of a small cannon, but was unable to manage it. There are about 1,000 head of stock on the run."

See the *South Australian Register*, Saturday, 8 October 1853, p. 2. See also John Nicholson, *The Incomparable Captain Cadell* (2004), p. 144. The cattle-station referred to by the "Special Correspondent" was the *Gol Gol* squatting run, located about 10 km downstream of what was to become Mildura. The "Mr. Williams" also referred to was Henry Thomas Williams. He was married to Elizabeth Williams (née Jenkins), John Clark Jnr's cousin. The *Gol Gol* run was established by Francis Jenkins, Elizabeth Williams' brother, in about 1848. Within a year or so, he transferred the management of it to his sister and brother-in-law: see *Australian Surname Group – Henry Thomas Williams* (https://tinyurl.com/yb9omy6e) (at 6 March 2023); State Library of South Australia: SA Memory, *Did you know – Captain Sturt's Cannon* (https://tinyurl.com/5brftyvh) (at 6 March 2023).

186 See New South Wales Legislative Council, *Report of Inquiry into the State of the Public Lands and the Operation of the Land Laws* (1883), p. 74. Henry Lewes went on to describe in more detail a "forestalled" attack by Aborigines on his own *Moira* run which occurred on 27 September 1843: *ibid*. See also Coulson, *op. cit.*, p. 119.

187 See Coulson, *op. cit.*, pp. 119-120.

188 See Coulson, *op. cit.*, p. 120.

in that year, a wool clip of 12 bales was sent by bullock wagon from *Perricoota* to Sydney.[189] In 1845, Bingham noted that there were around 600 head of cattle grazing on the run, with about 10 acres under cultivation. By 1847, *Perricoota* was carrying nearly 4,000 sheep and several hundred head of cattle. In all 13 people were living and working on the property.[190]

While John Clark probably made periodic visits to his *Perricoota* run, it is clear that he devoted most of his time and energies to his business interests in and around the New Crossing Place on the Goulburn River.

Surveying Seymour

By the middle of 1841, it was obvious that the New Crossing Place would be a more likely location for a township than the Old Crossing Place. Accordingly, the Surveyor in Charge of the Port Phillip District, Robert Hoddle, instructed Assistant Surveyor William Pickering on 22 July 1841 to undertake a survey of the land around the New Crossing Place, and from there downstream to the Old Crossing Place.[191] Because of the demands of his other surveying duties, Pickering did not complete his survey of the New Crossing Place and surrounds until October 1843.[192] Given that plans for a settlement at the Old Crossing Place had by this stage been abandoned, Superintendent Latrobe of the Port Phillip District suggested that the township in prospect at the New Crossing Place be named "Mitchell Town".[193] However, Sir Thomas Mitchell demurred, and the new settlement was named "Seymour" after Lord Seymour, the son of the eleventh Dule of Somerset.[194] The plans for the settlement were approved by the Executive Council in Sydney on 21 December 1843.[195]

A little before 13 February 1843, John and Martha Clark's fifth child was born in what was shortly to be called Seymour. The child, a daughter, was named Martha Clark after her mother.[196]

In the same year, 1843, John arranged for a new punt to be constructed to replace the original 1839 punt on the Goulburn River at the New Crossing Place.[197]

---

189 See Hearn, *op. cit.*, p. 50.
190 See Coulson, *op. cit.*, p. 120.
191 See Parris, *Early Mitchellstown*, p. 151.
192 See Parris, *Early Mitchellstown*, pp. 151-152; and Martindale, *op. cit.*, pp. 29-30.
193 See Parris, *Early Mitchellstown*, p. 152; and Martindale, *op. cit.*. p. 30.
194 See Martindale, *op. cit.*, p. 30.
195 *Ibid.*
196 See *New South Wales Births Register: Martha Clark* (1843) (No. 2877/1843, V18432877 27A).
197 See Martindale, *op. cit.*, p. 42. As will be seen in more detail below, John Clark's brother, William Clark, commissioned his own new punt in 1848 to convey travellers across the Ovens River: see Bill O'Callaghan, *The Wangaratta Story: Pre-settlement - 2009* (2009), p. 4. William Howitt reluctantly paid to cross the Goulburn River on John Clark's punt and the Ovens River on William Clark's punt when travelling to the goldfields in Victoria's North East in 1852. He observed that the latter punt was "precisely like that of the Goulburn": see William Howitt, *Land, Labour and Gold or Two Years in Victoria* (1858), Vol. 1, p. 109. According to Susan Priestley, William Clark's punt (and thus that of John Clark) was:
"built out of local hand-sawn red gum....It was thirty feet long and six feet wide, sufficient to take a loaded dray and a small team of bullocks or horses. At either end were windlasses for the hauling ropes, a boxed area for the operators and wooden flaps worked by chains and levers which became gangplanks to the shore."
See Susan Priestley, *The Victorians: Making Their Mark* (1984), p. 51. In 1853, Samuel Mossman and Thomas Banister observed that "large punts" such as those on the Goulburn and Ovens Rivers:

John and Martha's sixth and penultimate child, Rebecca Clark, was born at Seymour shortly prior to 10 March 1844.[198] 1844 was to prove to be a significant year for the Clarks in other ways as well.

Freehold Land Purchases in Seymour

On 20 March 1844, the first of the town allotments surveyed by William Pickering in Seymour were offered for sale in Melbourne. Further allotments were sold the following year. In all, five of the ten allotments bounded by Piper, Emily and Manners Streets were purchased by John Clark. The *Robert Burns Inn* stood on two of these allotments (allotments 9 and 10). John also purchased three of the ten allotments bounded by Manners, Emily and Robert Streets and Ballandella Place. Interestingly, his brother, Richard Clark, who was then living in Benalla, also purchased one of the latter ten allotments. In addition, John Clark further purchased three more allotments located on the north, or far, side of the Goulburn River.[199]

These sales of Seymour town allotments were among the earliest such sales made in the Port Phillip District outside Melbourne.[200] John Clark subsequently purchased other town allotments in Seymour, including allotments extending along most of what is now Station Street and on the site of the current Seymour Station.[201]

The Perricoota Punt

The difficulties presented by hauling wool bales from the *Perricoota* run to Sydney by bullock wagon led John Clark and James Maiden to the realisation that it would be preferable to move the wool out through Melbourne. However, this necessitated providing a proximate means to transport the bales across the Murray River. The means adopted was a punt. During 1844, John, fresh from securing the construction the previous year of a new punt to ferry travellers and produce across the Goulburn River, arranged for a punt to be built to convey the wool (and, no doubt, passengers and other cargo) from the right to the left bank of the Murray River.[202]

The punt designed for use on the Murray River was built at Seymour. It was almost

---

"are very clumsy, and are impelled across by means of a rope fastened on each bank of the river; at the same time they are admirably adapted for the purpose of ferrying heavy drays over."
See Samuel Mossman and Thomas Banister, *Australia Visited and Revisited* (1853), pp. 124-125.

198 See *New South Wales Births Register – Rebecca Clark* (1844) (No. 3299/1844, V18443299 28A).
199 See Martindale, *op. cit.*, p. 34 and Plate 4 on the page following p. 36. See also Parris, *Early Mitchellstown*, pp. 152-153; footnote 162 and its accompanying text above; and Seymour Village Plans (a) and (b) below.
200 See Martindale, *op. cit.*, p. 35.
201 See Martindale, *op. cit.*, pp. 43 and 52. According to Keith Turton, a barn owned by John Clark once stood on the site of the Railway Refreshment Rooms: see Keith Turton, *Six and a Half Inches from Destiny: The First Hundred Years of the Melbourne – Wodonga Railway 1873-1973* (1973), pp. 15-18; and Lorraine Huddle, *Mitchell Shire Stage Two Heritage Study* (2006), Vol. 5, p. 86.
202 See Hearn, *op. cit.*, p. 50.

certainly constructed of local red gum. Smaller than the Goulburn River punt in operation at the time at Seymour, the new punt was around 14 feet in length and six feet wide, flat bottomed and square ended. It was capable of ferrying about half a ton at a time.[203]

Two men, with a good supply of provisions, navigated the new punt down the Goulburn and Murray Rivers from Seymour to the *Perricoota* run over some five weeks; arriving at the latter property in November 1844. A line was attached to two stout trees on opposite banks of the Murray, apparently with considerable difficulty, and the punt was then ready for use.[204]

Maiden took the 1844 wool clip from *Perricoota* three bales at a time across the Murray River on the punt en route to Melbourne, and thence by sea to Sydney. The transporting wagon was dismantled on the right bank, taken across the Murray in sections and then reassembled on the left bank.[205] This crossing of the Murray River encouraged other Riverina squatters to re-route their wool via Melbourne.[206]

1844 also saw the erection of a double-storied inn constructed of stone on the right bank of the Goulburn River opposite, and in competition with, John Clark's *Robert Burns Inn*. This new inn, named the *Seymour Hotel*, was built and initially operated by Peter Young and Gilbert Nicol.[207]

Legal Problems

In contrast to 1844, 1845 proved to be a difficult year for John Clark. On 6 May 1845, he was prosecuted before local Justices of the Peace for breaching section 45 of the *Licensed Publicans Act 1838* (NSW) for employing one John Brunt, a Ticket of Leave convict, to serve alcohol on 8 or 9 April 1845 in the bar of the *Robert Burns Inn*.[208] John was duly convicted of the charge and fined £50, with the Justices observing in open court that they regretted feeling compelled to convict him.[209] John gave immediate notice of his intention to appeal his conviction. However, there is seemingly no record of whether he in fact pursued an appeal, and, if so, its outcome.

If the Justices were content to simply express a reluctance to convict John Clark of the offence, the *Port Phillip Gazette* was more scathing. It would seem that the offence which

---

203 See John Bushby, *Saltbush Country: History of the Deniliquin District* (1980), p. 19.
204 *Ibid.*
205 *Ibid.*
206 See Coulson, *op. cit.*, p. 13.
207 See Martindale, *op. cit.*, p. 32.
208 See the *Port Phillip Gazette*, Saturday, 10 May 1845, p. 2. The *Licensed Publicans Act 1838* (NSW) was formally entitled *An Act for Consolidating and Amending the Laws Relating to the Licensing of Public Houses and for Further Regulating the Sale and Consumption of Fermented and Spirituous Liquors in New South Wales 1838* (2 Vict. No. 18) (https://tinyurl.com/ycpcouuz) (at 6 March 2023). Section 45 of the Act rendered it an offence to employ a convict, including one holding a Ticket of Leave, in connection with the conduct of a public house.
209 See the *Port Phillip Gazette*, Saturday, 10 May 1845, p. 2.

John was convicted of was neither well regarded nor frequently invoked in the Port Phillip District. In its report of the hearing, the *Port Phillip Gazette* observed:

> "We think this the hardest case on record in the District; here is a respectable publican fined in the enormous sum of £50 for allowing a servant holding a ticket-of-leave to draw two glasses of rum. The clause in the Act was never intended to be enforced in this District...."[210]

The Robert Burns Inn – The Tolmie Lease

Even prior to his conviction, the unheard charge brought against John Clark could well have resulted in significant detriment to him. On 25 April 1845, his application for a renewed publican's licence was refused.[211] Although the *Robert Burns Inn* continued to provide food and accommodation to travellers, it presumably ceased to serve liquor for a time – at least legally. This detriment was part-rectified when, on 21 April 1846, a publican's licence for the Inn, under its true trading name of the *Robert Burns Inn*, was granted to Ewen Tolmie.[212] Since John continued to own the premises, Tolmie clearly applied for his licence as John's tenant and/or nominee.[213]

Things became even worse for John Clark as the year 1845 progressed. On 21 October 1845, he was committed by James Smith, a local Justice of the Peace, to stand trial on a charge of uttering a forged Bill of Exchange. John had used the Bill to pay a business debt owed to a Thomas Evans. The Bill was subsequently found to have been forged. In his defence, John gave evidence to Smith that he had been presented with the Bill by an Edward Hughes in payment for refreshments the latter had received at the *Robert Burns Inn*; and that, in turn, he had presented it to Evans not knowing that it had been forged.[214]

There is apparently nothing to suggest that John Clark was ever tried, let alone convicted, on the uttering charge preferred against him. Uttering was and remains a serious indictable offence which requires for a conviction proof beyond reasonable doubt of an intent on the part of the perpetrator to deceive the victim.[215] It would seem almost certain that the charge against John was dropped prior to trial upon the Crown prosecutors concluding that there was little or no chance of them proving that john had been aware of the forgery when he presented the Bill to Evans.

Some six months after John Clark was committed to stand trial on the uttering charge,

---

210 *Ibid.* See also the *Port Phillip Gazette*, Wednesday, 7 May 1845, p. 2.
211 See the *Port Phillip Gazette*, Wednesday, 16 April 1845, p. 2.
212 See the *Port Phillip Gazette and Settler's Journal*, Wednesday, 22 April 1846, p. 3.
213 See Martindale, *op. cit.*, p. 35. See also footnote 227 and its accompanying text below.
214 See the *Melbourne Courier*, Wednesday, 22 October 1845, p. 2.
215 See *R v Walker* [1851] NSWSupCMB 52 (https://tinyurl.com/5h3haj59) (at 6 March 2023); and the *Moreton Bay Courier*, Wednesday, 17 May 1851, p. 35.

he was again in court. On 7 April 1846, Edward Hughes appeared before a Justice of the Peace charged with forging the Bill of Exchange which John had earlier been accused of having uttered. John gave evidence to the Court against Hughes of the circumstances in which he had been presented with the Bill by the latter on 16 May 1845; asserting that it was the only Bill he had ever received from Hughes. He was seemingly not cross-examined on this evidence, and Hughes declined to say anything in his own defence. Hughes was duly committed to stand trial on the forging charge.[216] As in the uttering case brought against John, there appears to be no record of Hughes ever being tried on the charge for which he was committed.[217]

The Sale of Northwood

In July 1846, John Clark sold his interest in the *Northwood* run to W. H. Nicholson.[218] It is not currently known what consideration John received from Nicholson upon the sale. Nor is it presently known why John sold his interest in the property. It is possible, as Harold Martindale has suggested, that he wished to concentrate on innkeeping.[219] However, John seems to have taken no step at about this time to dispose of his *Perricoota* run, which could well have absorbed significant amounts of his time and energies by reason of its distance from Seymour, and which was presumably worth less than *Northwood*. It seems more likely that he sold the latter run in order to raise capital for future business ventures he had in mind.

On 18 December 1847, Martha Clark gave birth to the Clarks' seventh and last child, a daughter. She was named Margaret Emily Jane Victoria Clark. On 24 March 1848, the little girl was baptised by the Reverend Adam Thomson of St. James' Church in Melbourne.[220] It is interesting to note that in the Baptismal Register, Margaret Clark's parents' abode is said to be "Melbourne". Apart from this entry, there is nothing to suggest that the Clarks were in fact living in Melbourne at this time. It is possible that they travelled to Melbourne for the christening and that the entry was a mistake or the product of carelessness. However, it is more likely that Margaret Clark was baptised in Seymour whilst Thomson was moving through the area on circuit. This would still leave the entry as one made by mistake or carelessly.

---

216 See the *Port Phillip Patriot and Morning Advertiser*, Wednesday, 8 April 1846, p. 2.

217 Hughes was originally arrested on the forgery charge in Melbourne on 10 March 1846: see the *Port Phillip Gazette and Settler's Journal*, Wednesday, 11 March 1846, p. 2. He was held in gaol on remand for some three months until granted bail on 16 June 1846: see *The Argus*, Tuesday, 23 June 1846, p. 4. It may be that his case did not proceed to trial because the Crown concluded, in effect, that he had been punished sufficiently whilst on remand. See also the *Port Phillip Patriot and Morning Advertiser*, Friday, 3 April 1846, p. 2.

218 See Billis and Kenyon, *Pastoral Pioneers*, p. 191.

219 See Martindale, *op. cit.*, p. 15.

220 See *Victoria Births Register: Margaret Clark* (1848) (No. 15739/1848).

The Second Robert Burns Inn

By 1848, the slab-constructed and bark-roofed *Robert Burns Inn* would likely have been showing signs of its age.[221] John Clark was also faced with the competition posed by the more imposing *Seymour Hotel*, located on the right bank of the Goulburn River directly opposite John's inn.[222] John's answer was to commission the construction of a new Inn, located approximately 100 metres to the east of the original Inn on two of the allotments earlier purchased by him on the corner of Emily and Manners Streets (allotments 1 and 2).[223]

John Clark engaged the renowned Melbourne architect, Charles Laing, to design and supervise the construction of his new Inn.[224] In August 1848, Laing called for tenders for the erection of the Inn. Messrs. Lowe and Martin won the contract, and went on to construct the inn using local freestone and limestone.[225]

The Robert Burns Inn – The McLaurin Lease

During the second half of 1848, John Clark apparently leased the original *Robert Burns Inn* to Alexander McLaurin.[226] At about the same time, the publican's licence which Ewen Tolmie had held for the premises since 1846 was seemingly also transferred to McLaurin.[227] A member of a Scottish family which came to have squatting interests in the north of the Port Phillip District and in the Riverina, Alexander McLaurin joined his elder brother, Archibald McLaurin, in the Seymour area after the latter acquired a local squatting run in September 1848.[228]

In addition to leasing the *Robert Burns Inn*, Alexander McLaurin also took over the operation of John Clark's Seymour punt.[229] Whether he leased the punt from John, or operated it under a profit-sharing or other arrangement, is unknown. Like John before him, Alexander McLaurin probably charged those using the punt as much as he thought that the market would bear. This could well have annoyed some of his customers.

---

221 According to Harold Martindale, the inn was described by an unnamed commentator at about this time as an "ancient edifice": see Martindale, *op. cit.*, p. 29.

222 See footnote 207 and its accompanying text above.

223 See Martindale, *op. cit.*, p. 35 and Plate 4 on the page following p. 36.

224 Among many other buildings, Laing designed the still-standing *Royal Terrace*, in Nicholson Street, Fitzroy: see Huddle, *op. cit.*, p. 179; and J. L. O'Brien, "Laing, Charles (1809-1857)" in *Australian Dictionary of Biography* (https://tinyurl.com/y8gseb8z) (at 7 March 2023). See also Seymour Village Plan (a) below.

225 See Martindale, *op. cit.*, p. 35.

226 See Neil McLaurin, *1838 Settlers: A History of the Family of James McLaurin and his Descendants* (2017), pp. 57 and 175-176.

227 Tolmie's licence, having presumably been renewed in 1847, was again renewed in 1848: see the *Port Phillip Patriot and Morning Advertiser*, Wednesday, 19 April 1848, p. 2. There does not appear to be any surviving record of the licence transfer, or of a publican's licence issuing to Alexander McLaurin thereafter. However, by September 1849, Tolmie was to be found in occupation of a hotel in Lonsdale Street, Melbourne. Coincidentally or not, this new hotel also bore the name *Robert Burns*: see the *Melbourne Daily News*, Saturday, 22 September 1849, p. 3. See also *The Argus*, Friday, 7 September 1849, p. 2. Ewen Tolmie went on to become a substantial grazier in the Mansfield area. The Tolmie Plateau and the township of Tolmie, around 18 km to the north of Mansfield, are named after him: see *Wikipedia – Tolmie, Victoria* (https://tinyurl.com/y7lrrv9t) (at 7 March 2023).

228 See McLaurin, *op. cit.*, p. 57.

229 *Ibid*.

In October 1849, an unsuccessful attempt was made to sink the punt. An unknown person or persons had bored 13 holes through the vessel, cut its ropes and thrown the handles to its winch and pump into the Goulburn River. The punt was quickly recovered, repaired and returned to service. Alexander McLaurin immediately offered a reward of £20 for information concerning the perpetrator or perpetrators of the crime.[230] Some weeks later, he increased the reward to £50.[231] Still later, in November 1849, John Clark offered his own reward of £50, payable on the conviction of the person or persons responsible.[232] In the event, it seems that notwithstanding these large rewards, no person was ever convicted of the crime.

Immediately prior to the attempted destruction of the punt in October 1849, Alexander McLaurin moved from the old Inn to the partially completed new Inn, where he continued to trade under the *Robert Burns Inn* name.[233] He very likely continued to lease the new Inn, and to operate the punt, over the balance of John Clark's time as the owner of each of them.

Writing in *The Argus*, an unnamed "Seymour correspondent" observed of the new Inn at about the time of McLaurin's move:

> "This house is in every way superior to most houses on the road, and equal , with respect, in finish and durability, to any in the colony, reflecting great credit on the contractors, and also on the spirited proprietor (Mr. John Clark), who is determined to spare no expense to render it complete in every department. The house contains on the ground floor four sitting rooms, a bar, and [a] bed room; the attic story has ten bed rooms and a sitting room, the whole of which have been furnished in a superior manner, and afford excellent accommodation for families travelling. Messrs. Lowe and Martin are now engaged in building outhouses to the house, consisting of [a] kitchen and additional bed rooms, a twelve stalled stable, [a] shed, and a wash house, the whole will be built of free stone, taken from a quarry recently discovered by Mr. Lowe.[234]

To celebrate (and no doubt advertise) his move from the old to the new Inn, McLaurin hosted a dinner for locals on 9 October 1849. *The Argus* reported the event in the following flowery terms:

> "As it was understood that a dinner would be given by the host of the Robert Burns Inn on the 9th instant, a number of persons came to partake of the good cheer which they expected, and were not disappointed. A dinner was served up fit for an Alderman and quickly discussed; after which the usual attendants of those feasts, harmony,

---

230   See *The Argus*, Thursday, 18 October 1849, p. 2.
231   See *The Argus*, Wednesday, 31 October 1849, p. 4; and McLaurin, *op. cit.*, p. 57.
232   See *The Argus*, 30 November 1849, p. 3.
233   See *The Argus*, Thursday, 18 October 1849, p. 2.
234   *Ibid.*

and a deep devotion on the part of the bacchanals to the jolly god, was maintained to a late hour."[235]

According to Lorraine Huddle, the detached stables built for the new Inn were erected:

"using tree trunks for the main supporting structure, adzed logs in horizontal drop log construction and vertical adzed logs for the internal division of bays. The vernacular building is large with a gabled roof, dormer gable to the hayloft and a strong trellised design feature across the upper façade."[236]

At some stage in the early 1850s, a further two storey structure, attached to the Emily Street side of the original building, was erected to form a further part of the new Inn. According to Harold Martindale, the *Robert Burns Inn*, as John Clark would have known it early in 1853, was described by an unidentified source in that year as:

"having seven rooms on the ground floor, while on the first storey there were ten bedrooms and a sitting room. Attached was a two-storey stone building with cellars and storeroom, dining-room capable of containing thirty persons, servants' rooms and on the first floor five bedrooms holding from two to four beds each, and two flights of stairs; the whole flagged at bottom. On the opposite side of the yard were a large shed and kitchen store of stone, with stone-built stable containing eight stables and two loose boxes and a stone-built double water closet. The whole yard was pitched and the premises all guttered with case metal. There was a well with a constant supply of good water and a pump at the kitchen door."[237]

No sooner had the *Robert Burns Inn* been relocated in 1849 to its new premises than John Clark rented the old building to Henry O'Hara. O'Hara, "Seymour's shopkeeper" in the late 1840s, shifted his business into the old premises from the other side of the Goulburn River.[238]

The Robert Burns Inn and Social Life in Early Seymour

As the first of Seymour's 1840s hostelries, the original *Robert Burns Inn*, and later its grander nearby successor, were focal points for much of the social life of early Seymour and its

---

235 *Ibid.*
236 See Huddle, *op. cit.*, p. 191; and photo 13 below.
237 See Martindale, *op. cit.*, p. 35; and photos 14 and 15 below. It might be noted that this 1853 description of the *Robert Burns Inn* refers to there being seven rooms on the ground floor of the original structure. The 1849 description referred to above speaks of six rooms. Either one account was mistaken here, or there must have been a rearrangement of the internal walls of the building in the intervening period. It is also worth noting that the 1853 description appears to have been in error in describing the inn's stables as being "stone-built". As can still be seen, they were in fact built of wood.
238 See *The Argus*, Thursday, 18 October 1849, p. 2; and Martindale, *op. cit.*, pp. 34 and 36.

surrounds. In the words of Harold Martindale, the *Robert Burns Inn*, together with the rival *Seymour Hotel* across the Goulburn River:

> "were the centres at which the squatters of the surrounding areas met each other, and the squatters' servants, the shepherds and station hands, 'knocked down' their cheques there. The few public meetings necessary in that simple community were held in one or other of them."[239]

In 1847, the old *Robert Burns Inn* apparently sheltered upwards of 50 people when the Goulburn River was in flood.[240] The new inn served as Seymour's post office between 1849 and 1853.[241]

According to Harold Martindale, the Reverend William Singleton, the Anglican incumbent at Christ Church, Kilmore, and Father Charles Clarke, the Catholic priest serving at St. Patrick's Church, Kilmore, each periodically held services in the *Robert Burns Inn* during the 1840s. It is likely that the semi-itinerant Presbyterian minister, the Reverend Peter Gunn, also conducted services at the inn in the course of that decade. A Methodist minister, the Reverend John Symons, may have preached in the inn in 1846. Bishop Charles Perry, the first Anglican Bishop of Melbourne, almost certainly did when visiting Seymour in January 1850.[242]

It would further seem that throughout the 1840s, John Clark also earned income by allowing horse breeders to stand their stallions at stud on the grounds of the *Robert Burns Inn*.[243] No doubt horses were also bought and sold from the inn from time to time.

John Clark's Flour Mill

In addition to his other interests, John Clark established and operated the first flour mill in Seymour. A "slabbed and weatherboard" building, the mill was constructed during the 1840's on the allotment owned by John immediately to the east of the site where the second *Robert Burns Inn* was to be built (allotment 3). It was equipped with an overhead granary and apparently powered by four horses. It worked to grind grain for local squatters. The mill had ceased operating by 1853, and the building was seemingly referred to as "the old mill". Its millstones were still to be seen many years later in the grounds of the *Royal Hotel* (formerly the *Robert Burns Inn*).[244]

---

239 See Martindale, *op. cit.*, p. 36.
240 See Martindale, *op. cit.*, p. 35.
241 See Martindale, *op. cit.*, p. 36.
242 See Martindale, *op. cit.*, pp. 36 and 39. The Reverend Peter Gunn was the father of Aeneas Gunn, the husband of Jeannie Gunn of *We of the Never Never* renown.
243 See Martindale, *op. cit.*, p. 36; the *Port Phillip Patriot and Melbourne Advertiser*, Monday, 13 September 1841, p. 4; and *The Argus*, Saturday, 29 September 1849, p. 1. See also footnote 104 and its accompanying text above.
244 See Martindale, *op. cit.*, p. 37.

Further Squatting Runs

1850 was another pivotal year for John Clark and his family. Not content with overseeing his *Robert Burns Inn*, his *Perricoota* run and its associated Murray River punt, his Goulburn River punt and his Seymour flour mill, John saw fit to acquire at least two, and possibly three, new squatting runs over the course of that year. Whether he was stirred to do so by the loss of his publican's licence or, more likely, by a reinvigorated interest in pastoral pursuits and rewards, or by some other reason or reasons, would now appear to be lost to time.

On 11 May 1850, a "John Clarke" acquired the *Coonooer* run, located some 20 km north-east of St. Arnaud in the Wimmera, from a Charles Vaughan. The property covered some 49,280 acres and extended along both sides of the Avoca River. Whether the "John Clarke" who purchased *Coonooer* was John Clark of Seymour is presently unascertained. The run was certainly located a long way from both the Goulburn River and from *Perricoota*. However, Seymour's John Clark might have acquired *Coonooer* as a speculative venture. If so, he did not hold it for long. The property was sold to Henry Alexander and James Brock less than a month later on 7 June 1850.[245]

If there is uncertainty as to whether John Clark of Seymour purchased the *Coonooer* run, there seems little doubt that he acquired two other properties in December 1850. The first of these runs was the *Stewarts Plains* run, which John purchased from Joseph Sutherland and Daniel Mackenzie. This property was located near Corop, some 20 km to the south-east of Rochester. The run was approximately 20,000 acres in area, and fronted the eastern and northern shores of Lake Cooper. It lay around 50 km to the south-east of John's *Perricoota* run.[246]

Closer to Seymour, John Clark purchased the *Moranding* property from Joseph Sutherland on 31 December 1850. It's of interest to note that Sutherland was also one of the vendors of the *Stewarts Plains* run. It appears highly likely that John purchased both properties in the same transaction. Extending over some 28,000 acres, *Moranding* was located immediately to the north and west of Kilmore.[247] The run was bounded by the then-Boundary Road (now Willowmavin Road), the Forbes – Moranding Road, Allens Road and the Kurkuruc Creek.[248]

---

245 See Spreadborough and Anderson, *op. cit.*, p. 213; and Martindale, *op. cit.*, p. 54. See also Squatting Runs Map 3 below. Interestingly, Ralph Billis and Alfred Kenyon have written the John Clarke acquired *Coonooer* in January 1850, without specifying a specific day in that month when the acquisition was made: see Billis and Kenyon, *Pastoral Pioneers*, p. 193. However, given that Robert Spreadborough and Hugh Anderson are able to name a specific day in May 1850 for the date of acquisition, the latter authors appear to be more likely to be accurate.

246 See Billis and Kenyon, *Pastoral Pioneers*, p. 178; Spreadborough and Anderson, *op. cit.*, p. 186; Martindale, *op. cit.*, p. 54; and *The Australasian*, Saturday, 2 May 1936, p. 4. See also the Squatting Runs Map 4 below.

247 See Sreadborough and Anderson, *op. cit.*, p. 172; Billis and Kenyon, *Pastoral Pioneers*, p. 246; Martindale, *op. cit.*, pp. 54-55; and the *Kilmore Free Press*, Thursday, 12 March 1953, p. 6. See also Squatting Runs Maps 5 (a) and(b).

248 See Huddle, *op. cit.*, p. 31.

Moving Away From Seymour

It seems clear that John Clark purchased *Moranding* with the intention of moving onto that property with his family, and of winding up all of his affairs in Seymour. In 1851, he either moved into an existing homestead on the property or, more likely, into one constructed for him on the property. John's homestead was located on the crest of a hill to the north of Willowmavin Road and immediately to the east of the current Willowmavin Primary School.[249]

On 25 March 1851, the following advertisement appeared in *The Argus*:

> " £60 REWARD
> Whereas on the night of Sunday the second instant, some evil disposed persons entered the paddock of the undersigned, adjoining the special survey, Kilmore, and there maimed, by cutting his hamstring with an axe or some sharp instrument, a valuable grey harness horse, a reward of £25 will be paid by the undersigned, who is also authorised by Messrs. Mollison, Hamilton, Broadhurst, Tootal, Patterson and Mowat, to offer an additional reward of £35 to any party who shall give information leading to the conviction of the offenders.
> JOHN CLARK
> Moranding, Kilmore.
> March 22, 1851."[250]

The circumstances surrounding the crime which precipitated this advertisement are unknown. Whether it was a random offence, or one committed by a person or persons holding a grudge against John Clark, must remain a matter for speculation. What is perhaps most significant about the advertisement for present purposes is that it gives John's apparent residential address as being *Moranding* and not Seymour. The other men combining to offer the further reward of £35 were squatters with runs proximate to *Moranding*.

Less than a week earlier, on 19 March 1851, another advertisement in *The Argus* gave "preliminary notice" of a sale by auction in Melbourne "sometime about the middle of April" of:

> "the whole of MR. JOHN CLARK'S property at Seymour – Goulburn River, on the main road to Sydney, one of the greatest thoroughfares in the Colony."

The property to be sold was described in the advertisement as:

---

249 See Huddle, *op. cit.*, p. 32. See also photo 16 below. Although this homestead was never licenced, Lorraine Huddle has observed that weary travellers, who John Clark considered "respectable", were able to use it as an open house. She has also noted that "archaeological remnants" of the homestead are still extant: see Huddle, *op. cit.*, p. 32. See also Stuart Dodd, *Looking Back at Willowmavin* (1984), p. 3.
250 See *The Argus*, Tuesday, 25 March 1851, p. 3.

> "Those newly erected and substantially built Inn and premises, known as the Robert Burns (together with the Punt). Also the Old Inn and Premises, now let as a store, and about nine other allotments, on one of which is erected an excellent cottage, flour mill and granary, stabling, sheds, &c. &c.
>
> The Robert Burns Inn is a commodious and most superior two storied building, erected without regard to expense and universally admitted to be the best country Inn in the Colony."

The advertisement further advised that it was intended that John's Seymour properties would be sold "in suitable lots".[251]

In due course, two more advertisements, published in identical terms in *The Argus* on 23 April and 2 May 1851 respectively, advised that the sale by auction of John Clark's Seymour properties would take place in Melbourne on Saturday, 10 May 1851. These advertisements spruiked the forthcoming auction by proclaiming that:

> "To the capitalist seeking a safe and profitable investment for his capital, or desirous of entering into a most fortune making business, such an opportunity is rarely to be met with."[252]

It seems clear that few, if any, of John's Seymour properties were sold at the auction held in Melbourne on 10 May 1851. Those properties which remained unsold included both the *Robert Burns* Inn and John's punt. It may have been fortunate for John that he was unable to sell his inn and punt at auction in May 1851. Soon afterwards, the discovery of gold led to a great increase in traffic along the road between Sydney and Melbourne. In turn, this generated a significant increase in patronage of both the inn and the punt. Whether this led to any significant increase in income flowing to John Clark, as distinct from Alexander McLaurin, is not known.

Gold was first discovered in New South Wales, and the initial flow of miners was from Victoria northwards into New South Wales. However, the discovery of gold soon afterwards in Victoria reversed the flow, as northerners streamed south to the goldfields of Ballarat, Bendigo and Castlemaine. Still later, the flow was again reversed with the opening of new fields at Beechworth, on the upper Ovens River and at other sites in Victoria's North East.[253]

Not only did the many gold seekers cross the Goulburn River on John Clark's punt but so also did carriers carting supplies to the goldfields. As Harold Martindale noted:

---

251 See *The Argus*, Wednesday, 19 March 1851, p. 3.
252 See *The Argus*, Wednesday, 23 April 1851, p. 3; and *The Argus*, Friday, 2 May 1851, p. 3.
253 See Martindale, *op. cit.*, p. 41.

"These carriers conveyed all the great variety of materials and goods needed in the roaring canvass towns of the diggings...."[254]

As mentioned earlier, the charges levied for crossing on the punt probably angered many. In late 1852, William Howitt crossed, and noted both the volume of traffic seeking to use the punt and the high charges levied for its use. He observed:

"When we came down to the ferry on the Sunday afternoon [8 November 1852], we found a train of loaded drays, of about a mile long, all waiting to go over. When we went, early on the Monday morning, there was still a train of equal or greater length....
[We asked the drivers] 'why does not the Government see to this obstruction?'
'Government! [said a driver] Government ha'n't got nothing to do wi't. They only should; and then, I reckon, it wouldn't be no better.'
'Who, then, has to do with it?'
'Why, the publican here, to be sure. He put the ferry over; Government never troubles its head about sich things; and a pretty penny the man is making of it. Why, he sacks 100 l. a day, if he sacks a penny. Look, here's more nor fifty drays here now; not one on'em will get over under a pound a piece; and there's plenty more on the road.'
We watched the proceedings at this ferry (or punt, as they call it) with increasing astonishment. The lucky publican, who levied a good round tax for his liquors and entertainment at his house besides, not only laid on such incredible tolls here, but treated the people that he fleeced with the utmost contempt. Notwithstanding the pressure for transit, and the value of the passers' time, he could only employ two men to work the ferry-boat, who seemed quite resolved not to hurt themselves. They turned their winch very leisurely, stopping every now and then to gossip with bystanders...."[255]

Whether "the publican" referred to by Howitt was John Clark or Alexander McLaurin remains obscure.

In consequence of general dissatisfaction with the cost and level of service provided by John Clark in conveying persons, animals and drays across the Goulburn River, the Victorian Government purchased his punt in late 1852 or early 1853.[256]

Mary Clark's Marriage to Edward Argyle

On 10 January 1852, John and Martha Clark's eldest child, Mary Clark, married Edward Argyle in St. James' Anglican Church, Melbourne. Mary's mother, Martha Clark, was one

---
254 *Ibid.*
255 See Howitt, *op. cit.*, pp. 76-77. See also Martindale, *op. cit.*, pp. 41-42; and footnotes 229 and 230, and their accompanying texts, below,
256 See Martindale, *op cit.*, p. 42. See also Whittaker, *op. cit.*, pp. 36-37.

of the witnesses to the marriage. At the time of its occurrence, Mary was 15 years of age. Her bridegroom was 35 years old.[257]

Edward Argyle had been born in Derbyshire, England in 1818. Together with his friend and future brother-in law, Abraham Booth, he emigrated on *The Orient* as a bounty immigrant from England to Australia, disembarking in Melbourne on 13 December 1840.[258] In January 1841, he commenced employment as a shepherd on the Postlethwaites' *Burnewang* squatting run near Elmore.[259] Argyle probably worked on *Burnewang* for less than a year, after which he moved to the Seymour area where he worked for a short time as a stockman. While there is no apparent evidence that he ever worked for John Clark, the two became friends. It was during this period that Argyle would have first met Mary Clark – then a little girl.[260]

In 1842, Edward Argyle moved back to Melbourne where, together with Abraham Booth, he established butcher shops in Flinders Lane and in Collingwood.[261] Not content with retail butchering, and possibly with financial assistance from John Clark, Argyle and Booth formed a 115,000 acre squatting run near present day Pyramid Hill in January 1843. They named this property *Duck Swamp*. In 1849, the two acquired a further squatting run, *St. Agnes*, covering 19,200 acres. This run extended from the Campaspe River to the Coliban River, and from Carlsruhe to Malmsbury. It covered the whole of the Kyneton area.[262] In 1853, Edward Argyle bought out Abraham Booth's interests in both properties.[263]

Planning Retirement

At some point during or shortly prior to 1852, John Clark seemingly turned his mind not simply to leaving Seymour but to retirement. He was still a comparatively young man, turning 46 years old on 15 June 1852. What caused him to contemplate retirement is not now known. He had clearly made a lot of money from his various business pursuits, and he may have thought that he had amassed enough to see his days out in comfort. After living a

---

257 See *Victoria Marriages Register: Edward Argyle and Mary Clark* (1852) (No. 5829/1852); and Clarke and Argyle, *op. cit.*, pp. 268-269.

258 See Clarke and Argyle, *op. cit.*, pp. 156-157. It is, perhaps, of interest to note that Edward Argyle's sister, Ellen Argyle, married a Joseph Kirk in 1853. In turn, Ellen and Joseph Kirk's niece (the daughter of Joseph Kirk's brother, George Kirk Jnr), Eliza Rowdon Kirk, married Walter Russell Hall in 1874. Walter Hall died in 1911, leaving a substantial fortune to his widow. Soon after her husband's death, Eliza Hall used a large part of the monies she had inherited to establish the *Walter and Eliza Hall Institute of Research in Pathology and Medicine* (now the *Walter and Eliza Hall Institute*) in Melbourne. Mary Argyle (née Clark) maintained a close friendship with both Walter and Eliza Hall. On the latter's death in 1916, she left an annuity of £165 to Mary for life: see Clarke and Argyle, *op. cit.*, pp. 156, 348 and 394-398; Hazel King, "Hall, Eliza Rowdon (1847-1916)" in *Australian Dictionary of Biography* (https://tinyurl.com/2s3uzm4s) (at 9 March 2023); and *About the Walter and Eliza Hall Institute* (https://tinyurl.com/yy7cet8r) (at 9 March 2023).

259 See footnote 175 and its accompanying text above.

260 See Clarke and Argyle, *op. cit.*, pp. 201-204.

261 See "In Search of Victoria, Along the Gold Fields Road: No. V – The Story of Kyneton" in *The Age*, Tuesday, 1 February 1938, p. 12; and Clarke and Argyle, *op. cit.*, p. 204.

262 See Clarke and Argyle, *op. cit.*, pp. 267-258; Billis and Kenyon, "Pastoral Pioneers – The Booths and Argyles" in *the Australasian*, Saturday, 2 January 1937, p. 4; "In Search of Victoria, Along the Gold Fields Road: No. V – The Story of Kyneton" in *The Age*, Tuesday, 1 February 1838, p. 12; and Victorian Legislative Council, *Occupants of Crown Lands, Victoria 5th August 1852*, p. 23.

263 See Clarke and Argyle, *op. cit.*, p. 259; and "In Search of Victoria, Along the Gold Fields Road: No. V – The Story of Kyneton" in *The Age*, Tuesday, 1 February 1938, p. 12.

frontier existence for much of their lives, he and his wife Martha may have wished to savour some of the amenities offered by living in, or closer to, Melbourne. They may have thought that a move towards the growing Victorian capital city would present their younger children with greater opportunities than those offered by Seymour, Kilmore or their respective surrounds. It could also have been the case that John was aware that his health was failing. In any event, it appears likely that John, and probably Martha, began looking in early 1852 for a property near Melbourne on which to make a new home for themselves and their family.

According to Ralph Billis and Alfred Kenyon, John Clark sold his interest in the *Stewart's Plains* squatting run to James Murphy and William Robert Looker in June 1852.[264] It is not presently known what consideration he received from the purchasers on the sale.

The Sale of Perricoota

John Clark disposed of his remaining pastoral and other rural properties over the course of 1853. In that year, he sold the *Perricoota* run to Benjamin Holmes and Henry Bawtree for an undisclosed price.[265] In 1856, the run was subdivided, with the north-western end being sold by Holmes and Bawtree to John Capel. That portion of *Perricoota* was thereafter known as the *Tooringabby* run.[266] The residue of the original run retained the name *Perricoota*.

In April 1853, John Clark sought to sell eight allotments in Seymour which he had purchased in the township's first land sales.[267] It is not presently known whether he succeeded in selling any of them at this time. However, it seems likely that he was only able to sell some of the allotments later in the year.[268]

Moranding Subdivided

It would further appear that in March 1853, John Clark secured the approval of the Victorian Government to subdivide *Moranding* into two properties in preparation for the sale of

---

264 See Billis and Kenyon, *Pastoral Pioneers*, p. 178. Interestingly, Robert Spreadborough and Hugh Anderson state that the run was transferred by John to Murphy and Looker on 3 October 1853: see Spreadborough and Anderson, *op. cit.*, p. 186. It could well be that John concluded the sale of his interest in the property in June 1852, but that the run was not finally registered in the names of Murphy and Looker until October 1853.

265 See Hearn, *op. cit.*, pp. 49 and 50. The sale of *Perricoota* by John Clark to Holmes and Bawtree was apparently effected by James Maiden as John's agent: *ibid*. By about 1845, Maiden, while still working for John on *Perricoota*, was beginning to also pursue his own independent business interests. He acquired a run to the rear of *Perricoota* which came to be called the *Perricoota Back Block*. Towards the end of 1845, he began operating a new, larger punt across the Murray River near to the site of present day Moama: see Echuca Historical Society, *Maiden's Punt* (https://tinyurl.com/mr4behtk) (at 9 March 2023). By the end of 1846, he had constructed a two-storied hotel on the right bank of the River proximate to his punt. Calling this hotel the *Junction Inn*, he operated it in partnership with Robert Gemmell. This became the nucleus for the Moama township: see Hearn, *op. cit.*, pp. 50 and 52; Coulson, *op. cit.*, pp. 14-15; and Priestley, *op. cit.*, p. 14. Maiden subsequently made a lot of money through land dealings and the supply of meat to miners on the Victorian goldfields. However, he fell on hard times and ultimately lost most of his assets. He died on 28 December 1869 in the Bendigo Hospital of chronic bronchitis: see *Convict Records: James Maiden* (https://tinyurl.com/22cj4yzs) (at 9 March 2023).

266 See Hearn, *op. cit.*, p. 52.

267 See *The Argus*, Thursday, 14 April 1853, p. 8. See also footnotes 199 and 201, and their accompanying texts, above.

268 See footnote 278 and its accompanying text below.

the land.²⁶⁹ It would also appear that the Plan of Subdivision creating the two new properties was finally sealed on 26 April 1853. The new properties were named *Moranding and Moranding East* respectively.²⁷⁰ On 31 May 1853, John sold his interest in *Moranding East* to RearyMcDonald. Having a little earlier contracted to sell his interest in the reduced *Moranding* to Michael Flinn, John finally transferred the property to Flinn on 4 November 1853.²⁷¹

John Clark barely departed *Moranding* with his life. On 24 September 1853, he was on the property when it was attacked by two marauding bushrangers, Henry Bradley and Patrick O'Connor. Bradley and O'Connor were Van Diemonian Ticket of Leave convicts who hijacked a schooner near Wynyard and forced its crew to sail them to Victoria. On 15 September 1853, they landed on the Bass Strait coast of the Mornington Peninsula at what is now known as Bushrangers Bay. From there, they made their way north on a violent crime spree.²⁷²

On 24 September 1853, Bradley and O'Connor confronted W. J. Smith, John Clark's manager on *Moranding*. According to Smith, O'Connor:

> "asked me if I could give him a job hut-keeping or shepherding. I told him that Mr. Clark had just sold the station, but the new owner, a Mr. Flynn, had gone to the men's hut, and they could see him there."

Smith went on to state that Bradley and O'Connor then walked up to John Clark's house, where they met John as he was emerging from the building with a gardener. The bushrangers ordered John and the gardener to "bail up". According to Smith:

> "Mr. Clark rushed into the house, but O'Conner before he could close the door put his foot between it and the jamb. The gardener and Bradley had a struggle, in which the former tried to wrest Bradley's gun from him, but without succeeding. Mr. Clark then made an attempt to escape by running in the direction of the men's hut. Bradley followed him, and fired two shots at him, one of which passed through his hat, and the other through his whiskers. O'Connor shot the gardener through the body, so that we had to get a doctor."²⁷³

---

269 See Billis and Kenyon, *Pastoral Pioneers*, p. 246; and Huddle, *op. cit.*, p. 31.
270 *Moranding East* covered an area of around 8,500 acres, and the reduced *Moranding* of some 19,500 acres: see Dodd, *op. cit.*, p. 5; and Spreadborough and Anderson, *op. cit.*, p. 172.
271 *Ibid.* See also Billis and Kenyon, *Pastoral Pioneers*, p. 246.
272 See the *Tasmanian Colonist*, Thursday, 13 October 1853, p. 3; and James Maher, *The Tale of a Century: Kilmore 1837-1937* (1938), p. 34.
273 Smith's account of the incident can be found in Heather Knight, *Kilmore: Those That Came Before* (2007), pp. 22-23. Smith first recounted the story to a reporter from the *Kilmore Advertiser* in about November 1896 – some 43 years after the event. James Maher surmised that the two bushrangers had a grudge against John Clark: see Maher, *op. cit.*, p. 34. See also Martindale, *op. cit.*, p. 55. However, given Bradley and O'Connor's circumstances over the time leading up to the attack, this seems highly unlikely. See further the *Sydney Morning Herald*, Monday, 29 March 2010; and *Historical Facts – Mornington Peninsula: Bushrangers at Cape Schanck* (https://tinyurl.com/ya4jcj9u) (at 9 March 2023).

Bradley and O'Connor then made their escape. They were finally caught the following day, 24 September 1853, on another property near Kilmore.[274] The two bushrangers were tried, convicted and sentenced to death in the Supreme Court of Victoria at Melbourne on 20 October 1853.[275] They were hanged in the Melbourne Gaol four days later on 24 October 1853.[276]

It should be noted that John Clark saw fit to provide a reward of 200 guineas to the Victoria Police for distribution to those involved in the capture of Bradley and O'Connor.[277]

The Sale of John Clark's Remaining Seymour Properties

In about late August or Early September 1853, John Clark was able to sell his remaining Seymour assets. He was apparently paid a total of £11,500 for them. *The Argus* commented at the time that this amount was "a most inadequate price, those versed in these matters say".[278] The Seymour properties thus sold by John of course included his Hotel.

The Robert Burns Inn Becomes the Royal George Inn

By the time of its sale in 1853, John Clark had changed the name of his Inn from the *Robert Burns Inn* to the *Royal George Inn*.[279] This establishment was purchased from John by John Brooke.[280] The following year, Brooke, together with his brother, Thomas Collier Brooke, also acquired the *Worrough* run to the east of Seymour.[281]

During the latter years of John Clark's ownership of his Seymour Inn, or possibly shortly afterwards, it would appear that a likeness of him was painted on one of the interior walls of the premises. In an article on the inn entitled "Historic Seymour Walls That Speak", which was published in *The Argus* on 10 September 1938, C. R. C. Pearce wrote:

> "The walls of the original bar, which occupied about 16 ft. by 10 ft., form part of the present sitting-room. These walls are decorated with painted panels, depicting

---

274 See the *Tasmanian Colonist*, Thursday, 13 October 1853, p. 3; and Knight, *op. cit.*, p. 23.

275 See *Bell's Life in Sydney and Sporting Reviewer*, Saturday, 29 October 1853, p. 1; the *Maitland Mercury and Hunter River General Advertiser*, Wednesday, 2 November 1853, p. 4; and Knight, *op. cit.*, p. 23.

276 See *Bell's Life in Sydney and Sporting Reviewer*, Saturday, 29 October 1853, p. 1; *Historical Facts – Mornington Peninsula: Bushrangers at Cape Schanck* (https://tinyurl.com/ya4jcj9u) (at 9 March 2023); and Knight, *op. cit.*, p. 23.

277 Payment of the reward was accompanied by the following letter sent by John Clark to the Chief Commissioner of Police:
"I beg to hand you herewith a cheque for 200 guineas, the reward offered by me for the capture of the bushrangers O'Connor and Bradley, who made a murderous attack on me and my gardener, at my residence near Kilmore, and request that you will have the goodness to distribute the same among the captors and those who were instrumental in the capture, though not actually present at the arrest. And amongst the latter I would particularly point out Inspector Price, of Kilmore, whose vigilance and promptness in the matter deserves particular notice."
  See the *South Australian Register*, Monday, 31 October 1853, p. 3. It is of interest to note that John Clark's wife, Martha Clark, was allegedly also shot at in the early 1850s by the notorious bushranger, Francis Melville ("Captain Moonlight") from the far side of the Goulburn River as she stood in front of the *Robert Burns Inn*. Fortunately, she was not struck by the bullet: see John Jennings, *Seymour's Wooden Wonder and Other Stories* (2010), Chap. 28.

278 See *The Argus*, Tuesday, 6 September 1853, p. 5.

279 *Ibid.*

280 See Martindale, *op. cit.*, p. 54.

281 See *Letters [Manuscript]: Brooke, John* (https://tinyurl.com/2p93xyun) (at 9 March 2023).

incidents in the life of a shearer who was famous in the district in the late forties and early fifties. The paintings are on plaster, and they are the work of an artist who "went to the roads". On the walls of the bar in which he had witnessed some of the scenes, the artist first shows the shearer at work in the shed. In another panel, the shearer is flourishing his cheque before the hotel-keeper, John Clark. The cheque is signed by a squatter (Furlong), whose family helped to introduce merino sheep to Victoria."[282]

Unfortunately, the painted panels would appear to be long gone, and with them John Clark's portrait. No other portrait or photo of John is known to exist.

In 1859, John Brooke sold the *Royal George Inn* to William Shearer. Shearer renamed it the *Royal Hotel*.[283] Ownership of the premises has since passed through numerous hands. In 1891, a new front section was added to the hotel. The extension involved the construction of a façade, a bar, front upstairs bedrooms and a new verandah. These were built at a cost of £1,184.[284]

Between 1910 and 1951, the *Royal Hotel* was owned and operated by Eliza Moody and her children, Leslie and Bessie Moody. During this period, it came to be known as "Moody's Pub". The artist Russell Drysdale lodged in it with his father on several occasions during the 1920s and 1930s. In about 1941, Drysdale depicted the hotel in his oil painting, "Moody's Pub". This work currently hangs in the National Gallery of Victoria.[285]

The Purchase of Gooparl

In 1854, and with his rural properties sold, John Clark, together with his wife Martha and their younger children, moved to a house on land which John had acquired in that year near to Melbourne. The property acquired by John was a portion of Allotment 31, Section 3 in the Parish of Doutta Galla. The latter allotment comprised some 48 acres of land bounded by the Saltwater River (now the Maribyrnong River) to the west; and with what later became Epsom and Langs Roads, Ascot Vale also forming boundaries to the property.

Allotment 31 had been first purchased on 3 June 1846 by Charles Payne and his wife, Elizabeth Payne. Charles Payne was a Melbourne merchant, grazier and magistrate. He built a homestead on that portion of the property which was subsequently acquired by John Clark. The Paynes named their land and homestead *Gooparl*.[286]

In November 1852, the Paynes offered their *Gooparl* estate for sale "in whole or in

---

282 See *The Argus*, Saturday, 10 September 1938, p. 7.
283 See Martindale, *op. cit.*, p. 55.
284 See Huddle, *op. cit.*, p. 179.
285 See Jennings, *op. cit.*, Chap. 11; *Moody's Pub 1941* (https://tinyurl.com/bpayn546) (at 9 March 2023); and *Wikipedia – Moody's Pub* (https://tinyurl.com/mpbscjx5) (at 9 March 2023). See also photo 17 below.
286 See Lenore Frost (ed.), *The Fine Houses of Essendon and Flemington: 1846-1880* (2010), p. 35. See also Land Victoria's general law conveyancing records for Allotment 31, Section 3, Parish of Doutta Galla ; and photos 18 and 19 below.

partitions".[287] In an advertisement published in *The Argus* on 6 November of that year, the property was described in the following terms:

> "The Gooparl Estate is the property of Charles Payne, Esq. comprising 48 acres of Land, five of which are in a high state of cultivation, as a flour, fruit, and kitchen garden. Also ten acre cultivation paddock, and two grass paddocks of 33 acres. The whole is substantially fenced with post and three rails, and dividing fences, with very superior gates. The buildings consist of a neat verandah cottage, of seven rooms, kitchen and scullery; the out buildings comprise, stabling, harness room, coach-house, open shed, and fowl house, and sleeping apartments, and store-room over. There is a large water tank, built of stone, and cemented, the yard is paved, and everything in first-rate order."[288]

John Clark acquired the central portion of the *Gooparl* estate, fronting what is now Langs Road. He purchased the land in two parts. On 30 January 1854, he acquired the western section of it from Charles and Elizabeth Payne for £10,000. The *Gooparl* homestead and outbuildings were located on this section. The Clarks almost certainly moved into the homestead very soon after John's acquisition of the section. Later in the same year, on 29 November 1854, he purchased the smaller, eastern section from a John Wilson for £2,492.15.9. Interestingly, Wilson had himself only acquired the eastern section from the Paynes on 18 November 1854. In all, John Clark purchased around 12 acres of land. He and Martha continued to call their portion of the original estate *Gooparl*.

It seems unlikely that John Clark ever worked again after his move to *Gooparl*. A liquor licence for the *Stanley Arms Hotel* in Footscray was granted to a John Clark in 1854.[289] However, this would appear to have been a different John Clark.[290] It is, perhaps, also significant that in his last Will, executed by him on 25 September 1856, John Clark of *Gooparl* described himself as a "Gentleman".[291] Then, and sometimes still now, the description "gentleman" was and is used as a synonym for "male retiree".

The Death of John Clark

Unfortunately, John Clark did not live to enjoy his retirement for long. He died on 10 April 1857 at the comparatively young age of 50 years. On his Death Certificate, his causes of death were said to be:

---

287 See *The Argus*, Saturday, 6 November 1852, p. 7.
288 *Ibid.*
289 See Victorian Heritage Database Report, *Saltwater River Crossing Site and Footscray Wharves Precinct* (2017), p. 5 (https://tinyurl.com/ykkefpjb) (at 9 March 2023). See also *The Argus*, Wednesday, 22 April 1857, p. 5.
290 The obituaries column in *The Argus* on 3 March 1860 recorded the following death:
   "On the 25th ult., at his residence, Stanley Arms, Footscray, Saltwater River, Mr. John Clark. Late of Peel, Isle-of-Man, aged 46 years."
   See *The Argus*, Saturday, 3 March 1860, p. 4.
291 See *John Clark's Will* (PROV, VPRS 7591/P0001, Unit 000005, Item 2/151).

"Hydrothorax 2 years, Disease of the heart 3 months."[292]

Hydrothorax is a type of pleural effusion in which an excessive quantity of fluid (blood, lymph or pus) accumulates in the sufferer's pleural cavity. It is most likely to develop as a consequence of heart failure. However, in a minority of cases, hydrothorax can develop in those suffering from cirrhosis or other diseases of the liver.[293] In John Clark's case, according to his Death Certificate, his heart disease was said to have had an onset after that of his hydrothorax. It may be that the heart disease had an earlier, undiagnosed onset, and that it did precipitate John's hydrothorax. If not, and given John's background as a publican, it is reasonable to suppose that his hydrothorax was likely to have been a pathology secondary to "Publican's Disease" – cirrhosis of the liver.

Following an Anglican funeral, John Clark was interred in a plot at the Melbourne General Cemetery on 15 April 1857. A memorial column was subsequently erected over his grave.[294]

John Clark's Will

John Clark died leaving a Will executed by him on 25 September 1856.[295] The Will, although long in form and complex in nature, was a fairly standard one for a man of some substance in his day and age.

By his Will, John appointed his widow, Martha Clark, and an Andrew Brown to be his executors and the trustees of his estate.[296] Probate of the Will was granted in the Supreme Court of Victoria on 14 May 1857.[297] The Will went on to provide that Martha was to receive all of her late husband's household effects and an immediate legacy of £100. The balance of John's real and personal estate was to be held in trust by Martha and Brown. They were empowered to sell estate assets and to invest estate monies. Trust funds were to be first used to pay John's debts and his funeral and testamentary expenses. Income earned by the trust was to be paid to Martha "so long as she continues to be my widow."[298]

Under John's Will, if Martha did not remarry, she was entitled to dispose of the capital assets held in the trust at her death, by Deed or by her Will, to whomsoever she thought fit. However, if she was to remarry, the residue of John's estate then held in trust was to be divided equally between Martha and each of John and Martha's children.[299]

---

292 See *Victoria Deaths Register: John Clark* (1857) (No. 2568/1857).
293 See *Wikipedia – Hydrothorax* (https://tinyurl.com/ysx48cvf) (at 10 March 2023).
294 See *The Age*, Tuesday, 14 April 1857, p. 1. John's remains lie buried in Church of England Compartment F, Grave 201. See also photos 20 and 21 below
295 See footnote 291 and its accompanying text above.
296 Nothing is presently known of Andrew Brown, or of his relationship with John Clark.
297 See *John Clark's Will: Probate* (PROV, *VPRS* 7591/P0001, Unit 5).
298 *Ibid.*
299 *Ibid.* On 2 August 1865, John and Martha Clark's son, Thomas John Clark, obtained an order from Mr. Justice Molesworth in the Supreme Court of Victoria requiring his mother and Andrew Brown to account to the Court and to John and Marth's children for their administration of John's estate: see *Thomas John Clark v Martha McIntosh and Andrew Brown: Order for an Account of John Clark's Estate* (PROV, *VPRS* 259/P1, Unit 68, Item 759). The account provided would appear to have disappeared. However, it must have satisfied Thomas John Clark as no further litigation seemingly ensued.

It is unfortunate that an inventory of John Clark's assets and liabilities as at the date of his death has not survived on his probate file presently held by the Public Records Office of Victoria, or, apparently, anywhere else. However, Martha Clark is on record as asserting in May 1862 that John had left her property to an annual value of "£400 or £500".[300]

It should be noted that *Gooparl* did not fall into John Clark's estate. On 19 September 1856, and perhaps conscious of the fact that he might not have had long to live, John transferred his title to the property to Martha.[301]

Martha Clark's Marriage to William McIntosh

As matters eventuated, Martha Clark remarried on 17 April 1858, a little over a year after John Clark's death. Her new husband was a William McIntosh.[302] Very shortly prior to the marriage, and no doubt in order to protect her entitlement to *Gooparl*, Martha arranged for the property to be vested in two trustees, T. P. Stone and H. Hunter; with herself as the beneficiary of the trust. On 18 January 1862, and following Stone's death and Hunter's retirement, John Clark's younger brother, Richard Clark, and a James Campbell Grassie, of *Poon Boon* station north of Swan Hill, were appointed as replacement trustees.[303]

Martha McIntosh's second husband, William McIntosh, had been born in Nairn, Scotland, and was about 41 years old at the time of his marriage to Martha. A pastoralist from the Heathcote area at that time, McIntosh subsequently moved into *Gooparl* with his new wife and members of her family.[304]

Martha McIntosh's marriage to McIntosh proved to be a very unhappy one. McIntosh struck his wife on a number of occasions, inflicting injuries on her. Martha left him in January 1861. Soon afterwards, Richard Clark and James Grassie, as the trustees of the *Gooparl* trust, instituted an action in the Supreme Court of Victoria to secure the ejection of McIntosh from *Gooparl*. Their action was heard in Melbourne on 21 May 1862 before Mr. Justice Williams and a Special Jury of four men. George Higinbotham appeared for Clark and Grassie, with James Martley appearing for McIntosh. The Court ruled in favour of Clark and Grassie. McIntosh was ejected and Martha regained possession of *Gooparl*.[305] She lived in the property for the balance of her life.

At about the same time as Richard Clark and James Grassie launched their ejectment action against McIntosh, Martha filed a Petition in the Victorian Supreme Court at Melbourne by which she sought a decree of judicial separation from McIntosh on the grounds of cruelty

---

300 See *The Age*, Tuesday, 27 May 1862, p. 6.
301 See *The Argus*, Thursday, 22 May 1862, p. 5.
302 See *Victoria Marriages Register: William McIntosh and Martha Clark* (1858) (No. 2162/1858).
303 See *The Argus*, Thursday, 22 May 1862, p. 5.
304 See Frost, *op. cit.*, p. 35.
305 See *The Argus*, Thursday, 22 May 1862, p. 5.

and drunkenness. The proceeding was one of the first brought under section 5 of the newly-enacted *Divorce and Matrimonial Causes Act 1861* (Vic).[306]

Martha McIntosh's Petition was heard by Mr. Justice Chapman on 26 May 1862, with McIntosh contesting her entitlement to the decree she sought.[307] The following day, Mr. Justice Chapman found that the charge of cruelty made by Marsha against McIntosh had been substantiated to his satisfaction. He accordingly granted Martha her decree of judicial separation from McIntosh.[308]

The Death of Martha McIntosh

Martha McIntosh died on 21 March 1868.[309] She was subsequently buried under that name in John Clark's plot at the Melbourne General Cemetery.[310]

Martha McIntosh's Will and Codicil

Martha McIntosh left a Will executed by her on 6 January 1868, together with a Codicil to that Will executed on 19 March 1868. By her Will, she appointed her late husband's brother, Richard Clark, and James Grassie to be her executors and the trustees of her estate.[311] What Grassie's connection with Martha might have been is presently unknown. In any event, he renounced probate of the Will and Codicil on 14 April 1868.[312] In consequence of his renunciation, probate of the Will was granted to Richard Clark alone in the Supreme Court of Victoria on 30 April 1868.[313]

By Martha McIntosh's Will, her household provisions, together with her wines, spirits and other liquors, were left, subject to the exercise of her executors' discretion, to be consumed by those living in her former household. Martha further provided that her wearing apparel was to be divided, again at her executors' discretion, between her children, her sister, Jane Maiden, and the Latter's two daughters, Jane and Hannah Maiden.

The Will went on to provide that the residue of Martha's estate was to be held in trust by her trustees; firstly, to pay Martha's debts and her funeral and testamentary expenses; and secondly, to pay the income generated by the trust in equal shares to:

- Martha's sister, Jane Maiden;
- Jane Maiden's daughters, Jane and Hannah Maiden;

---

306 See *An Act to Amend the Law Relating to Divorce and Matrimonial Causes 1861* (Vic.) (25 Vict. No. 125) (https://tinyurl.com/tyy3xvp5) (at 10 March 2023).
307 See *The Age*, Tuesday, 27 May 1862, p. 6.
308 See *The Age*, Wednesday, 28 May 1862, p. 7. It may be that Martha sought a decree of judicial separation from McIntosh rather than a divorce decree because as an Anglican, she had a religious objection in principle to divorce.
309 See *Martha McIntyre's Will* (PROV, *VPRS* 7591/P0001, Unit 28B).
310 See footnotes 163 and 294, and their accompanying texts, above. See also photo 21 below.
311 See *Martha McIntyre's Will* (PROV, *VPRS* 7591/P0001, Unit 28B). See also footnote 163 above.
312 See *James Grassie's Renunciation of Probate* (PROV, *VPRS* 28/P0000, Unit 73).
313 See *Martha McIntyre's Will: Probate* (PROV, *VPRS* 28/P00001, Unit 15).

- Martha's daughters, Martha, Rebecca and Margaret Clark;
- Marth's grand-daughter, Lily Bull; and
- Martha's grandsons, Hebden and Harold Smith.

Upon the death of the last of these beneficiaries, the assets remaining in trust were to be gifted to the Melbourne Hospital.[314]

The daughters provided for by Martha McIntosh in her Will, Martha, Rebecca and Margaret Clark, were her youngest children. Each was unmarried at the time Martha executed her Will. She made no provision in that Will for her three older daughters, Mary Argyle, Elizabeth Smith and Jane Bull, who were all married, or for her son, Thomas Clark, who was then unmarried. Perhaps she thought that her married daughters would be adequately supported by their respective husbands, and that her son could look after himself.[315]

As can be seen above, Martha McIntosh made provision by her Will for a grand-daughter, Lily Bull, and for two grandsons, Hebden and Harold Smith.[316] However, she made no provision by it for Reginald, Charles or Stanley Argyle; the three sons of her eldest daughter, Mary Argyle. All three had been born prior to the Will's execution, Again, perhaps she thought that Mary's husband, Edward Argyle, could well support his three sons as well as his wife. Alternatively, Martha may have had "issues" with Mary Argyle.

It may be that Martha McIntosh anticipated that the provisions in her Will could lead to disputation within her family. In any event, a clause in the Will provided that any beneficiary under it who sought to dispute its provisions in any manner was to forfeit all entitlements provided by its terms.[317]

Two days prior to her death, on 19 March 1868, Martha McIntosh executed a Codicil to her Will. By this Codicil, Martha:
- left a legacy of £300 to her son, Thomas Clark;
- left two other legacies, of £100 each, to be used by her trustees as they saw fit for
- the maintenance and education of, respectively, a Janet Fortune, "now staying at my
- house", and a Alfonso Tierney; and
- included two of the three of her then married daughters, Mary Argyle and Jane Bull,
- in the cohort of persons entitled to equal shares in the income generated by the
- assets in the testamentary trust established by Martha under her Will.[318]

Who Janet Fortune and Alfonso Tierney were, and what their respective connections were with Martha McIntosh, remain mysteries. Also not know is the reason why Martha's

---

314 See *Martha McIntyre's Will* (PROV, VPRS 7591/P0001, Unit 228B).

315 It is also possible that Martha McIntosh bore a degree of animus towards her son, Thomas John Clark: see footnote 269 above.

316 See footnote 314 and its accompanying text above. As it turned out, Lily Bull died on or slightly prior to 13 January 1868: see *Victoria Deaths Register: Lily Bull* (1868) (No. 465/1868). She thus died after Martha McIntosh executed her Will, but before Martha herself died and before probate of Martha's Will was granted.

317 See *Martha McIntyre's Will* (PROV, VPRS 7591/P0001, Unit 28B).

318 *Ibid.*

other married daughter, Elizabeth Smith, continued after the Codicil to be excluded from any meaningful benefit from Martha's estate.

Unfortunately, there appears to be no record now extant of Martha McIntosh's assets and liabilities at the time of her death.

John and Martha Clark's Children: Mary Argyle

As mentioned above, John and Martha Clark's eldest child, Mary Clark, married Edward Argyle in 1852.[319] Following her marriage, Mary moved her abode for a few years periodically between homesteads located on her husband's *Duck Swamp* and *St. Agnes* squatting runs. However, during 1855, work began on a grand, two-storey stone house on the *St. Agnes* run. The completed building was given the name *Rock House*. As always intended, it thereafter became the Argyles' principal home.[320]

Edward Argyle proved to be a successful squatter and businessman. Over time, he secured part interests in a number of other pastoral runs. These included *Pental Island, Murrabit, Bael Bael, Tittybong, Long Lake, Gunbower, L'Albert, The Terricks, Gerahmin* and *Tragowell Plains*.[321]

In all Edward and Mary Argyle had five children. Reginald Ivon Argyle was born in 1859, Charles Alfred Argyle in 1862, Stanley Seymour Argyle in 1867, Thomas Cyril Willington Argyle in 1870 and Raymond Hubert Argyle in 1872.[322] However, only three survived to reach adulthood. Thomas Argyle died when only nine months old.[323] Raymond Argyle drowned in a dam at the age of two years.[324]

Mary Argyle's relationship with her husband broke down during the late 1860s and early 1870s. It would appear that their estrangement was largely the product of Edward Argyle's heavy drinking. Matters reached the stage where he repeatedly, and almost certainly wrongly, accused his wife of infidelity; asserting that she had committed adultery with many of his relatives, friends and associates.[325]

Edward Argyle died on 11 February 1875 following the rupture of a blood vessel in his stomach.[326] He left an estate valued in total at about £17,000.[327] His last Will, executed by him in 1873, patently reflected the bitterness he felt towards his widow. By it, he directed

---

319 See footnote 257 and its accompanying text above.
320 See Clarke and Argyle, *op. cit., p. 273*; *The Age*, Friday, 19 May 1972; and *Victorian Heritage Database Report – Rock House* (https://tinyurl.com/yacujut5) (at 11 March 2023). See also photos 22 and 23.
321 See Clarke and Argyle, *op. cit.*, pp. 315 and 333.
322 See Clarke and Argyle, *op. cit.*, pp. 334, 351, 359, and 366. See also "Clark, Mary (1836-1918)" online in the *Moore Considine Family Website* (https://tinyurl.com/58ntx5sc) (at 12 March 2023).
323 See Clarke and Argyle, *op. cit.*, p. 334.
324 See Clarke and Argyle, *op. cit.*, p. 345
325 See Clarke and Argyle. *op. cit.*, p. 333.
326 See Clarke and Argyle, *op. cit.*, pp. 336-339; and the *Bendigo Advertiser*, Saturday, 13 February 1875, p. 2
327 See *The Argus*, Tuesday, 7 October 1875, p. 6.

that all of his assets be sold, with the net proceeds to be held in trust for his surviving sons equally. Mary Argyle was left nothing.[328]

Mary unsuccessfully challenged the grant of probate of her late husband's Will on the ground that he had been insane at the time of the Will's execution. Her Application was heard by Mr. Justice Molesworth in the Supreme Court of Victoria on 4 October 1875. Notwithstanding that he reached a very negative view of Edward Argyle's drunken behaviour, and assessed Mary Argyle to have been blameless in the marriage, Mr. Justice Molesworth held that he was unable to infer that Edward Argyle had been insane when he executed his Will. He accordingly dismissed Mary's application.[329]

Mary Argyle appealed Mr. Justice Molesworth's decision. However, before her appeal was heard, a settlement appears to have been negotiated by which she retained an entitlement to remain living in *Rock House*, and possibly also secured an annuity to be paid to her from the testamentary trust fund established by her late husband.[330]

Mary Argyle lived on in *Rock House* with her unmarried younger sister, Rebecca Clark, until the latter's death in 1902. She then retired to a property she had acquired in Punt Road, South Yarra, where she died on 4 March 1918.[331]

Edward and Mary Argyle's three surviving children were all accomplished and successful men.

Reginald Argyle, the eldest, was educated at Mr. Hinsby's Collegiate School in Kyneton, and then as a boarder at Wesley College in Melbourne. A civil engineer by profession, he unsuccessfully tried his hand as a pastoralist in Queensland with his younger brother, Charles Argyle. He then played a prominent part in the founding of the Kyneton Butter Factory in 1891. It would seem that Reginald was fondly known by Kyneton locals as "roaring Reggie from Bleak Hill". He sat as a councillor on the Kyneton Shire Council from 1897 until 1901. He served as the Liberal Party member for the Victorian Legislative Assembly seat of Kyneton from November 1901 until May 1904, and then for the successor seat of Dalhousie from June 1904 until November 1914. During this period, Reginald Argyle was Government Whip and Secretary to the Cabinet. He died on 3 September 1936.[332]

Charles Argyle also attended Mr. Hinsby's Collegiate School in Kyneton before boarding at Wesley College in Melbourne. He qualified as a lawyer in England, returned to Victoria

---

328 See Clarke and Argyle, *op. cit.*, p. 341

329 See "In re Edward Argyle" in *The Argus*, Thursday, 7 October 1875, p. 6; and Clarke and Argyle, *op. cit.*, pp. 342-344. Of Edward Argyle, Mr. Justice Molesworth concluded:
 "Argyle was an extreme drunkard [and] suffered repeated attacks of *delirium tremens*. According to the evidence of several witnesses, of ample means of observation and unquestionable truth, when sober he was a reasonable, intelligent man, with considerable capacity for business, as appears by his having accumulated a fortune of about £17,000. When drunk he was like a raging maniac, applying the coarsest epithets to his wife as an adulteress with various men, and speaking of her children, sometimes one, sometimes another, as really those of other men....Argyle was most absurd in his charges...."
 See "In re Edward Elgar" in *The Argus*, Thursday, 1 October 1875, p. 6.

330 See Clarke and Argyle, *op. cit.*, p. 344.

331 See Clarke and Argyle, *op. cit.*, p. 348. See also footnote 342 and its accompanying text below.

332 See Parliament of Victoria, *Re-Member (Former Members) – Reginald Ivon Argyle* (https://tinyurl.com/2p88fdek) (at 12 March 2023); *The Argus*, Friday, 4 September 1936, p. 10; and the *Kilmore Free Press*, Thursday, 24 September 1936, p. 2.

and commenced practice as a solicitor in Tatura. Following the failure of the pastoral venture in Queensland he had embarked on with his older brother, Reginald Argyle, he moved to Western Australia for a time, where he continued to work as a solicitor. He then returned to Tatura. In 1909, he moved to work as a solicitor for Mallesons in Melbourne. Charles Argyle died on 20 July 1918.[333]

Like his two older brothers, Stanley Argyle was initially schooled at Mr. Hinsby's Collegiate School in Kyneton. However, unlike his brothers, he next attended Hawthorn Grammar School and then Brighton Grammar School; boarding in both cases. On leaving school, Stanley entered the Medical Faculty at Melbourne University. He graduated in 1890. After postgraduate studies in England, he returned to Victoria and established a general medical practice in Kew. In 1898, he founded the Willsmere Certified Milk Company; becoming its first Chairman of Directors.

Stanley Argyle was elected to the Kew City Council in 1898. In all, he served 12 years on the Council, and was Mayor of the City from 1903 until 1909. A well-read man, he was said to have possessed a photographic memory.

In about 1908, Stanley obtained an appointment as a specialist "medical electrician and skiagraphist" (a radiologist) at the Alfred Hospital in Melbourne. He became the Director of Radiology at that Hospital in 1924. Stanley was elected to the Council of the Victorian Branch of the British Medical Association in 1918; becoming its President in 1925.

During the First World War, Stanley served as a medical officer with the Australian forces in the Middle East. He returned to Australia in 1917 with the rank of Lieutenant-Colonel.

In 1920, Stanley Argyle won the seat of Toorak in the Victorian Legislative Assembly as an independent Nationalist. As a parliamentarian, he served as Minister for Health, Treasurer and Chief Secretary. In 1930, he was knighted for his services to medicine and the State of Victoria. Later in that year, he was elected as Leader of the Parliamentary Nationalist Party. Sir Stanley Argyle served as Premier of Victoria from 1932 until 1935. He was then Leader of the Opposition until his death on 24 November 1940.[334]

Numerous portraits and photos of Sir Stanley Argyle remain extant.[335] A bronze bust of Sir Stanley is also to be found in the Parliament of Victoria.[336]

---

333 See Clarke and Argyle, *op. cit.*, pp. 359-365.

334 See A. G. L. Shaw, "Argyle, Sir Stanley Seymour (1867-1940)" in *Australian Dictionary of Biography* (https://tinyurl.com/yf6ee7ej) (at 12 March 2023); Geoff Browne, "Stanley Argyle: The Incidental Premier" in Paul Strangio and Brian Costar, *The Victorian Premiers: 1856-2006* (2006), pp. 204-214; Clarke and Argyle, *op. cit.*, pp. 366-376; *The Argus*, Friday, 20 December 1901, p. 6; the *British Medical Journal*, Saturday, 7 December 1940, p. 813; and *The Argus*, Monday, 25 November 1940, p. 5.

335 See, for example, *National Portrait Gallery, Canberra – Stanley Argyle* (https://tinyurl.com/54muwavk) (at 15 March 2023); and *Brighton Grammar, Hall of Fame – Sir Stanley Argyle KGB* (https://tinyurl.com/3x34s4uy) (at 15 March 2023).

336 On 3 June 1992, *The Age* published a photo of retired Judge Michael Argyle, formerly of the Central Criminal Court in London (the "Old Bailey"), posing beside the bust of his cousin, Sir Stanley Argyle, in the Victorian Parliament: see *The Age*, Wednesday, 3 June 1992, p. 3; and *Wikipedia – Stanley Argyle* (https://tinyurl.com/3kxausmj) (at 15 March 2023). As a barrister, Michael Argyle appeared for Ronnie Biggs in the trial arising out of the Great Train Robbery. As a judge, he presided in the notorious Oz obscenity trial: see *Wikipedia – Michael Argyle (Judge)* (https://tinyurl.com/sbzcx57a) (at 15 March 2023). As their surnames indicate, Michael Argyle's relationship with Sir Stanley Argyle must be traced through their respective fathers.

In *The Victorian Premiers: 1856-2006*, Geoff Browne summed up Sir Stanley Argyle, the politician, thus:

> "The particular strengths that enabled Argyle the politician to endure and achieve were a high level of administrative competence; a great capacity for work; dogged self-belief, sometimes bordering on arrogance; and a certain mystique attaching to his role as a medical man in politics. This last quality was burnished by the only truly radical side to his character. In matters relating to health Argyle was a constant advocate of reform, including State intervention, if necessary."[337]

John and Martha Clark's Children: Elizabeth Smith, Thomas Clark, Jane Bull, Martha McGill, Rebecca Clark and Margaret Savage

John and Martha Clark's second daughter, Elizabeth Clark married Charles Smith in 1857. She had three children with the latter. Elizabeth Smith died in Prahran in 1899.[338]

The Clarks' next child and only son, Thomas John Clark, married Alexina Duncan in 1870. They moved to Nilma near Warragul in Victoria, where Thomas became a Director of the Bloomfield Butter Factory. Thomas an Alexina Clark had a total of seven children. Thomas died at Nilma in 1917.[339]

Jane Susanah Clark was the fourth of John and Martha Clarke's seven children. She married Frederick Bull in 1861. They also had seven children together. Jane died in New South Wales on 12 April 1924.[340]

The Clarks' next child, Martha Clark Jnr, married Oliver Armstrong in 1869. She had two children with the latter. Following Oliver Armstrong's death, Martha married James McGill in 1886. They had no issue together. Martha McGill died on 19 February 1921 in South Yarra.[341]

John and Martha Clark's penultimate child, Rebecca Clark, remained a spinster all her life. She died at Kyneton on 26 August 1902.[342]

---

337 See Browne, *op. cit.*, p. 205.
338 See "Clark, Elizabeth (1837-1899)" online in the *Moore Considine Family Website* (https://tinyurl.com/58ntx5sc) (at 15 March 2023).
339 See "Clark, Thomas J. (1839-1917)" online in the *Moore Considine Family Website* (https://tinyurl.com/58ntx5sc) (at 15 March 2023).
340 See "Clark, Jane S. (1940-1924)" online in the *Moore Considine Family Website* (https://tinyurl.com/58ntx5sc) (at 15 March 2023).
341 See "Clark, Martha (1843-1921)" online in the *Moore Considine Family Website* (https://tinyurl.com/58ntx5sc) (at 15 March 2023).
342 See "Clark, Rebecca (1844-1902)" online in the *Moore Considine Family Website* (https://tinyurl.com/58ntx5sc) (15 March 2023). See also footnote 331 and its accompanying text above.

The Clarks' youngest child, Margaret Emily Jane Victoria Clark, married William Savage in 1869. The Savages had a total of nine children together. Margaret Savage died in Clifton Hill on 21 October 1908.[343]

---

[343] See "Clark, Margaret E. J. (1847-1908)" online in the *Moore Considine Family Website* (https://tinyurl.com/58ntx5sc) (at 15 March 2023).

6. The main entrance to "Northwood Park".

7. The Muse Restaurant, Mitchelton Winery.

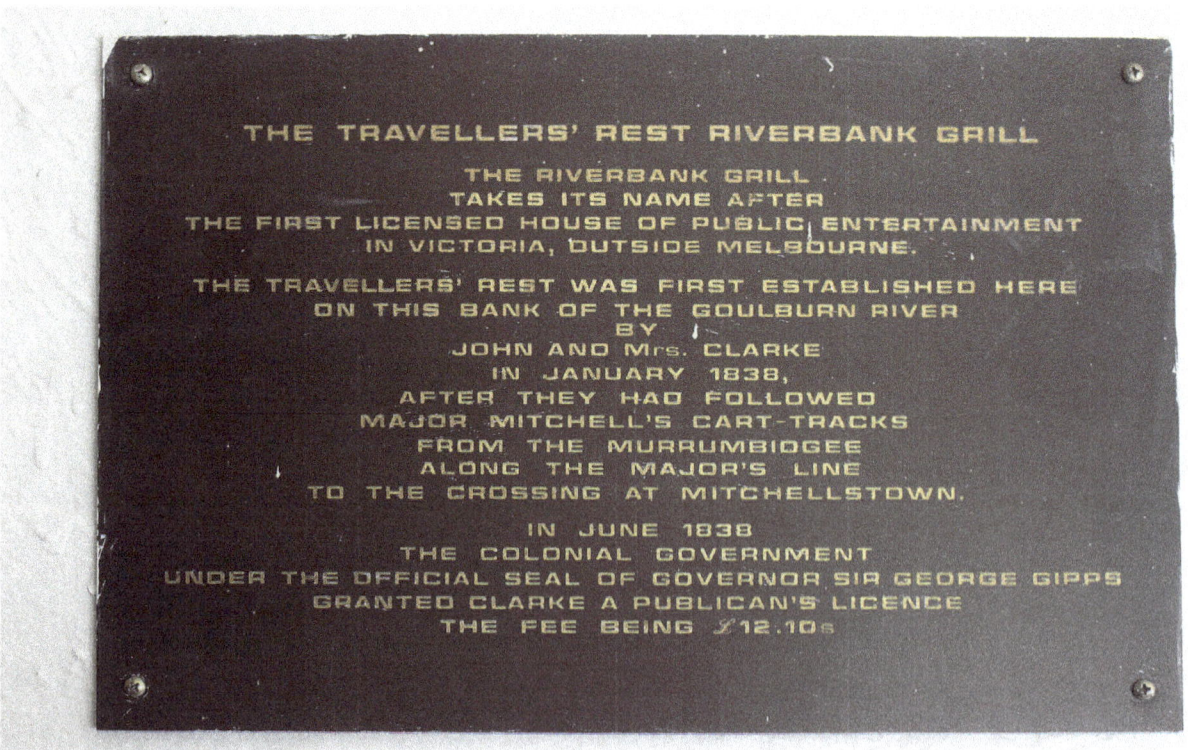

8. History plaque within the Muse Restaurant, Mitchelton Winery.

9. The approximate site of the Faithfull Massacre.

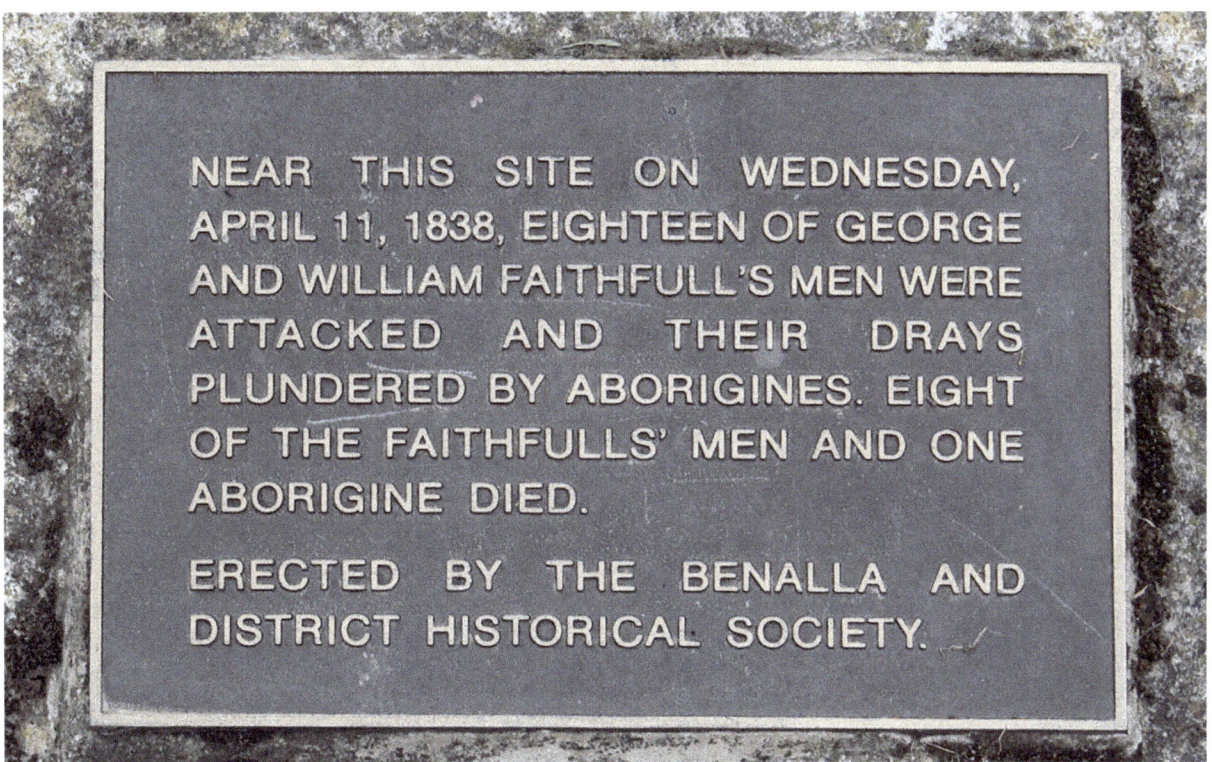

10. History plaque at the approximate site of the Faithfull Massacre.

11. The site of the first Robert Burns Inn.

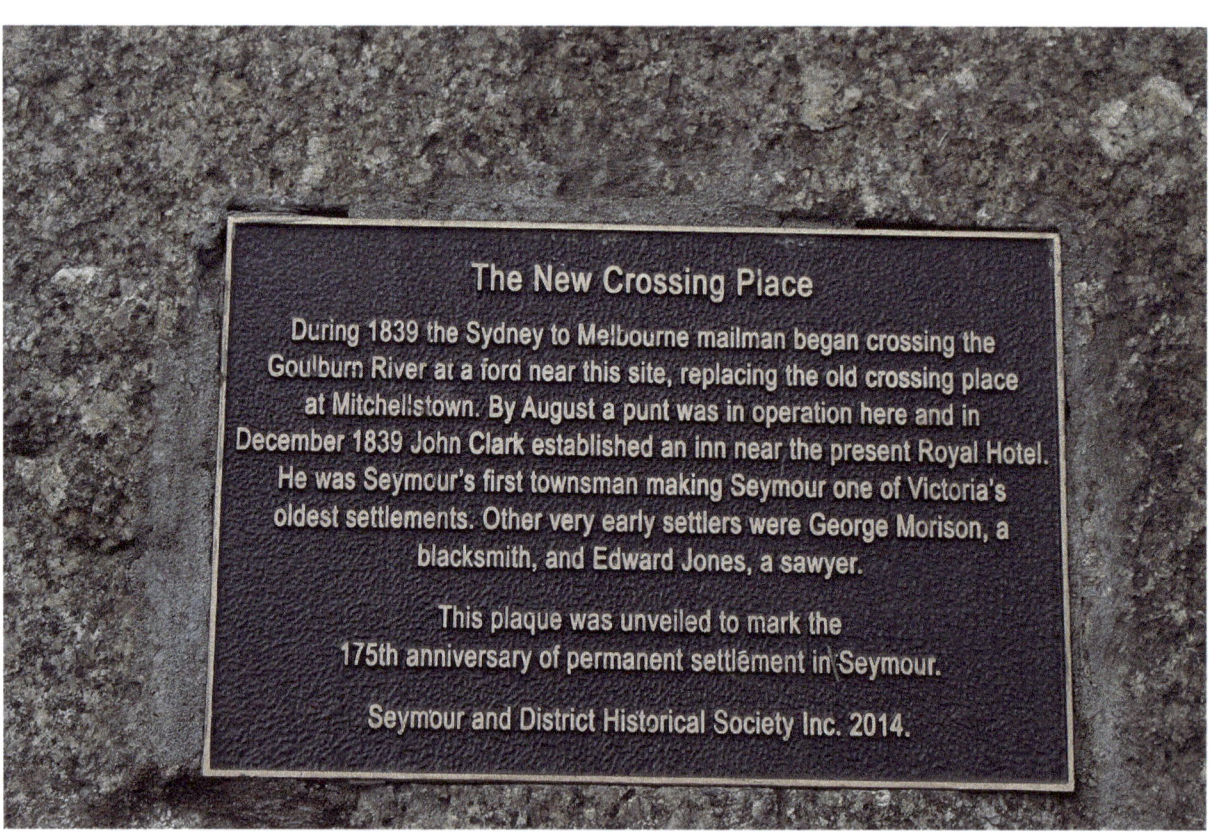

12. History plaque commemorating the first Robert Burns Inn.

13. The stables of the second Robert Burns Inn.

14. A front view of the Royal Hotel. The lower wing on the left of the photo is the second Robert Burns Inn.

15. A side view of the Royal Hotel. The lower two-storey rendered wing at the left of the photo is the second Robert Burns Inn.

16. The likely site of John Clark's Moranding homestead, looking north-east.

17. *"Moody's Pub" by Russell Drysdale.*

18. *The Gooparl homestead in the 1890s, looking north.*

19. The site of the Gooparl homestead in February 2016.

20. A panoramic view of John Clark's grave, Melbourne General Cemetery.

21. A close-up view of the inscription on John Clark's grave monument.

22. The entrance of the driveway leading to the Rock House homestead.

23. A front view of the Rock House homestead.

WILLIAM HENRY CLARK

William Clark's Marriage to Elizabeth Harris

There is a measure of controversy surrounding the year of William Clark's first arrival in the Port Phillip District: 1838 or 1839. What is certain, however, is that in an Anglican service conducted by the Reverend Charles Brigstocke on 22 June 1839 at Bowning near Yass, William married Elizabeth Harris. William was 29 years old at the time of the marriage. Elizabeth was around 15 years of age.[344]

Elizabeth Harris was likely born in 1824 in, or in close proximity to, the village of Mayfield in East Sussex.[345] She was the second child and eldest daughter of Jonathan Harris and Elizabeth Harris Snr (née Baker). The two senior Harrises were married on 17 November 1821 in St. Dunstan's Church, Mayfield.[346]

Elizabeth Harris Jnr's early years were marked by hardship and dislocation. At the time of her birth, her father worked as an agricultural labourer. However, at or around that time, he was also reputed to be a thief.[347] Whatever be the truth of that contention, Jonathan Harris was in fact arrested in Brighton on 21 February 1825 with his mother and a brother. Jonathan, his brother and two other men were subsequently charged with breaking and entering the house of Thomas Cobham at Uckfield on 18 or 19 February 1825 and stealing goods therefrom.[348]

At the Lent Assizes in Horsham, Jonathan Harris was convicted on 23 March 1825 of the breaking and entering charge and sentenced to death. However, this death sentence was

---

[344] See *New South Wales Marriages Register: William Clark and Elizabeth Harris* (1839) (Vol. 23B, No. 420).

[345] It would seem that Elizabeth Harris was never baptised. She may have been born in Mayfield or in either of the surrounding villages of Crowsborough or Hadlow Down: see Garry Moore, *A Problematic Patriarch: Jonathan Harris* (2022), p. 9; and *WikiTree – Elizabeth (Harris) Clark (abt. 1823-1888)* (https://tinyurl.com/32bxvz7p) (at 13 March 2023).

[346] See Family Search: *Parish Registers and Poor Law Records for Mayfield – Jonathan Harris and Elizabeth Baker* (https://tinyurl.com/y3qdt88p) (at 13 February 2023).

[347] On 3 March 1825, the *Brighton Gazette* reported that Jonathan Harris had previously been in gaol for "fowl-stealing": see the *Brighton Gazette*, Thursday, 3 March 1825, p. 3. Particulars of this alleged offence and consequent imprisonment have not as yet been ascertained.

[348] See the *Sussex Advertiser*, Monday, 28 February 1825, p. 3; and the *Brighton Gazette*, Thursday, 3 March 1825, p. 3.

subsequently commuted to transportation "for Life Beyond the Seas".[349] After a period of some three and a half months incarcerated in a prison hulk moored in Portsmouth Harbour, Jonathan was conveyed on the *Marquis of Hastings* from Portsmouth to Port Jackson in New South Wales. He landed at Sydney on 9 January 1826 and was promptly assigned to work for Charles Tompson on an estate at Marsden Park.[350]

Jonathan Harris' arrest, sentence and transportation for life in Australia would have left his wife and family devastated and bereft. How they managed the loss of his support is not now known. It may be that Elizabeth's parents or one of her siblings took them in or otherwise assisted them. Alternatively, they may have been forced to seek refuge and sustenance in a local workhouse. Making matters worse, Elizabeth Harris Snr was pregnant at the time of her husband's arrest.

It would seem that Jonathan Harris initially bloomed in New South Wales. In 1828, and with the active support of Charles Tompson, he successfully petitioned Governor Ralph Darling of New South Wales and the Colonial Office in London for permission to have his wife and children join him at Government expense in the Colony.[351] They finally arrived on 11 March 1831 in Sydney on board the *Kains,* and were subsequently united with Jonathan.[352]

Jonathan Harris moved with his growing family, including Elizabeth Harris Jnr, from Marsden Park to the Parramatta District towards the end of 1831.[353] From there, they moved to the Goulburn Plains in 1834 or 1835; where Jonathan both worked for, and rented land from, William Shelley.[354]

On 30 March 1836, tragedy struck the Harris family when Elizabeth Harris Snr was killed after the cart she was travelling in overturned and crushed her.[355] Following his wife's death, Jonathan Harris no doubt relied to a very significant extent on Elizabeth Harris Jnr in caring for the younger Harris children.

It is not known how William Clark met Elizabeth Harris Jnr. Whilst working for William Shelley on the Goulburn Plains and also at Shelley's other cattle runs on the Tumut River, Jonathan Harris probably got to know the members of the Clark family as he travelled in the region of nearby Yass. Indeed, Jonathan Harris and William Clark may have had something

---

349   See Ancestry: *Harris Jonathan – Trial Manuscript Notes* (https://tinyurl.com/y8aozndw) (at 13 March 2023); Ancestry: *England and Wales, Criminal Registers, 1791-1892 – Jonathan Harris* (https://tinyurl.com/yxolnu2c) (at 13 March 2023); and the *Sussex Advertiser*, Monday, 28 March 1825, p. 3.

350   See Ancestry: *United Kingdom, Prison Hulk Registers and Letter Books, 1802-1849 for Jonathan Harris* (https://tinyurl.com/y2jqssch) (at 13 March 2023); the *Sydney Gazette and New South Wales Advertiser*, Thursday, 12 January 1826, p. 3; and *New South Wales Convict Indents, 1788-1842 for Jonathan Harris* (https://tinyurl.com/y5jonf9h) and (https://tinyurl.com/y68vy9dc) (both at 13 March 2023).

351   See Ancestry: *Harris, Jonathan 1800-1891 & Baker, Elizabeth 1802-1836 – Petition to Come to Colony* (State Records New South Wales: Colonial Secretary's Correspondence, 26/6419 – 4/1989) (Image 3 of 3) (https://tinyurl.com/be3se3fh) (at 13 March 2023).

352   See *Convict Records – Kains Convict Ship* (https://tinyurl.com/y5l4eusa) (at 13 March 2023).

353   See Ancestry: *Approved Ticket of Exemption Location Transfer Application for Jonathan Harris, September 1831* (https://tinyurl.com/ybn6mmhr) (at 13 March 2023); and Ancestry: *Exemption from Government Labour for Jonathan Harris, 1832* (https://tinyurl.com/y6t2pwyh) (at 13 March 2023).

354   See Ancestry: *St. John's Church, Parramatta, Baptism Record for George Jarvis Harris* (https://tinyurl.com/y6c63h7t) (at 13 March 2023); and Ancestry: *Letter from Edmund Lockyer to the Colonial Secretary dated 28 December 1842* ("the Lockyer Letter") (https://tinyurl.com/y7k5dqxp) (at 13 March 2023).

355   See the *Sydney Gazette and New South Wales Advertiser*, Saturday, 2 April 1836, p. 2.

in common which drew them and their respective families together. Like William and the latter's older brother, John Clark, Jonathan Harris was suspected by local authorities of "sly grog selling".[356]

Jonathan's life following his eldest daughter's marriage to William Clark remained an eventful one. He married twice more and, in all, fathered a total of 17 children.[357]

In August 1842, Jonathan Harris was arrested for robbing a shepherd, Alfred King, of £47.[358] On 10 September 1842, he was convicted of the robbery at the Parramatta Quarter Sessions sittings and sentenced to be transported to Van Diemen's Land for 15 years.[359] In all, Jonathan Harris spent around 14 years in Van Diemen's Land; returning to the mainland with his third wife in about 1856 or 1857.[360]

Arriving on the Ovens River

In *Worthy of Mention*, the anonymous author claimed that William Clark's father, John Clark Snr, gave him 100 sovereigns, a wagonette and livestock, and advised him to travel south to the Port Phillip District. The author went on to assert that that William and his new wife Elizabeth spent some time in the tiny settlement of Albury before travelling on to the Ovens River.[361] If William did first arrive in the Port Phillip District in company with Elizabeth, this would necessarily put the date of that arrival in the second half of 1839.[362]

However, a number of other authorities have William Clark arriving on the Ovens River, and then taking up a run on its left bank, in 1838. Of these authorities, perhaps the most authoritative is Ralph Billis and Alfred Kenyon's historical survey of Victorian squatting runs, *Pastoral Pioneers*.[363]

It should also be noted that on crossing the Ovens River on 16 April 1839, Lady Jane Franklin, on her way overland from Melbourne to Sydney, noted in her diary on that day:

> "Coming to Ovens, saw Rattray's unfinished hut – [Rattray] was tipsy at Clarke's when we were there – is said to sell grog here, but has no licence – 2 poles for milking

---

356   See the *Lockyer Letter* (https://tinyurl.com/y7k5dqxp) (at 15 March 2023).

357   See Moore, *op. cit.*, passim.

358   See the *Australasian Chronicle*, Tuesday, 23 August 1842, p. 2.

359   See Ancestry: *Parramatta Quarter Sessions Trial Register for 1842 – Jonathan Harris* (https://tinyurl.com/y835fbny) (at 15 March 2023).

360   See the *Sydney Morning Herald*, Tuesday, 6 October 1891, p. 5; and the *North Eastern Ensign*, Friday, 16 March 1934, p. 3.

361   See *Worthy of Mention*, p. 14. The anonymous author of this work cited no authority for his or her account of John Clark Snr's asserted advice and gifts to his departing son and daughter-in-law. The account seems most unlikely. In the first place, William almost certainly did not need, or rely on, his father's advice before moving to the Port Phillip District: see footnote 86 and its accompanying text above. In the second place, by the late 1830s, William Clark probably earned more than, and had accumulated as many or more assets as, his father: see footnotes 71 and 72, and their accompanying texts, above. See also the *Wangaratta Chronicle*, Monday, 4 January 1893, p. 21.

362   See footnote 344 and its accompanying text above. It might also be observed that the author of *Worthy of* Mention, in apparent ignorance of the date of William and Elizabeth's marriage, has them arriving together at the Ovens River in 1838: see *Worthy of Mention*: p. 14. See also W. H. Edwards, "Early Wangaratta": (1920) 8(1) *The Victorian Historical Magazine* 38.

363   See Billis and Kenyon, *Pastoral Pioneers*, pp. 46 and 262. See also Whittaker, *op. cit.*, p. 23; and O'Callaghan, *op. cit.*, p. 4.

cows. Determined to cross the Ovens at once – a herd of 40 to 50 cattle or so with 2 stock keeper belonging to Mr. Docker 5 miles off were down into the river before us.... Descended the bad bank of the Ovens where only 2 or 3 feet of water; were told we should only find water holes, but it had risen by rain, embarked on the other side."[364]

The reference to "Clarke's" in Lady Franklin's diary entry strongly suggests that William Clark had already constructed a rough hut of some sort at the Ovens River by the time of Lady Franklin's crossing; the latter at a time prior to William Clark's marriage to his wife at Bowning and his subsequent return to the Port Phillip District.

Given the weight of authority, and Elizabeth Harris' age at the time of her marriage to William Clark, it appears highly likely that William in fact travelled down to the Ovens River and established his run there in 1838; returning north across the Murray River the following year to marry Elizabeth, and to bring her south to his Ovens River run.

If William Clark did establish his run on the Ovens River in 1838, it is conceivable that he may have accompanied his elder Brother, John Clark Jnr, down from the Yass Plains. However, this seems unlikely as neither Edward John Eyre nor John Conway Bourke, who each travelled overland between Melbourne and the Murray River shortly after the time of John Clark's arrival at the Goulburn River in January 1838, made any mention in their accounts of their journeys of William Clark's presence on the Ovens River. Accordingly, it seems probable that William first arrived in the Port Phillip District sometime later in 1838 after John Clark had already settled on the Goulburn River.

Settling on the Ovens River

William Clark was not the first European to occupy a squatting run in the area of present day Wangaratta. The *Tarawingi* run was taken up by William Bowman in 1837. George Faithfull and William Pitt Faithfull briefly settled on *Bontharambo* in February 1838 before moving upstream along the Ovens River to take up the *Oxley Plains* run. At about the same time as William Clark took up his run, Dr George Mackay settled on *Myrrhee* and later on *Warouley*, Joseph Docker settled on the abandoned *Bontharambo* run and David Reid occupied the *Carrargarmungee* run.[365]

The nature of William Clark's title to his lands, like those of John Clark and Richard Clark to their lands respectively, changed over time. In 1825, the Secretary of State for the Colonies in London, Lord Bathurst, instructed Governor Brisbane of New South Wales to divide the settled lands in the Colony into surveyed counties. On 14 October 1829, Brisbane's successor, Governor Darling, proclaimed the division of the settled regions of New South Wales into

---

364 See *Lady Franklin's Diaries*; diary from 3 April to 20 April 1839, p. 52.
365 See John Faithfull and Jim Lewis, *From 16,000 to 5* (2003, 2nd ed.), p. 17; and *Worthy of Mention*, p. 2.

19 counties centred around Sydney. Settlement beyond the bounds of these counties (the *"Limits of Location"*) was prohibited.[366]

Notwithstanding Governor Darling's Proclamation, squatters quickly moved with their herds and flocks to the north, west and south to occupy lands beyond the *Limits of Location*.[367] Initially these squatters occupied their runs illegally as trespassers. However, in late 1836, squatters were permitted by law to occupy lands beyond the *Limits of Location* upon payment of a flat annual licence fee £10, irrespective of the sizes of their runs.[368]

According to Ralph Billis and Alfred Kenyon, the run taken up by William Clark on the Ovens River in 1838 was in its earliest days known as the *Wangaratta* run, or alternatively as the *Junction* run.[369] The northern boundary of the original run extended south-west in a straight line from the Ovens River, commencing about 2.5 km to the south-east of the current Warby Tower Road and continuing across the Warby Range to a point about 3 km to the south-east of present day Thoona and near to the current junction of the Glenrowan – Boweya Road with Sayers Road. The western boundary ran roughly south from here in a jagged line to a point just south of the current Taminick Gap Road, From there, the boundary ran in an east-south-easterly direction, re-crossing the Warby Range some 3 km north of present day Glenrowan, to a point about 3 km north-east of the latter. The boundary then ran roughly north and then to the north-east until it met the Ovens River just downstream of the latter's junction with the King River. The eastern boundary of the run was, of course, the Ovens River itself.[370]

William Clark's original run covered approximately 39,000 acres. It encompassed the greater part of the southern Warby Range(then known as Futters Range), together with most of what was later to become the township of Wangaratta to the west of the Ovens River. It seems likely that William would have immediately stocked his new run with cattle and/or sheep driven down from across the Murray River. No doubt when he returned north across that River to marry Elizabeth Harris, , he would have left the care of his run and his stock in the hands of a man or men hired by him for that purpose.[371]

---

366 See C. J. King, *An Outline of Closer Settlement in New South Wales: Part 1, The Sequence of Land Laws 1788-1956* (1957), p. 40; and Thomas Perry, *Australia's First Frontier: The Spread of Settlement in New South Wales 1788-1829* (1957), Appendix 1.

367 In a dispatch dated 19 December 1840 from Governor Gipps of New South Wales to Lord John Russell, the Secretary of State for the Colonies, the Governor observed:
"As well might it be attempted to confine the Arabs of the desert within a circle, traced upon their sands, as to confine the Graziers or Wool-growers of New South Wales within any bounds that can possibly be assigned to them…"
See *Historical Records of Australia* ("*HRA*"), Ser.1, Vol. 21, p. 127.Revealing his disagreement with the reasoning behind the *Limits of Location*, Gipps went on to say:
"and as certainly as the Arabs would be starved, so also would the flocks and herds of New South Wales, if they were so confined, and the prosperity of the Country be at an end."
Ibid.

368 See *An Act to Restrain the Unauthorised Occupation of Crown Lands 1836* (NSW) (7 Wm. 4 No. 4) (https://tinyurl.com/2zrntu8p) (at 15 March 2023); and the "Crown Lands Proclamation 1836" in *New South Wales Government Gazette No. 242*, 5 October 1836, p. 745.

369 See Billis and Kenyon, *Pastoral Pioneers*, p. 262. The junction which gave the run one of its early names was undoubtedly the nearby junction of the Ovens and King Rivers.

370 See Faithfull and Lewis, *op. cit.*, p. 19. See also Squatting Runs Map No. 6 below.

371 In her Blog *Life on Spring Creek*, Jacqui Durrant has remarked that:
"It should be obvious that none of the 'pioneers' who 'settled' North East Victoria (the 'squatters' who took out licenses to 'depasture flocks and herds' on Crown Lands, establishing the first pastoral stations of the region) did so single-

First Years at Wangaratta

At the time William Clark first settled on its bank, much of the Ovens River would have reflected the fact that the River then largely ran free from the deleterious effects of European occupation. In 1842, James Demarr, who crossed the Ovens a little upstream of what was to become Wangaratta, described it in the following terms:

> "In due time we reached the Ovens River, which, being a comparatively small and shallow stream, compared with the Murray, we crossed without difficulty. I remember that the banks of the Ovens consisted of thick shrubs, in which disported themselves, great numbers of bell-birds, and occasionally a coachman-bird was to be heard.
> The bell-bird, has a note like the tinkling of small bells; and the coachman-bird, a note like the crack of a whip. I had never, to my recollection, heard these birds before, but frequently after this time, I have heard with delight the bell-bird's note, always a pleasant sound to thirsty travellers, for where the bell-bird is, there is sure to be water."[372]

However, William Clark was not the first European to settle on the banks of the Ovens River in the Wangaratta region near to that River's junction with the King River. The first white man to build on the site of the future Wangaratta township would seem to have been Thomas Rattray. It would appear that in about March 1838, Rattray constructed a rough bush hut some 45 metres inland of the left bank of the Ovens and a short distance downstream from the junction of the two Rivers. He used this hut to accommodate overlanders crossing the Ovens River. He constructed another hut nearby and used it as a store. In addition to accommodating overlanders, Rattray seemingly used his premises as an unlicensed "sly grog" shop.[373]

Rattray further attached a cable to sturdy trees on either side of the Ovens River in the immediate vicinity of his huts, secured a punt by a moving rope to the cable and used the punt to ferry overlanders and others across the river for a fee.[374] The punt was probably a

---

handedly.... They not only had to establish head-stations and out-stations from which stock could be managed, but do so while simultaneously dispossessing the original inhabitants. Such a feat could only be managed with the assistance of a labour force. Each station commonly had a manager or overseer, and various stockmen, shepherds, bullock drivers, and sometimes their wives (who worked as hut-keepers)."

See Jacqui Durrant, *Life on Spring Creek – Don't Mention the 'C' Word*, Tuesday, 8 January 2019 (https://tinyurl.com/mv278p2m) (at 21 March 2023). That said, nothing now appears to known as to how William Clark managed his run or who he may have employed for that purpose. In 1929, *The Age* noted with respect to squatters during this period:
"Persons holding runs were supposed to have sufficient stock to occupy them, but many of the pioneers did very much as they liked."
See *The Age*, Saturday, 3 August 1929, p. 3.

372 See James Demarr, *Adventures in Australia Fifty Years Ago* (1893), p. 78. The coachman-bird referred to by Demarr was very likely the bird now commonly known as the eastern whipbird (Psophodes olivaceus): see *Wikipedia – Eastern Whipbird* (https://tinyurl.com/mr2ffpf4) (at 21 March 2023).

373 See Whittaker, *op. cit.*, p. 28; and *Worthy of Mention*, pp 4-5. It seems clear that Rattray was himself partial to a tipple: see footnote 364 and the accompanying text above.

374 J. C. Byrne, who crossed the Ovens River with others in Rattray's punt, observed of his crossing:
"At the time, the river was swollen with rain and the passage was no easy matter. It was effected by means of a small punt made fast to, and traversing on, a cable which was attached to a tree on either bank. One by one, each rider entered

profitable venture for Rattray. Assistant Surveyor Thomas Townsend crossed on it in early September 1839 and wrote of being aggrieved at being charged £1 for the privilege.[375]

William Clark almost certainly returned with his new bride to his squatting run on the Ovens River at some time between late June and early October 1839. During October of that year, he purchased from Rattray the latter's premises and punt. Rattray left the district for parts north very shortly after the sale. It is not presently known what William paid for the premises, but it has been asserted that he paid Rattray 20 sovereigns for the punt.[376]

Soon after acquiring Rattray's premises and punt, William Clark saw to the construction of a new building to house both Elizabeth and himself, and also to provide accommodation at a fee for travellers. He apparently constructed the new building in close proximity to the huts built by Rattray. Years later, one of William and Elizabeth's daughters, Charlotte Sophia Cusack (née Clark), described the construction of the new building as follows:

> "Father built a place of split slabs, 3 rooms in a line, and the roof was of bark; he was afraid to put windows in for fear of the blacks, so he had slits cut in the slabs about 1½ inches wide, and then put the bark well over the walls; the doors were of hand-sawn boards and the fastenings were strong wooden bars."[377]

There is very little recorded with respect to William Clark and his immediate family's relations with the original custodians of the land on which they settled – the Pangerong Aborigines. Whether William had real reason to fear the local blacks is not now known. There is no record of any large scale confrontation between whites and blacks in and around the little group of buildings constructed by the Europeans on the bank of the Ovens River. However, unreported confrontations could well have occurred.[378]

---

the punt, and leading his horse, swam him with the punt, supporting his head with a collar above the water."
  See J. C. Byrne, *Wanderings in the British Colonies from 1835 to 1847* (1848), Vol. 1, pp. 170-171. See also Whittaker, *op. cit.*, pp. 28-29; *Worthy of Mention*, p. 4; and photo 24 below.

375 Rattray added insult to financial injury by not permitting Townsend to load his dray onto the punt. The dray had to be towed across the River: see *Worthy of Mention*, p. 5. See also O'Callaghan, *op. cit.*, pp. 2-3.

376 See *Worthy of Mention*, p. 14.

377 See Whittaker, *op. cit.*, p. 29.

378 According to James Demarr, who crossed the Ovens River a little upstream of present day Wangaratta in 1842:
  "Conflicts with the blacks were common enough at this time, but the blacks were never numerous....
  [T]he white men had been flowing into this newly-discovered country with their flocks and herds from the older colonies of New South Wales and Van Diemen's Land, during the last four or five years, and many of the men they brought with them were the scum of the earth, so that collisions with the blacks were inevitable.
  The blacks were driven away from their ancestral possessions, their hunting grounds taken possession of, their game either destroyed or driven away, and they themselves driven back into mountain fastnesses; the consequence was, the blacks sought every opportunity of revenge, killing the solitary shepherd and stockman whenever they had the opportunity of doing so, and scattering, and partly destroying, the flocks and herds, as I have described like occurrences on the Devil's river. The settlers retaliated in their own way, and old colonists know what that means. Their superiority in their horses and their arms, as might be expected, were all in their favour, and there were no Government regulations to check these irregular proceedings.
  Many of the settlers were well disposed towards the blacks, and their were men also like-minded, but the ruffian element mixed up with them, brought on conflicts with the blacks which the kindly-disposed were powerless to prevent, and when these conflicts came, individual self-preservation was the first thought of all."
See Demarr, *op. cit.*, p. 132. "Devils River" is an area lying to the east of present day Alexandria and on the western side of Lake Eildon. See also letter from Edward Bell to Lieutenant Governor Latrobe dated 12 August 1853 in Bride, *op. cit.*, pp. 296-297; and footnote 605 and its accompanying text below.

There is, however, one recorded incident of confrontation between William Clark and a local Aborigine. A currently unattributed and unsourced family typescript entitled *William Henry Clark: Pioneer and Settler Wangaratta ("First Known as "Ovens Crossing")* ("the *Family Typescript*") states with respect to William the following:

> "He knew the advantage of maintaining good relationships with the Aboriginals who then lived & roamed the district, and provided them with meat at times. Later at his Homestead an aboriginal woman was employed to care for the children. Her husband became disturbed that his wife spent more time at the house than his own camp, & wearing only his spear he arrived at "The One Mile" to remonstrate with her and anyone else who was willing to do battle. The women were terrified & when Clark arrived he saw on the kitchen range a grid iron, having just been used and still very hot. It proved a most effective weapon when applied to the behind of the black fellow who of course left at once."[379]

The businesses acquired by William Clark from Rattray prospered. In 1843, William perceived the need to construct a larger and more advanced accommodation building. This was built on the site of the later *Sydney Hotel* (now the Wangaratta RSL building). Charlotte Cusack (née Clark) described the erection of the new structure in the following terms:

> "The second house was on the corner of Ovens and Templeton Streets. It was built with five rooms each way, of split slabs and had a shingle roof, a verandah, skillions at the back, with wooden shutters at the window openings. There was glass only in the front, seven inches wide and ten inches long. The doors were made of lighter wood but of boards, not of panels. Father called this the *Hope Inn*."[380]

The Final Years of John Clark Senior and Elizabeth Clark Senior

It might be recalled that by no later than 20 August 1839, John Clark Snr and Elizabeth Clark had left the Yass Plains and joined their eldest son, John Clark Jnr, at his Goulburn River establishment.[381] How long they remained on the Goulburn River is not now known. However, it would seem that at some stage in the early to mid 1840s, they moved from the Goulburn to the Ovens River to see out their days either with, or in close proximity to, their second son, William Clark. What precipitated this move is also unknown.

John Clark Snr died at Wangaratta on 10 November 1848 at the age of 62 years.[382] His

---

[379] The incident is recorded on the first page of the *Family Transcript*; a copy of which is in the possession of the author. If, in fact, the incident did occur, it would likely have happened in the 1860s after the Clarks had moved to a home near to the One Mile Creek.
[380] See Whittaker, *op. cit.*, p. 29.
[381] See footnotes 136, 137 and 138, and their accompanying texts, above.
[382] See the *Moore Considine Family Website* (https://tinyurl.com/58ntx5sc) (at 27 March 2023)..

wife, Elizabeth Clark, followed him to the grave six months later; dying on 20 April 1849.[383] It is likely that each was initially buried on a site on Ovens Street, Wangaratta which was subsequently the location of the municipal market yards. However, following the opening of the current Wangaratta Cemetery in 1851, their bodies were apparently exhumed and were among the first to be interred in the new graveyard.[384]

Pastoral Contraction and Expansion

In addition to managing the *Hope Inn* and his punt business, William Clark continued to pursue his pastoral interests. He was required to do so in a changing legislative and regulatory environment.

In August 1844, Governor Gipps of new South Wales, in an effort to constrain squatting in the Colony, issued an Order-in-Council requiring separate licences for each squatting run occupied by a squatter; setting a maximum run size of 20 square miles (12,800 acres) and mandating that no single run could carry more than 4,000 sheep or 500 head of cattle.[385]

In August 1844, William Clark divided his squatting run in two along a line commencing in the north near the junction of the current Adams and Wangaratta – Devenish Roads, and then extending south along the eastern foothills of the Warby Range to the southern boundary of the run.[386] The western section, covering approximately 23,000 acres, was acquired by Benjamin Warby and variously called the *Taminick* or *Punkard's Island* run.[387] It is not now known whether William received any financial compensation from Warby by reason of the division. However, given the former's acute business acumen (later amply evidenced), it seems likely that William would have received some payment from Warby.

William Clark retained the eastern portion of his original run. At around 16,000 acres, it was smaller than the western section. But whereas a substantial proportion of the latter encompassed the steep, wooded hills of the southern Warby Range, the eastern section retained by William extended along the richer and more open flat lands fronting the Ovens River. This eastern section gained and retained the name *Ovens Crossing Place*; a name which it shared with the nascent settlement on the River which later was to become Wangaratta.[388]

It may be that the division of William Clark's original run was at least in part effected in response to Governor Gipps' Order-in-Council of April 1844. However, this seems unlikely

---

383 *Ibid.*

384 In 1919, it was observed of John Clark Snr and Elizabeth Clark Snr in an article published in the *Yackandandah Times* that following their respective deaths:
"their burial ground was the site of the present market yards, but the bodies were removed when the present cemetery was established and were amongst the first interments there."
See the *Yackandandah Times*, Thursday, 8 May 1919, p. 1. See also Whittaker, *op. cit.*, p. 98; and *Australian Cemeteries: Wangaratta Cemetery Trust* (https://tinyurl.com/y3lzvul8) (at 27 March 2023).

385 See S. C. McCulloch, "Gipps, Sir George (1791-1847)" in *Australian Dictionary of Biography* (https://tinyurl.com/2jurpx26) (at 28 March 2023); and Boyce, *op. cit.*, p. 155.

386 See Faithfull and Lewis, *op. cit.*, p. 19.

387 See Billis and Kenyon, *Pastoral Pioneers*, p. 262.

388 *Ibid.*

as both of the successor runs were larger in area than was ostensibly permitted under the Order. More likely, the division was the product of William's wish to divest himself of the burden of his less productive land, and thus ease his way to acquiring further, more well-watered property for pastoral purposes. This hypothesis appears to gain support from the fact that in 1845, William acquired a new squatting run fronting the King River upstream of his *Ovens Crossing Place* run.[389]

William initially called his new run *Whitefield*. However, it later became known as *Whitfield*.[390] The run, which covered 59,250 acres, extended southwards up the King River valley on the left bank of that River from a point adjacent to present day Edi to the current site of the hamlet of Cheshunt.[391] It covered the location of what is now the village of Whitfield.

Thomas and George Clark's Arrival At, and Lives In, Wangaratta

Thomas Kent Clark, the third son of John Clark Snr and the latter's wife, Elizabeth Clark, was discharged from the British Army on 1 November 1842, shortly after his father wrote to him at Newcastle-upon-Tyne from John Clark Jnr's establishment on the Goulburn River.[392] By 1845, Thomas was apparently at the small settlement of Ovens Crossing Place (soon to be renamed Wangaratta) where, on 3 June 1845, he was appointed pound keeper on the Ovens River by Henry Smythe, the Commissioner of Crown Lands for the Murray District, pursuant to section 12 of the *Crown Lands Unauthorised Occupation Act 1839* (NSW).[393]

On 1 December 1851, Thomas Clark was appointed a petty constable in the police contingent at Wangaratta following the drowning of his predecessor, Charles Potter.[394]

In 1855, Thomas married Elizabeth Watson in Melbourne. There was no issue from

---

389 See Billis and Kenyon, *Pastoral Pioneers*, p. 300.

390 *Ibid*. It has been asserted that William Clark originally named the new run *Whitefield* when he first inspected it in the winter of 1845 and found it to be heavily laden with snow: see *Worthy of Mention*, p. 14. Unfortunately, no authority has been cited for this assertion.

391 See Billis and Kenyon, *Pastoral Pioneers*, p. 300. See also G. J. Wilson, *Back To Whitfield: Whitfield Ramblings 1875-1975* (1975), p. 2; and Squatting Runs Map 6 below.

392 See UK National Archives, *Service records for Thomas Clark – Attestation Page* (RC3368989-67293f21-4eda-49ac-b739-3b95b1c69435/WO 69_8_001.jpg). See also footnote 52 above.

393 See *An Act Further to Restrain the Unauthorised Occupation of Crown Lands and to Provide the Means of Defraying the Expense of a Border Police 1839* (NSW) (2 Vic. No. 27) (https://tinyurl.com/yatb9lcj) (at 29 March 2023). Thomas Clark's appointment was advertised twice in the *Port Phillip Government Gazette*: No. 75 at p. 339, published on Wednesday, 11 June 1845 (see https://tinyurl.com/yb3ojoge) (at 29 March 2023); and No. 76 at p. 341, published on Wednesday, 18 June 1845 (see https://tinyurl.com/y8rxvvnn) (at 29 March 2023). See also *Lorraine Key's manuscript*, p. 12; and O'Callaghan, *op. cit.*, p. 6. At the time of Thomas' appointment as pound keeper on the Oven River, Commissioner Smythe was based in Seymour. Smythe may well have been friendly with Thomas' older brother, John Clark; and that friendship could have led directly to Thomas' appointment.

It is interesting to note that on his 1879 Death Certificate, Thomas Clark was recorded as having spent 30 years in the Australian colonies prior to his death. This would have placed his arrival in Australia in 1849. However, the death Certificate was witnessed by Thomas' nephew, William Clark of Bundalong. The latter may only have been roughly aware of the date of his uncle's arrival. Thomas Clark's Death Certificate also records that Thomas had spent "several years" in New Zealand. It does not go on to specify which years these were: see *Victoria Deaths Register: Thomas Clark* (1879) (No. 3289/1879).

394 See Whittaker, *op. cit.*, p. 49.

their union.³⁹⁵ Elizabeth died in Wangaratta on 26 November 1873 and was buried in the Wangaratta Cemetery.³⁹⁶

At some time prior to 1867, Thomas Clark was appointed as the Borough of Wangaratta's rate collector and lamplighter.³⁹⁷ There is, perhaps, some irony in the fact that Thomas was employed in Australia to light lamps, whilst his uncle, John Jenkins, had originally been sentenced to death in England, and then had his sentence commuted to transportation for life to Australia; in part for stealing a pair of snuffers – instruments used for trimming candle wicks.³⁹⁸

Thomas Clark died on 24 January 1879 aged 67 years old. He was buried in his late wife's grave in the Wangaratta Cemetery.³⁹⁹ The *Ovens and Murray Advertiser* had the following to say about his passing:

> "Mr. Thomas Clark, a very old resident of Wangaratta, was found dead in his bed early on last Friday morning. He occupied the position of rate collector and lamplighter for the borough of Wangaratta for over 12 years; he had not been altogether well for some time, but on Thursday night he lit the lamps, and the following morning he was discovered dead by his nephew. The deceased was brother to the late Mr. William Clark, one of the earliest, if not the very earliest, pioneers of Wangaratta; and as a rate collector of the borough he gained the esteem of nearly everyone in the place for doing his duties in an obliging and pleasant way...."⁴⁰⁰

Little appears to be known about John and Elizabeth Clark's fourth son, George Clark. It appears that at some now unknown time, he returned from New South Wales to live in the country of his birth, England; and that he had also worked for some unknown time as a sailor.⁴⁰¹ In about 1848, he seemingly arrived in Victoria. He settled in Wangaratta, where he worked as a labourer. He never married. George clearly had an excessive fondness for alcohol. He died on 9 June 1854, at the early age of 36 years, "in the bush near Wangaratta". The cause of his death recorded on his Death Certificate was "exhaustion consequent of delirium tremens".⁴⁰² A very sad end for a young man! George was buried in the same grave as his parents in the Wangaratta Cemetery.⁴⁰³

---

395 Thomas Clark's Death Certificate erroneously records that he married Elizabeth Watson in Melbourne when he was 40 years old. Had it been correct, this would have put the year of the marriage at around 1852. It also incorrectly states that Thomas had been employed as a clerk immediately prior to his death: see *Victoria Deaths Register: Thomas Clark* (1879) (No. 3289/1879).

396 See *Victoria Deaths Register: Elizabeth Clark* (1873) (No. 11366/1873).

397 See *Victoria Deaths Register: Thomas Clark* (1879) (No. 3289/1879).

398 See footnote 43 above.

399 See *Victoria Deaths Register: Thomas Clark* (1879) (No. 3289/1879); and the *Moore Considine Family Website* (https://tinyurl.com/58ntx5sc) (at 29 March 2023).

400 See the *Ovens and Murray Advertiser*, Saturday, 25 January 1879, p. 4.

401 See *Inquest Deposition Files – George Clark* (PROV, VPRS 24/P0, Unit 20).

402 *Ibid*; *Victoria Deaths Register: George Clark* (1853) (No. 3603/1853); and Jenny Coates, "George Clark and his unfortunate end" in *Conversations with Grandma* (https://tinyurl.com/y44gv9nd) (at 29 March 2023).

403 See footnote 384 above.

William Clark and Land Law Changes

Squatter agitation, both in New South Wales and in Britain, led in 1847 to further changes to New South Wales law with respect to squatting runs. In Britain, the passage of the *Waste Lands Occupation Act 1846* (Imp.) led to the promulgation of an Imperial Order-in-Council o 9 March 1847. This Order was officially proclaimed in New South Wales by Governor FitzRoy on 5 October 1847. For the purposes of the Order, New South Wales was divided into three lands districts: the settled, intermediate and unsettled districts respectively. Squatting runs in the Ovens and King Rivers valleys fell within the unsettled district.[404]

By virtue of the Imperial order, squatters in the unsettled district were entitled to apply for leases of their runs of up to 14 years in duration on the proviso that such runs were each capable of carrying not less than 4,000 sheep or "the equivalent" number of cattle. In the case of each run, the rent payable by the squatter was to be proportionate to the run's stock carrying capacity; with such rent in any event to be not less than £10 per annum. The squatter was given a pre-emptive right (or option) during the term of the lease to purchase any part or parts of the run, provided that each such part was not less than 160 acres in area and that the purchase price was not less than £1 per acre.[405]

In essence, the Order was designed to provide a mechanism by which squatters could convert their licensed runs via leases into freehold holdings.

In the Port Phillip District of New South Wales, Superintendent Latrobe, who was opposed to what he saw as squatters "locking up" large areas of land under his jurisdiction, took the view that although they could apply for leases of their runs under the Imperial Order, he was not obliged by that Order to grant such leases to them. Accordingly, he refused to do so; both in his capacity as Superintendent of the Port Phillip District and, following the separation of Victoria from New South Wales in 1851, in his capacity as Lieutenant Governor of Victoria. Notwithstanding his refusal to grant leases to the squatters, Latrobe announced in August 1852 that thenceforth, they would be permitted to purchase their "homestead" blocks of up to 640 acres. The remainders of their runs would continue to be held under licences, and not leases.[406]

The passage of the *Land Act 1862* (Vic) ("the *Duffy Act*") saw squatting licences thereafter reduced to being renewed from year to year only. This state of affairs continued until all of

---

404 See the *Supplement to the New South Wales Government Gazette* (No. 87), Thursday, 7 October 1847, pp. 1070-1077 (https://tinyurl.com/2s4d58z3) (at 30 March 2023).

405 *Ibid.* See also John Quick, *The History of Land Tenure in the Colony of Victoria* (1888), pp. 6-15; and Faithfull and Lewis, *op. cit.*, p. 17. It is interesting to note in this context that in 1849, William Clark's *Whitfield* run was assessed as having a carrying capacity of 10,000 sheep or 1,500 head of cattle. In the same year, his *Ovens Crossing Place* run was estimated to be capable of carrying 600 head of cattle : see *The Squatter's Directory* (1849) (https://tinyurl.com/yt6u7dsb) (at 30 March 2023); and Wilson, *op. cit.*, p. 2.

406 See Richard Brown, "Unlocking the Land" in *Looking at History*, 6 April 2013 (https://tinyurl.com/lqrhu7v) (at 30 March 2023); A.G. L. Shaw, "Victoria's First Governor" in (2003) 71 *The Latrobe Journal* 85 at p. 94 (https://tinyurl.com/k4pcovb) (at 30 March 2023); and *The Argus*, Saturday, 21 August 1852, p. 2.

the remaining licensed lands had been resumed by the Victorian Government or sold to selectors and other freeholders.[407]

Where did these statutory and regulatory changes leave William Clark? One can reasonably assume that during the second half of the 1840s and into the 1850s, he used his *Ovens Crossing Place* and *Whitfield* runs to pursue his pastoral interests. However, it is worth noting that in 1846, and on a site a short distance to the west of his *Hope Inn* now predominantly occupied by the *King George V Memorial Gardens*, William grew Wangaratta's first wheat crop. The initial area he placed under cultivation was some five or six acres, and the harvested wheat was apparently ground to flour by hand.[408] Although William may not have grown wheat on this particular site for long, it seems quite likely that he continued to grow cereal on other parts of his *Ovens Crossing Place* run in subsequent years.

In their manuscript *From 16,000 to 5*, John Faithfull and Jim Lewis have asserted that William Clark was granted a lease of his *Ovens Crossing Place* run in about 1848 and, further, a lease of his *Whitfield* run at some unspecified time between 1845 and 1853.[409] However, they cite no authority for these assertions, and given the stance taken by Superintendent (and later Lieutenant Governor) Latrobe with respect to squatters' leases, it appears highly unlikely that either run was ever leased to William Clark.

From Ovens Crossing Place to Wangaratta

In or about 1849, an area including and surrounding William Clark's *Hope Inn*, and designated by the New South Wales Government to be the site of a new town, was excised from William's *Ovens Crossing Place* run. The area in question had first been surveyed by Assistant Surveyor Thomas Townsend in 1839.[410] In 1848, Robert Hoddle, the Surveyor-in-Charge of the Port Phillip District, instructed Assistant Surveyor Thomas Wedge to survey and mark out allotments for the proposed town.[411] Wedge completed his survey by October 1848, marking out some 200 allotments on the left bank of the Ovens River.[412]

On 11 April 1849, the New South Wales Government announced that the new town, given the name "Wangaratta" by Superintendent Latrobe, had been gazetted, and that the approved survey plans for it were open for inspection in both Sydney and Albury. The first sale of allotments in Wangaratta took place in Melbourne on 28 June 1849.[413]

---

407 See Quick, *op. cit.*, pp. 6-15.
408 See *The Age*, Saturday, 3 August 1929, p. 5; and O'Callaghan, *op. cit.*, p. 7. The furrows left from the planting of this first wheat crop were apparently still visible for many years afterwards: see Whittaker, *op. cit.*, p. 33. See also photo 25 below.
409 See Faithfull and Lewis, *op. cit.*, p. 94.
410 See Whittaker, *op. cit.*, p. 34. See also footnote 375 and its accompanying text above.
411 See Whittaker, *op. cit.*, p. 34. Prior to issuing his instructions to Wedge, Hoddle had noted in a letter dated 23 May 1848: "...during the last two years, there have been many applications for allotments at [*Ovens Crossing Place*] and I consider that if there were 60 allotments marked out they would sell readily."
    Ibid.
412 *Ibid.*
413 See *The Argus*, Tuesday, 8 May 1849, pp. 1 and 4. See also Whittaker, *op. cit.*, p. 35.

In the years immediately following William and Elizabeth Clark's arrival at the crossing on the Ovens River, the little settlement was, as one local pioneer, Rowland Vincent, put it, "a small affair". Vincent arrived there as a child with his family in 1847. In 1925, he described the early township as consisting of:

> "... a few houses scattered about in the area between Reid, Ovens and Faithfull Streets; also some over the Ovens River."[414]

Another early settler apparently recalled that the howls of native dogs were a nightly occurrence.[415]

Punt Operator

Notwithstanding the rude state of the early Wangaratta settlement, more and more people were both passing through and settling in the area as time passed. William Clark's businesses at the *Hope Inn* and with his punt traversing the Ovens River prospered. In the early days, crossing the River could be a complicated matter. It has been noted that:

> "Teamsters unloaded their goods and sent them across in William's boat. The dray wheels would be taken off and sent across, then the dray would be floated over held by the chains attaching the boat to the crossing rope. The bullocks would swim across."[416]

A combination of increased traffic over the Ovens River and deterioration in the fabric of the punt he had purchased from Rattray led to William Clark commissioning a new punt in 1848.[417] According to David Whittaker, William's new punt was constructed locally for him by a Phillip Keighran at a cost of £500. Whittaker went on to describe this new vessel as follows:

> "It was made of hand-sawn red gum, 30 feet long and 6 feet wide. There was a windlass, with several lines of strong rope at each end, to haul it across the river. Little boxed-in areas at the ends protected the men from injury while working the punt – this usually

---

414 See "Reminiscences from Pioneers – Wangaratta Chronicle Wednesday April 29, 1929" in *Kaye's Greta, Myrrhee and Winton Webpages* ("*Kaye's Webpages*"), p. 14 (https://tinyurl.com/2rzcmuc9) (at 30 March 2023).

415 See O'Callaghan, *op. cit.*, p. 6. Bill O'Callaghan wrote further that:
"As early as 1839, the Reverend Joseph Docker, on behalf of Dr Mackay, Messrs Cropper, Bowman, Chisholm, Faithfull, the Reids, Livingstone, Ellis, Warby, Gray and Clark, had written to Superintendent Latrobe requesting the appointment of a police magistrate, but it was not until 1852 that G. M. Harper was appointed at a salary of £600 per annum."
See O'Callaghan, *op. cit.*, pp. 11-12. According to David Whittaker:
"At one time before the advent of police in Wangaratta, Clark was issued with a pair of handcuffs by the Government and no doubt made good use of them."
See Whittaker, *op. cit.*, p. 39, n. 21.

416 See *Worthy of Mention*, p. 14.

417 See O'Callaghan, *op. cit.*, p. 4.

taking two men. Railing along the sides, and a wooden flap with chains and levers at each end to act as gangways, completed the equipment."[418]

The rush of people to the Woolshed, Nine Mile and Beechworth goldfields in 1851 and 1852 proved to be a boon to William Clark's businesses on the Ovens River, and it would appear that William took full advantage of the increased traffic that came his way.[419] Although a competitor, John Crisp, had established another punt upstream, it seems that most cross-river passengers still utilised William's punt. However, he soon acquired an adverse reputation for charging high fees for the crossing: from 12 shillings to £1 per passage.[420] It has been asserted that he earned up to £100 per day during this period.[421]

A measure of the anger which William generated by his high charges for river crossings may be gathered from the reaction of one distinguished passenger, William Howitt. Howitt crossed the Ovens River on William Clark's punt on 14 November 1852. He wrote of this passage:

> "On the 14th we crossed in the punt over the river, which was about twenty yards wide, and the punt was precisely like that of the Goulburn. Exactly as in that case, the Government had not taken a single thought for the passage of the public, but had left it to be accommodated and fleeced, according to the conscience of any man who chose to make the speculation. The man who did undertake it was on the punt himself, and charged us 12/- for the passage of our cart and ourselves. The descent to the ferry, and the ascent from it, were so steep that it was highly dangerous to heavily laden drays."[422]

In late December 1852 or early January 1853, the Victorian Government purchased William Clark's punt.[423] It is not now known what purchase price William received for his punt. However, shortly after purchasing the punt, the Government fixed charges for

---

418 See Whittaker, *op. cit.*, p. 36. Whittaker continued:
"There was a law suit in Melbourne over the payment for the punt, but apart from the fact that Clark won the case, nothing else is known."
Ibid. Bill O'Callaghan has observed that an unknown contemporary of William Clark described this punt as "a floating bridge": see O'Callaghan, *op. cit.*, p. 4. A model of the punt is to be found in the Wangaratta Museum: see photo 26 below. See also photo 27 below.

419 See the *Wangaratta Chronicle*, Saturday, 28 November 1914, p. 1; and *Worthy of Mention*, p. 14. The operation of the punt during this period was coloured by tragedy when two of its passengers in 1851 were drowned whilst alighting from it: see Whittaker, *op. cit.*, p. 36.

420 See *Worthy of Mention*, p. 14.

421 See "About Clark, William Henry" in the *Moore Considine Family Website* (https://tinyurl.com/58ntx5sc) (at 30 March 2023).

422 See Howitt, *op. cit.*, p. 109. See also footnotes 197 and 255, and their accompanying texts, above. The Goulburn River punt was, of course, owned by John Clark Jnr, William's brother. Given the similarity between the two punts, William may well have borrowed the design for his punt from John.

423 See Whittaker, *op. cit.*, pp. 36-37. It might be recalled that at about the same time, the Government also purchased John Clark Jnr's punt on the Goulburn River: see footnote 256 and its accompanying text above. In both cases, the acquisitions were apparently instigated by Henry Smythe, the Victorian Commissioner of Crown Lands for the Murray District: see Whittaker, *op. cit.*, pp. 36-37.

passengers and vehicles using the vessel which appear to have been significantly cheaper than those earlier charged by William, and let the operation of the punt out after tender.[424]

The Sale of Whitfield

In July 1853, William Clark sold his interest in his *Whitfield* squatting run to John Evans.[425] What motivated him to do so is unclear. It is unlikely that the run's distance from Wangaratta would have been a factor. More likely, William was simply freeing up capital and concentrating his business interests closer to Wangaratta. It is not now known what Evans paid to William for his licence for the run.[426]

A Short Stay at Eaglehawk Gully Near Bendigo?

There is an intriguing report possibly placing William Clark at Eaglehawk Gully near Bendigo in late 1853 or early 1854. The report is to be found in an unpublished autobiographical manuscript dictated by a James McLaurin in 1888. McLaurin was a member of a Scottish family of squatters, with runs in northern Victoria and the Riverina.[427] His manuscript, entitled *Memories of Early Australia*, covered his life in Australia between 1838 and 1857. In it, he described a journey he made with a companion from Seymour to Bendigo via Eaglehawk Gully in late 1853 or early 1854; observing:

> "We arrived at Eaglehawk Gully just about dark. In making inquiry for McKinnon's store, we came across old Bill Clarke from the Ovens and he made us both comfortable for the night and had plenty for the horses – oats and chaff and plenty of new bags and blankets to sleep on."[428]

If an accurate reference to William Clark, this account would seemingly have him residing

---

424 By way of example, whereas William Clark charged William Howitt twelve shillings to cross the River with his cart, the fee fixed by the Government for an equivalent crossing was one shilling: *ibid*. See also O'Callaghan, *op. cit.*, p. 14. It would seem that William may have again operated the punt for a short period of time in 1854 and early 1855 under a licence from the Victorian Government: *ibid*.
 William's erstwhile punt was subsequently sunk in the Ovens River on about 15 February 1855 – the day the first bridge over the River was opened for traffic: see Whittaker, *op. cit.*, p. 38. It was substantially salvaged by military engineers in the mid 1960s and mounted as an historical memorial in nearby *Apex Park*. There, it was unfortunately allowed to deteriorate to the point where the remains were removed and disposed of: see generally Pressreader, *Evolution of a River Crossing* (https://tinyurl.com/43w8xf7m) (at 30 March 2023).

425 See Billis and Kenyon, *Pastoral Pioneers*, p. 300. A few months after purchasing the run in 1853, Evans on-sold it to Charles Payne. However, Evans bought the property back from Payne in 1857: see Wilson, *op. cit.*, p. 2.

426 However, an anonymous author of an article published in the *North Eastern Ensign* on 8 September 1893 briefly asserted rather cryptically that:
 "Mr W. Clark, of Wangaratta sold the King River station and the cattle thereon for 35s per head, yearlings and calves given in."
 See the *North Eastern Ensign*, Friday, 8 September 1893, p. 3.

427 See, with regard to John Clark Jnr's relations with a member of this family, Alexander McLaurin, footnotes 226, 227 and 228, and their accompanying texts, above.

428 Extracts from James McLaurin's *Memories of Early Australia* are to be found in Neil McLaurin, *1838 Settlers: A History of the Family of James McLaurin and his Descendants* (2017). See here at p. 64.

in Eaglehawk Gully at the time of McLaurin's reported encounter with him. Indeed, the report may carry an implication that William was operating an inn at Eaglehawk Gully when his meeting with McLaurin occurred. Eaglehawk Gully was a thriving gold mining area in 1853 and 1854.[429] Moreover, as will be seen below, William held shares in a goldmining company operating a mine at Eldorado in and after 1859. It is not inconceivable that he tried his luck with gold (or at least goldminers) at Eaglehawk for a short time during the period in question here.

However, there would not appear to be any other reference to William Clark living at Eaglehawk Gully in 1853, 1854 or at any other time. Furthermore, his interests in and around Wangaratta in the mid 1850s would have left him little time to dally in the Eaglehawk Gully area. In consequence, it could well be that James McLaurin's "old Bill Clarke" was not William Clark, but simply another Clarke he had met on the Ovens River. Alternatively, it may be that McLaurin's memory was simply faulty here.

Freehold Land Acquisitions and the Commercial Hotel

Agitation for the construction of a bridge across the Ovens River seemingly commenced soon after the formation of the little settlement at the Ovens Crossing Place.[430] For his part, William Clark was of the perhaps unwise belief that such a bridge would not be built, and that cross-river traffic would continue to use his punt adjacent to the *Hope Inn* and in line with what had become the main thoroughfare of Ovens Street. To cope with accommodating the increasing traffic, William began construction of a new hotel on the corner of Ovens and Faithfull Streets diagonally opposite to the *Hope Inn* in 1853.

There are some indications that William Clark's proposed new hotel diagonally opposite to the *Hope Inn* may never have been completed. An obituary published in the *Ovens and Murray Advertiser* on 15 September 1906 for a local Wangaratta builder, Samuel Ashworth, observed in relation to the *Commercial Hotel* built by William in Murphy Street, Wangaratta in 1855:

> "It may be interesting in connection with the erection of this hotel to recall the fact that the site first chosen for it was where Mr. T. Laidler's residence now stands, opposite the old 'punt', and excavations were even made for cellars."[431]

Further, in their *Wangaratta: old tales and tours*, Judy Bassett and Edna Harman have written with respect to William Clark:

---

429 See eGold, *A Nation's Heritage – Eaglehawk, VIC* (https://tinyurl.com/5n72rytc) (at 1 April 2023).
430 See O'Callaghan, *op. cit.*, p. 14.
431 See "Death of an Old Resident" in the *Ovens and Murray Advertiser*, Saturday, 15 September 1906, p. 1.

> "He began a new hotel on the corner diagonally opposite [the *Hope Inn*], then abandoned the site. Rain-water filled the cellars...."[432]

That said, Jenny Coates has forcefully argued that William Clark's proposed hotel on the corner of Ovens and Faithfull Streets was not only completed but was also operated by William as a hotel under the name "*The Grape Inn*" for a short period in 1854. She has noted that during the course of 1854, two local inquests were conducted by Wangaratta's doctor and coroner, William Dobbyn, in a structure identified in each case at the time as "*The Grape Inn*". The first of these inquests was held in June 1854 into the death of William's younger brother, George Clark.[433] The second of the inquests related to the death of one Denis Sullivan in October 1854. After thorough searches, no other possible site for *The Grape Inn* other than on the corner of Ovens and Faithfull Streets has come to light.[434]

The reason why William Clark's proposed hotel on the corner of Ovens and Faithfull Streets was either not completed or, if completed, only functioned as a hotel for a short period of time was that William became aware that contrary to his expectations, the Victoria Government planned in fact to construct a bridge over the Ovens River. The Government called for tenders for the construction of this bridge in early 1854. It was not to be built in line with Ovens Street, but rather with Murphy Street upstream to the east. In the event, the new bridge was opened for traffic on about 15 February 1855.[435]

Two different stories have been advanced as to why the bridge was built in line with Murphy Street rather than with the original main thoroughfare, Ovens Street. The first has James Meldrum, a hotel proprietor in competition with William Clark, successfully using his political influence to have the bridge sited in close proximity to his new *Wangaratta Hotel* on the right bank of the Ovens River facing what is now Clements Street.[436] The second story has Thomas Wedge, the surveyor who laid out Wangaratta, staying at William's *Hope Inn* whilst effecting his survey. After a session at the inn during which Wedge over-indulged in whiskey and argued with his host, William threw him out. Wedge subsequently took his revenge on William by successfully recommending that the main road through the township be Murphy Street, and that the bridge accordingly be in line with this thoroughfare.[437]

Not to be outdone by the location of the new bridge, William Clark moved to construct

---

432 See Judy Bassett and Edna Harman, *Wangaratta; Old Tales and Tours* (1983), p. 99.

433 See footnote 402 and its accompanying text above.

434 See Jenny Coates, "William Henry Clark and his hotels – a new chapter" in *Conversations with Grandma* (https://tinyurl.com/3b3wtmfb) (at 1 April 2023)

435 See Whittaker, *op. cit.*, p. 39.

436 See the *Ovens and Murray Advertiser*, Saturday, 25 February 1865, p. 3.

437 *Ibid.* See also footnotes 411 and 412, and their accompanying texts, above. On this matter, Bill O'Callaghan has sagely written:
> "Why Murphy Street not Ovens Street was chosen as the main street is a question that has never been satisfactorily answered. In the 1938 centenary booklet the editor wrote: 'The intention of the early surveyors were sadly perverted by local influences.' As no documentation is available to provide a satisfactory answer, the reason why remains a mystery."
>
> See O'Callaghan, *op. cit.*, p. 15. The note in the 1938 centenary booklet does, however, suggest that the first, rather than the second, of the two stories for the siting of the bridge is more likely to be the correct – albeit less colourful – version of events.

a new hotel, which he called the *Commercial Hotel*, on two allotments of freehold land on Murphy Street which he had purchased on 23 May 1850 during the New South Wales Government's third sale of Wangaratta allotments.

By the time the *Commercial Hotel* was constructed, William was already the owner of substantial amounts of freehold land in and about the township of Wangaratta. In the first freehold land sale on 28 June 1859, he had purchased three allotments of town land. In the second and third sales, held on 15 and 23 May 1850 respectively, he purchased a total of 10 town allotments. In 1852, he purchased a further two allotments of town land and two allotments of "suburban" land from the Victorian Government. 1854 saw him purchase another five "suburban" allotments, and 1855 a total of six town allotments and two allotments of "suburban" land.[438]

Undoubtedly, William Clark's biggest freehold land acquisition in 1855 was his pre-emptive purchase of 640 acres from his *Ovens Crossing Place* squatting run. Although the Crown Grant of this land to William only issued on 21 January 1858, his application to purchase it had in fact been approved much earlier by the Victorian Government on 17 January 1855. The land, located in the vicinity of the intersection of what are now Sessions and the Warby Range Roads, was subsequently identified on the Victorian cadastre as *Pre-Emptive Section E*. William Clark paid £1 per acre for it: a total of £640.[439]

William purchased his two allotments on Murphy Street in 1850 for a total of £37. The allotments occupied the whole of the street frontage on the south side of the road from Reid to Ely Streets.[440] He called for tenders for the construction of the *Commercial Hotel* on 17 February 1855. The building was constructed during that year, at a cost of £7,000 and likely using the same plan as had been drawn up for William's planned hotel on the corner of Ovens and Faithfull Streets.[441]

There is some uncertainty as to where the bricks for the *Commercial Hotel* were sourced. One version of events has it that the bricks had been made for William Clark by a Samuel Calvert to be used in the construction of the hotel on the corner of Ovens and Faithfull Streets. These bricks were then carted from that site to the site of the new hotel on Murphy Street.[442] A second version of events has the bricks brought up from Melbourne.[443] Perhaps

---

[438] See Whittaker, *op. cit.*, p. 35; and Faithfull and Lewis, *op. cit.*, p. 95. During this period, town allotments in Wangaratta ranged in size from a quarter of an acre to one and a half acres, and suburban allotments from five to nine acres: *Ibid*.

[439] See Faithfull and Lewis, *op. cit.*, pp. 20, 96 and 98. See also footnote 406 and its accompanying text above.

[440] See Whittaker, *op. cit.*, p. 35.

[441] See Whittaker, *op. cit.*, p. 40.

[442] See "The Sydney Hotel" in *Wangaratta Historical Society Files: Hotels* ("the *Sydney Hotel file*"), p. 230. It seems that on 1 February 1854, Calvert saw fit to confront and insult William Clark in the *Hope Inn* for refusing to pay Calvert what the latter considered was appropriate for his labours. When William's barman, Thomas Coates, tried to reason with Calvert, Calvert called Coates "a bloody, snotty thing" whose breeches were too big for him. Calvert was subsequently fined for creating a disturbance: see the *Sydney Hotel file*, pp. 230-231. How Calvert's claim against William finally played out is unknown. However, it seems unlikely that the former would have got all that he wanted.

It might be added that if Jenny Coates is correct in her argument that the hotel on the corner of Ovens and Faithfull Streets was completed and at least used for the purposes of coronial inquests, and if the bricks for the new *Commercial Hotel* were sourced from that building, then it would have had to have been demolished to that end. Any such demolition would presumably have left the cellars exposed to the elements, potentially allowing them to fill with rain water: see footnotes 432 and 434, and their accompanying texts, above.

[443] See *Worthy of Mention*, p. 15.

the truth was that Calvert made the bricks, or had them made, in Melbourne and then transported them up to Wangaratta for the construction of the hotel on the corner of Ovens and Faithfull Streets.

The carpentry work for the *Commercial Hotel* was effected by Samuel Ashworth and James Ellis. In the words of the *Ovens and Murray Advertiser* of 15 May 1906:

> "When the Commercial Hotel was sufficiently advanced for the carpenters, Messrs Ashworth and Ellis secured the contract for the whole of the woodwork, of which there was £800 worth in the building. Redgum in those days was £5 per 100 feet."[444]

As constructed, the *Commercial Hotel* was effectively three stories high, with a steep, hipped roof behind which apparently lay small, windowless attic rooms. The building originally had a small verandah fronting Murphy Street.[445]

On the hotel's completion, William Clark is said to have proposed christening it by hoisting his wife up to the roof to break a bottle of champagne on a chimney. Elizabeth Clark, then pregnant, apparently demurred at the prospect. The Clarks' eldest son, William John Clark (who was then all of five years old), did the honours in his mother's stead.[446]

According to David Whittaker, on completion of the hotel, William Clark sent a man with a tomahawk to mark trees so as to show the new route from the Sydney to Melbourne road at One Mile Creek on the then-outskirts of Wangaratta, past the *Commercial Hotel* and onwards to the bridge.[447]

Children

William and Elizabeth Clark raised a large family together. Although William John Clark was the eldest of their two surviving sons, he was in fact the seventh of at least 12 children in all born to them.[448]

William and Elizabeth's first child was a son whom they named George Clark. According to a note accompanying a family bible formerly belonging to George Arthur Clark, William

---

[444] See "Death of an Old Resident" in the *Ovens and Murray Advertiser*, Saturday, 15 September 1906, p. 1. This article conveyed an interesting story as to how Ashworth and Ellis came to be in Wangaratta:
"The two young Lancashiremen struck off for the goldfields shortly after landing at Sandridge, and were on their way when they saw a waggon load of building material being travelled on the same road. Being carpenters, the two men took more than passing notice of the waggon as indicating that work for them was probably available at its destination, and they kept the vehicle in view until it reached Wangaratta. The timber proved to be material for the present Commercial Hotel, then in the course of construction for Mr William Clark....":
Ibid.

[445] See Whittaker, *op. cit.*, p. 40. It has been said that:
"The attic rooms of the third storey were probably intended as servants' rooms, but originally served a very different purpose. There, women prisoners were detained and, if necessary, were handcuffed to their iron bedsteads, by none other than publican Clark himself (the handcuffs were specially issued to Clark by the police)."
See Bassett and Harman, *op. cit.*, p. 99. See also footnote 414 above; and photos 28 and 29 below.

[446] See Whittaker, *op. cit.*, p. 40.

[447] *Ibid.*

[448] See the *Moore Considine Family Website* (https://tinyurl.com/58ntx5sc) (at 3 April 2023).

and Elizabeth's second last child, and currently in the possession of Colin Clark (a descendant of George Arthur Clark), the firstborn George Clark was born on 6 December 1840 at the Ovens River and died as an infant on 8 March 1841.

William and Elizabeth Clark's second child, Sarah Ann Clark, was born at the *Hope Inn* in 1842. Sarah married twice. Her first husband was a George E. Davies whom she married in Wagga Wagga, New South Wales in 1862. Sarah's second husband was John G. Baker. She married the latter on 27 June 1864 at Three Mile Creek near Wangaratta. Sarah had seven children in all. She died on 10 February 1899 in Wellington, New Zealand.

William and Elizabeth Clark's third child was Elizabeth Mary Clark. She was born at the *Hope Inn* a short time prior to 30 June 1843, and baptised on that date. On 1 February 1864, she married John Moore Jnr. The latter was the eldest son of John Moore Snr and Margaret Moore (née Considine). Like William Clark, John Moore Snr was born in Kent. The two were friends over many years. John Moore Jnr and Elizabeth Mary Moore had a total of 10 children. Elizabeth died in Carlton on 19 December 1898.

William and Elizabeth Clark's fourth child, Charlotte Sophia Clark, was born shortly before 24 September 1844 at the *Hope Inn*, and baptised on that date. Charlotte married Patrick Cusack on 12 December 1864. Patrick and Charlotte Cusack produced 10 children in all. Charlotte died on 29 September 1912 in Wangaratta.

The Clarks' fifth child, Emily Jane Clark, like her older surviving siblings, was born at the *Hope Inn*. Born a little before 6 December 1846, Emily was baptised on the latter date. She married twice. Her first marriage was to James Willett at Wangaratta on 9 October 1862. Emily's second husband was John W. Sullivan, whom she married at Wangaratta on 1 December 1880 some 15 years after James Willett's death. Emily also gave birth to 10 children in all. She died in Wangaratta on 11 December 1927.

William and Elizabeth's sixth child was Margaret Clark. Margaret was born in 1849 at the *Hope Inn*. She died in infancy in Wangaratta on or about 2 May 1850.

William and Elizabeth's seventh child was William John Clark. He was born in 1850. Like his older surviving siblings, he was born at the *Hope Inn*. William John Clark married Ellen Smith on 9 October 1875. They produced four children together. William John Clark died on 5 May 1912 in Wangaratta.

The eighth child born to William and Elizabeth Clark was Alice Rebecca Clark. She was born at the *Hope Inn* a little before 12 December 1851 and baptised on that date. Like her older sister, Elizabeth Mary Clark, Alice also married a Moore – in her case, John Moore Jnr's younger brother, William Moore. William and Alice were married in Benalla on 1 May 1872. They raised 10 children in all. However, it appears that the eldest of those 10 children, Alice Rosetta Moore, may have been fathered by another, unidentified man. Alice Rebecca Moore died in Wangaratta on 2 August 1919.

William and Elizabeth's ninth child was Rosetta Gertrude Clark. Rosetta was born shortly before 24 July 1853 at the *Hope Inn*. She was christened on 24 July 1853. In 1873, Rosetta married David Knox in Wangaratta. Together, they had seven children. Rosetta Knox died in Wangaratta on 14 January 1931.

The Clarks' tenth child, Jemima Maria Clark, was born at the *Hope Inn* a little before 26 April 1855. She was baptised on the latter date. Jemima had two marriages. In 1878, she married Denis Sullivan. They had three children together. Following Denis Sullivan's death in 1884, Jemima married William T. Kett on 16 July 1886 in Brisbane. She had two further children with William Kett. Jemima Kett died in Toorak on 13 November 1933.

William and Elizabeth Clark's second surviving son and penultimate child was George Arthur Clark. He was born at the *Commercial Hotel* shortly prior to 16 June 1859, and baptised on that date. George Arthur Clark married Margaret Hargreaves in Wangaratta on 14 April 1884. They had three children in all. George Arthur Clark died in Kensington, Victoria on 13 August 1927.

William and Elizabeth's last child, Florence Amelia Margaret Clark, was also born at the *Commercial Hotel*. She was born a little before 9 February 1861 and baptised on the latter date. In 1883, Florence Clark married John Schofield. They produced a total of nine children. Florence Schofield died in East St Kilda on 29 April 1936.[449]

Wangaratta Homes

Immediately following their arrival at Ovens Crossing Place in 1839, William and Elizabeth Clark made their first home either under canvass or possibly in a rough hut which William probably built in 1838 prior to his marriage to Elizabeth.[450] However, following William's construction of a more substantial structure shortly after that arrival, the couple made the new building their home.[451] 1843 saw the construction of the *Hope Inn*. For some time thereafter, the Inn was home for William, Elizabeth and their growing family.[452] But it appears that the Clark family were living in other premises in Wangaratta in 1853 and 1854.

On or shortly prior to 26 April 1851, William Clark was granted a liquor licence for the *Hope Inn* by the newly-established Court of Requests in Wangaratta.[453] It was a requirement of that licence that William, as the licensed publican, live on the premises. Yet less than three years later, on 4 February 1854, he was brought before the Wangaratta Court of Requests on a charge of:

---

449 *Ibid.* See also Faithfull and Lewis, *op. cit.*, pp. 90-92.
450 See footnote 364 and its accompanying text above.
451 See footnote 377 and its accompanying text above.
452 See footnote 380 and its accompanying text above.
453 See Whittaker, *op. cit.*, p. 51. According to David Whittaker, "the Commissioner" unsuccessfully opposed William's application for the licence on the ground that the *Hope Inn* was located on Crown land. William was represented by an Albury solicitor at the hearing: *ibid.* It would appear that William only gained freehold title to the *Hope Inn* land and its surrounds on 30 October 1857: see Faithfull and Lewis, *op. cit.*, p. 95. It would also seem that prior to the grant of the liquor licence in 1851, William had been selling liquor illegally from the *Hope Inn*: cf. footnote 71 and its accompanying text above.

"abandoning the business of his licensed house, the 'Hope Inn', at Wangaratta, and permitting another person to manage, superintend and conduct the business of the said house."[454]

The case against William Clark in the Court of Requests was prosecuted by Sub-Inspector Samuel Furnell, who had only recently arrived at his Wangaratta police post.[455] Furnell alleged that William had turned the business of the Hope Inn over to a manager, Thomas Coates.[456] He further alleged that for a considerable time, William had "virtually abandoned" the occupation of the *Hope Inn* as his usual place of residence. Furnell gave evidence to the Court that:

"Some months ago, I mentioned to [William Clark] that he was infringing on the Licensed Publicans' Act in so doing, and pointed out to him the clause, of which he seemed ignorant. He was then living in a house at the furthest end of the township from the Inn, about ¼ mile. He said he supposed he must come up and live in the house. Some time since, he moved up with his family to another house in the vicinity of the Inn, about 200 yards away from it on the opposite side of the street, where I believe he usually lived except during the temporary absence of Mr Coates to Melbourne."[457]

Giving corroborative evidence, Sergeant Charles Meyer stated with respect to William: "He usually resides (and his family) about 50-100 yards from the Inn across the road."[458]

The evidence was clearly enough to satisfy the Court, which declared the liquor licence for the *Hope Inn* to be "absolutely void" for the remainder of the year.[459]

Given that Furnell apparently warned William Clark "some months" prior to this hearing that William was in breach of his liquor licence by not residing in the *Hope Inn*, one might reasonably wonder why Furnell left it as long as he did before bringing his application in the Court of Requests. The answer almost certainly lies in the fact that at about 11.00 pm on 1 February 1854, Furnell had been unable to find a bed at the *Hope Inn* for an associate, and had been refused entry into the premises by William's barman/manager, Thomas Coates. At the time, those within the hotel bar (seemingly including William Clark) were said to have been making "a great noise". In apparent retaliation for his treatment, Furnell prosecuted William on 3 February 1854 for conducting the *Hope Inn* in a disorderly manner and for refusing Furnell entry on demand. William was duly convicted and fined £4, with 4s 6d in costs.[460] The complaint brought by Furnell the following day against William in

---

454 See the *Sydney Hotel file*, pp. 230 and 232.
455 See Whittaker, *op. cit.*, p. 50.
456 See footnote 442 above.
457 See the *Sydney Hotel file*, pp. 230 and 232.
458 *Ibid*.
459 *Ibid*
460 See the *Sydney Hotel file*, pp.230 and 231. No doubt Furnell's anger on the night of 1February 1854 was exacerbated by

the Court of Requests for abandoning his occupation of the *Hope Inn* would appear to have been a further vengeful act on Furnell's part.

It is unclear where precisely the two private Clark residences in Wangaratta which were referred to by Furnell and Meyer in their Court of Requests evidence were located. What is clear is that after the completion of the *Commercial Hotel* in 1855, William Clark and his family took up residence in that establishment.[461]

Following the de-licensing decision of the Court of Requests, the *Hope Inn* remained unlicensed for some time. It has been said that it was used as a private residence for a number of years.[462] However, the identity or identities of its resident or residents during this period is or are presently unknown.

Be that as it may, on 5 December 1859, the hotel building was burned to the ground, with only its outbuildings being saved.[463] It was then rebuilt by William Clark and re-named the *Sydney Hotel*. In or shortly prior to 1864, William leased the premises to William Painter.[464] In turn, Painter applied for, and was granted, a liquor licence for the hotel in 1864. However, William retained the freehold of the property up until the time of his death.

After the completion of the *Commercial Hotel*, William Clark was left to run that establishment and to attend to his pastoral and agricultural interests. However, these activities by no means exhausted his business pursuits.

Further Freehold Land Acquisitions

Not content with the freehold land purchases he made between 1849 and 1857, William Clark continued to buy, and also to sell, land for most of the remainder of his life. Indeed, it is noteworthy that in his Will, he described himself as a "Landowner". The most comprehensive outline of his land dealings are to be found in *From 16,00 to 5*.[465] However, in that work, John Faithfull and Jim Lewis are at pains to point out that their account of those dealings may well be incomplete, and that William could well have bought and sold other freehold properties during the latter part of his life.[466] The following summary of William's land dealings is based on the results of their searches to be found in *From 16,000 to 5*.

It would seem that in addition to purchasing the freehold interest in the land on which the *Hope Inn* was located, William Clark bought a further four town allotments in Wangaratta in 1857. In that year, he also purchased seven rural allotments on the outskirts of the town.

Coates telling him to "go about his business" and calling him "a great long ghost", and by William Clark subsequently shutting the door in his face: see the *Sydney Hotel file*, p. 231.

461 See Whittaker, *op. cit.*, p. 40.
462 See "Death of an Old Resident" in the *Ovens and Murray Advertiser*, Saturday 15 September 1906, p. 1.
463 See the *Ovens and Murray Advertiser*, Tuesday, 6 December 1859, p. 2; and *The Age*, Wednesday, 14 December 1859, p. 5. See also Graham Jones, *On This Day in the North East* (1989), p. 252; and Whittaker, *op. cit.*, p. 40.
464 See Jenny Coates, "Sepia Saturday: a quartet of hotels" in *Conversations with Grandma* (https://tinyurl.com/bdehxjdp) (at 3 April 2023). See also photo 30 below.
465 See Faithfull and Lewis, *op. cit.*, Appendices H and R.
466 See Faithfull and Lewis, *op. cit.*, p. 100.

These rural allotments, totalling some 670 acres in area, lay between the Ovens River in the east and the Wangaratta-Yarrawonga Road in the west, and extended almost from the southern end of William's *Pre-Emptive Section E* in the north to Boundary Road (now Phillipson Street) in the south. Although not entirely contiguous with each other, or with *Pre-Emptive Section E*, the seven rural allotments were undoubtedly used by William for pastoral and agricultural purposes in conjunction with *Pre-Emptive Section E* and with the residue of his *Ovens Crossing Place* run still held by him under licence from the Victorian Government.

In 1858, William Clark purchased a further 16 town allotments in Wangaratta. 1860 saw him buy a further two such allotments. Still later, he acquired most of the land on the Merriwa Park side of Ely Street and on Murphy Street to the south of Ely Street, two allotments on Chisholm Street, two on Faithfull Street, two on Templeton Street, two on Ryley Street and two in "suburban" Wangaratta.

In 1866, William purchased some 50 acres from John Jones in close proximity to his other rural properties. In 1869, he further purchased one half of a close-by rural allotment from Jones. Outside Wangaratta and its immediate environs, he also purchased five "suburban" allotments in Benalla extending over 25 acres, and a town allotment in Bundalong on the Murray River.[467]

During his later years, William Clark sold some 25 town allotments in Wangaratta and a further two in its "suburbs". However, perhaps his biggest sale of land occurred in 1866. In that year, he sold 207 acres from *Pre-Emptive Section E* to his son-in-law, John Moore Jnr.

Flour Miller

For a time, William Clark was also a flour miller. In the early 1860s, it would seem that Wangaratta was blessed with three flour mills. One of the largest of these mills was established by William in conjunction with John Evans.[468] Initially known as *Victoria Flour Mills*, the mill was constructed on land acquired by William on the south-eastern corner of Murphy and Ely Streets. It used water taken from the King River.[469] The mill commenced operation on 3 March 1861.[470] In an article published in the *Ovens and Murray Advertiser* in January 1863, it was described as containing:

"machinery for working four pairs of stones, and is second to none in the colony."[471]

It appears that William Clark's involvement in the *Victoria Flour Mills* was brief. Indeed,

---

467 It is possible that William Clark's connection with Bundalong has been commemorated with "Clarke Street" in that town.
468 See Whittaker, *op. cit.*, p. 167. John Evans was also the man to whom William sold his Whitfield squatting run in July 1853: see footnote 425 and its accompanying text above. It might also be recalled that William Clark is said to have grown Wangaratta's first crop of wheat: see footnote 408 and its accompanying text above.
469 *Ibid*. See also Faithfull and Lewis, *op. cit.*, p. 95.
470 See Whittaker, *op. cit.*, p. 167
471 See the *Ovens and Murray Advertiser*, Thursday, 22 January 1863, p. 2.

he could well have sold his interest in the enterprise shortly after John Evans' accidental death in January 1862. It would seem that William's interest in the venture was purchased for £1,330 by a Daniel Hugh Evans (who, notwithstanding his surname, was unlikely to have been a relative of John Evans.[472]

Brewer

William Clark was also a shareholder in a short-lived Wangaratta brewery. The first brewery in Wangaratta was established by James Meldrum. Meldrum's "Pale Ale" was consumed in considerable quantities over a number of years in Wangaratta and surrounding areas. However, by the early 1860s, Meldrum had apparently been forced out of the brewing business by Beechworth- based competition.[473]

With the aim of restoring brewing to Wangaratta, a meeting of subscribing shareholders in a new brewing company was held in Wangaratta's *Royal Victoria Hotel* on 2 June 1868. Henry Kett was duly elected to be the chairman of the company which, on William Clark's motion, was given the name the *Wangaratta Brewing and Malting Company*. The meeting further agreed, not without some dissention, to purchase land on which to construct the brewery from William. The land in question was located on the corner of Chisholm and Ely Streets.[474]

The foundation stone for the brewery was laid on 19 September 1868.[475] Notwithstanding the high hopes held for the venture, it was apparently not a success and had failed by 1877.[476] Possibly because he was unable to sell them, William Clark retained his four shares in the *Wangaratta Brewing and Malting Company* until his death.

Gold Miner

In addition to his shares in the *Wangaratta Brewing and Malting Company*, William Clark held 20 shares at his death in the *National Insurance Company*, and a further 22 shares in

---

472   See Jenny Coates, "Trove Tuesday – Wangaratta 1863 – Part 1" in *Conversation with Grandma* (https://tinyurl.com/3dtf456c) (at 4 April 2023); and footnote 557 and its accompanying text below.

473   See Jenny Coates, "Trove Tuesday – Wangaratta 1863 – Part 2" in *Conversations with Grandma* (https://tinyurl.com/59a52yru) (at 4 April 2023). See also footnote 436 and its accompanying text above.

474   See the *Ovens and Murray Advertiser*, Thursday. 4 June 1868, p. 3. One of William Clark's fellow shareholders, Francis Mitchell, although finally voting in favour of purchasing the land from William, advised the meeting that he considered the latter's price "high and exorbitant", and that he thought that William should reduce his price "a little". William apparently responded by asserting that:
   "he considered the land well worth the money he asked for it, and he would not be doing justice to himself if he had charged less."
   Ibid.

475   See the *Ovens and Murray Advertiser*, Tuesday, 22 September 1868, p. 2. The newspaper account of the ceremony stated that at its conclusion, Henry Kett asked all present:
   "to partake of some refreshments which had been provided by the company. This suggestion appeared to be a welcome one. After champagne, brandy, sherry and beer had been partaken of, the various speakers waxed more eloquent, and it was astonishing how many virtues were discovered by everybody in everybody. Speechifying was indulged in very extensively until dusk."
   Ibid.

476   See Whittaker, *op. cit.*, p. 168. Part of the old brewery buildings is still standing behind a Wangaratta house: see photo 31 below.

the *Kneebone Gold Mining Company*. This corporation successfully worked a deep lead gold mine at Eldorado between 1859 and 1872.[477]

The life of the mine was marred by a bitter miners' strike in 1869. This strike was ultimately broken by the company bringing in scab miners from Ballarat and elsewhere.[478] The gold won from the mine gradually petered out despite the company sinking a new shaft through hard rock in 1870.[479] There is nothing to suggest that William Clark took any active part in the company's management. Its corporate shell lingered on after the end of mining and was not dissolved until 28 July 1964.[480]

William Clark's investment in the *Kneebone Gold Mining Company* was unlikely to have earned him much income. Although the Eldorado mine did produce payable gold, the overheads of the company would likely have been high, and the productive life of the mine short. Nor were William's flour milling, brewing and insurance interests likely to have generated much wealth for him – or, indeed, occupied much of his time.

A Rural Move

William Clark did not operate the *Commercial Hotel* for long. In July 1861, he leased it to William Murdoch, and at the same time transferred the liquor licence for the premises to the latter. William finally sold the hotel to Murdoch in October 1870.[481] As mentioned above, he leased the *Sydney Hotel* to William Painter in or prior to 1864.[482]

After leasing the *Commercial Hotel* to Murdoch in 1861, William Clark left "urban" Wangaratta with his family and moved into a homestead he had built on nearby rural land he owned. William was to live in this homestead for almost all of the rest of his life.

There is considerable uncertainty as to precisely where the homestead was located and when it was constructed.

On 27 June 1864, Elizabeth and William Clark's oldest surviving child, Sarah Ann Clark, married John George Baker. Their marriage record notes that the marriage was solemnised "At the house of Mr Wm Clark Three Mile Creek Wangaratta."[483] At this time, William Clark owned a number of allotments with frontages on the Three Mile Creek to the north-west

---

477 See the *Historic Mining Sites Assessment Project: Eldorado Goldfield*, p. 42 (https://tinyurl.com/3buxfaas) (at 6 April 2023).
478 See *The Argus*, Thursday, 14 October 1869, p. 5.
479 See "Beechworth Mining District" in *Reports of the Mining Surveyors and Registrars: Quarter Ending 31st March 1870*, p. 25 (https://tinyurl.com/k9zdnyb) (at 6 April 2023).
480 See *Victoria Government Gazette* (No. 70), Wednesday, 5 August 1964, p. 2254. Open cut hydraulic sluicing for gold after 1870 gradually washed away most of the *Kneebone Gold Mining Company*'s mine at Eldorado. However, the remains of an exposed side of the mine's main shaft may still be seen: see photo 32 below.
481 See Faithfull and Lewis, *op. cit.*, p. 112. The *Commercial Hotel* continued to be a notable and important Wangaratta institution for over 100 years. After it passed out of William Clark's hands, it provided accommodation for a number of illustrious persons, including the soprano Dame Nellie Melba, the pianist Ignace Paderewski and the composer Percy Grainger. It was finally demolished in December 1969: see Bassett and Harman, *op. cit.*, p. 100; and Whittaker, *op. cit.*, pp. 153-154.
482 See footnote 464 and its accompanying text above.
483 See *Victoria Marriages Register: John George Baker and Sarah Ann Clark* (1864) (No. 1461/1864).

of the Wangaratta township. John Faithfull and Jim Lewis, after closely examining possible alternative sites with such frontages for the homestead, reasoned that:

"Section 16, Crown Allotment 2 appears, albeit on somewhat flimsy evidence, to be the most likely location for William Henry Clark's rural residence."[484]

If correct, this would probably put the homestead somewhere in the vicinity of the intersection of the present day Wangaratta-Yarrawonga and Old School Roads, Waldara. Although William purchased this allotment with six other allotments in 1857, it had earlier formed part of his *Ovens Crossing Place* squatting run.

However, Faithfull and Lewis also noted that William Clark's first executor and trustee, James Willett, sold the allotment in February 1874 after William's death to John Parnell Jones for £183, and that this amount appeared to be an inadequate consideration if it encompassed the land on which the Clark homestead was located.[485] Moreover, the sale of the allotment in 1874 would seemingly have left William's widow, Elizabeth Clark, without her own home if this land had been where she had been living. These considerations may be seen to cast some doubt as to whether it was this allotment where the Clark homestead was situated.

Another possible site for the homestead could have been on the portion of *Pre-Emptive Section E* which William devised by his Will to his second daughter, Elizabeth Mary Moore (née Clark).[486]

It should also be noted that the *Family Transcript* asserts that the Clark homestead was at least informally known as *The One Mile*.[487] If correct, this could place the structure as having been located by, or close to, the junction of the One Mile Creek with the three Mile Creek – perhaps somewhere on the present day grounds of the Wangaratta Golf Club or close to the eastern margin of those grounds. William Clark certainly owned a number of allotments around the junction of the two creeks.[488]

Churchman

In an obituary for William and Elizabeth Clark's third daughter, Charlotte Sophia Cusack (née Clark), published in the *North Eastern Despatch* on 2 October 1912, the anonymous author observed that William had disposed of the *Commercial Hotel*:

> "in order to devote his attention to his extensive holding of lands, the Ovens Crossing station, an area that included the western portion of Wangaratta, 'Waldara' and the greater portion of what is now known as Wangandary."[489]

---

484 See Faithfull and Lewis, *op. cit.*, p. 186.
485 *Ibid.*
486 See *William Clark's Will* (PROV, *VPRS* 28/P0, Unit 103).
487 See footnote 379 and its accompanying text above.
488 See Faithfull and Lewis, *op. cit.*, p. 55.
489 See the *North Eastern Despatch*, Wednesday, 2 October 1912, p. 2.

In truth, William's primary interests were his pastoral and agricultural pursuits, and the buying and selling of real estate. However, it is also true that his intensive engagement in those pursuits did not preclude him from an extensive involvement in Wangaratta community affairs.

First and perhaps foremost, William Clark was long active in the church life of Wangaratta. Like a number of other local pioneers, he was a committed Anglican. In the early years of the Ovens Crossing Place settlement, itinerant Anglican clergymen conducted services in William's *Hope Inn*.[490] William was also one of several prominent local Anglicans who pressed for the construction of a dedicated church in Wangaratta. In 1849, he joined Bishop Perry from Melbourne and another local identity, Dr Thomas Murphy, in a search to find a suitable location for the proposed church. The site finally chosen was at the present day intersection of Ovens and Docker Streets.[491]

The arrival of the Reverend Cooper Searle in Wangaratta in 1855 as the district's first resident Anglican clergyman led to a Crown Grant from the Government of the Port Phillip District to the Church of England of two and a half acres of land for the construction of a church. Prominent Anglican residents in and around the township, including William Clark, promptly formed a building committee to raise funds for building the church. William was himself one of a number of "liberal" donors.[492] The building was completed in early 1856, and opened for services in May of that year as "Holy Trinity Church". However, it was not formally dedicated until 19 May 1858, and only then on a petition to which William was one of a number of signatories.[493]

In 1860, William Clark was one of two donors who individually donated substantial lands abutting Holy Trinity Church to the Church of England.[494] In William's case, the donation was effected in two tranches.

Firstly, by a Conveyance dated 26 June 1860 between Samuel McGhee, William Clark and the Bishop of Melbourne, Charles Perry, McGhee conveyed the lands in Crown Allotments 2 and 3, Section 20 to Bishop Perry at William's direction. The Conveyance records that

---

490 See the *Wangaratta Despatch*, Wednesday, 4 June 1924, p. 3. Although a committed Anglican, William Clark almost certainly gave rooms over in the *Hope Inn* to visiting clergymen from other denominations for accommodation and in which to conduct services. As Paul McGuire put it:
"When priest or parson came [William Clark] gathered the appropriate flock in his parlour."
See Paul McGuire, *Inns of Australia* (1952), pp. 166-167. As early as 1845, Father Charles Lovat, a Catholic priest stationed in Goulburn and Yass, who probably first met William during the latter's time in the Yass district, was likely welcomed by William during an early pastoral visit to the Ovens River valley: see Peter Murray, *As the Spirit Leads* (2013), p. 3.

491 See Whittaker, *op. cit.*, p. 108. David Whittaker, probably relying on a story handed down in the Clark family, wrote of this search and its outcome:
" 'We have chosen a site for the church', said William Clark one day in 1849 when he returned to the Hope Inn for lunch. 'Where?', asked his wife Betty. 'Up on the hill where the cows camp', was the reply."
Ibid.

492 See Canon Percy Dicker, "The Church in the North-East" in (Sept. 1949) 7(5) *The Witness*, p. 2; and Whittaker, *op. cit.*, p. 108.

493 See the *Wangaratta Despatch*, Wednesday, 4 June 1924, p. 3.

494 See "Holy Trinity Cathedral: History of the Church" in the *Wangaratta Chronicle (Special Edition)*, Wednesday, 4 June 1924, p. 1; Colin Holden, *Church in a Landscape* (2002), p. 9; and Faithfull and Lewis, *op. cit.*, pp. 125-127. The second donor, of one allotment, was a Charles William Hughes.

McGhee had first acquired the allotments by way of a Crown Grant on 10 March 1858. On a date not provided in the Conveyance, but implied by it to have been shortly prior to 26 June 1860, William had contracted to purchase the lots from McGhee for £32. He had then directed the latter to convey them to Bishop Perry rather than to himself.

Secondly, by a Conveyance dated 13 July 1860 between William Clark and Bishop Perry, William conveyed the lands in Crown Allotments 4, 15, 16 and 17, Section 20 to Bishop Perry in consideration of a fairly nominal payment of 10s by the Bishop to William. These allotments had earlier been purchased by William from the Crown on 30 October 1857.[495]

Following the creation of the Diocese of Wangaratta in 1902, the Bishop's Lodge was constructed in 1904 on part of the lands donated by William Clark. Holy Trinity Church itself was demolished and replaced by Holy Trinity Cathedral, built in stages between 1908 and 1965. The Church of England further constructed a number of other buildings between 1939 and 1950 along Cathedral Close on other parts of the lands donated by William.[496]

In about 1927, the remaining two allotments conveyed by William Clark to the Church of England were in turn conveyed by the Church of England Trust Corporation of the Diocese of Wangaratta to the Victorian Government to become part of the grounds of the Wangaratta Technical School. The two allotments concerned, Crown Allotments 2 and 17, Section 20, were located on the corners of Mackay and Docker Streets and Mackay and Cusack Streets respectively.[497]

Local Politics

William Clark also turned his hand to local government. Following the lodging of a petition signed by 160 Wangaratta householders with the Victorian Chief Secretary pursuant to the provisions of the *Municipal Institutions Act 1854* (Vic) (No. 15), the Victorian government proclaimed the establishment of the Municipal District of Wangaratta on 18 June 1863.[498]

The election for the first Wangaratta Municipal Council was held on 15 July 1863. Sixteen men were nominated for the seven Council positions. William Clark was nominated as a candidate by his friend, John Moore Snr, the future father-in-law of two of William's daughters. On being so nominated, William apparently observed, to cheers from a gathered

---

495 See Faithfull and Lewis, *op. cit.*, p. 95. Following the establishment of the Anglican Diocese of Wangaratta in 1902, a further Conveyance, between the Bishops of Melbourne and Wangaratta, executed on 4 December 1903 saw the allotments conveyed by the Bishop of Melbourne to the Church of England Trust Corporation of the Diocese of Wangaratta: see Faithfull and Lewis, *op. cit.*, p. 125. Crown Allotments 3, 4, 15 and 16, Section 20 are currently held in trust by the Corporation pursuant to the *Wangaratta Church of England Land Act 1930* (Vic) (21 Geo. 5 No. 3924) (https://tinyurl.com/2raccjxj) (6 April 2023).

496 See Dicker, *op. cit.*, p. 2; and Heritage Council of Victoria, *Holy Trinity Anglican Cathedral Close* (https://tinyurl.com/ksmmcrs) (at 7 April 2023).

497 See Faithfull and Lewis, *op. cit.*, p. 126. See also Whittaker, *op. cit.*, p.123.

498 See *An Act for the Establishment of Municipal Institutions in Victoria 1854* (Vic) (18 Vict. No. 15) (https://tinyurl.com/58bf6m8s) (at 7 April 2023); *Victoria Government Gazette* (No. 121), Friday, 10 October 1862, p. 1952; *Victoria Government Gazette* (No. 64), Friday, 19 June 1863, p. 1362; and Whittaker, *op. cit.*, pp. 64-65. As can be seen from the 1862 *Victoria Government Gazette* referred to earlier in this footnote, William Clark was one of the first to sign the Wangaratta petition.

crowd, that if elected, he would do his best for the interests of the town. He said that he was a very old resident, that he imagined he knew a few of the requirements of the place, and that he would discharge his duties to the best of his abilities.[499]

At the declaration of the poll on 15 July 1863, Michael Cusack was first elected with 89 votes. William Clark, with 88 votes, was the second councillor elected. After his election, William said that the electors must not expect a long speech from him, as public speaking was not his forte. He thanked the electors for placing him second on the poll, and stated that he would do his best for the good of the township.[500] At the first Council meeting held the following day, 16 July 1863, William declined to accept nomination as the Council's first Chairman.[501]

At the second election for the Wangaratta Council held in August 1864, William Clark was defeated. Undeterred by his defeat, he successfully stood again in 1866; taking his Council seat on 28 February 1866.[502] He thereafter held office on the Council until his death.

Little is recorded of William's activities as a councillor. On 3 July 1867, he apparently complained of the inferior quality of the material being used in building the first Wangaratta Town Hall, which was then under construction.[503] On 16 December 1867, he seconded a motion that the building of a privy at the municipal offices be delayed.[504] William's motive for seconding this motion no doubt had a fiscal, rather than a sanitary, basis.

In the context of colonial, rather than municipal, political affairs, it might be noted that in about July 1853, William Clark, like his friend John Moore Snr, signed an Address emanating from Wangaratta residents and declaring the signatories' loyalty to the new Lieutenant Governor of Victoria, Sir Charles Hotham.[505] Three years later, in September 1856, both William Clark and John Moore Snr were signatories to a Notice published in *The Argus* and calling on James Stewart to stand for election to the Victorian Legislative Council for the Eastern Province (which included Wangaratta) in the forthcoming Victorian Parliamentary elections. Stewart stood and was duly elected. He remained in office until his early death in August 1863.[506]

---

499 See Whittaker, *op. cit.*, p. 68.
500 See the *Ovens and Murray Advertiser*, Saturday, 18 July 1863, p. 3. See also Whittaker, *op. cit.*, p. 70; and O'Callaghan, *op. cit.*, p. 24.
501 See Whittaker, *op. cit.*, p. 71. Councillor Edward Lucas was elected in his stead: *ibid*.
502 See Whittaker, *op. cit.*, p. 81.
503 See Whittaker, *op. cit.*, p. 74.
504 See Whittaker, *op. cit.*, p. 74, n. 22.
505 See *Address of Loyalty to Lieutenant Governor Hotham* (PROV, *VPRS* 1095/Po, Unit 7A, Bundle 3, No. 72, pp. 1 and 2). See also Jenny Coates, "Sir Charles Hotham and the good citizens of Wangaratta" in *Conversations with Grandma* (https://tinyurl.com/bdf75euk) (at 7 April 2023).
506 See *The Argus*, Saturday, 6 September 1856, p. 6. To judge from his published political manifesto, Stewart was a man of liberal persuasions: *ibid*. See also Jenny Coates, "1856 politics Wangaratta style" in *Conversations with Grandma* (https://tinyurl.com/yc5dmbvv) (at 7 April 2023). It might also be noted that William Clark's younger brother, Richard Clark in Benalla, was also a signatory to this published Notice.

Education

Whilst William Clark probably received little formal schooling in England, events were to show that he took a close interest in education once he became established in Wangaratta.

The first school in Wangaratta was opened by a Mr Bendall in a little slab hut in 1848. Among the initial 16 students attending the school were Elizabeth and William Clark's first two daughters, Sarah Clark and Elizabeth Clark Jnr. The school only had a short life due to Bendall's early death. A successor private school established by a William Peacock was also short-lived.[507]

The year 1848 also saw the creation of a National Schools Board of New South Wales charged with establishing a public education system in the Colony. In order to secure the construction of National Schools in their areas, local patrons were required to raise a quarter of the building costs, superintend the erection of the school buildings and take a share in their conduct.[508]

At a meeting convened in Wangaratta on 29 August 1849, William Clark was chosen as one of five local patrons for the purposes of constructing and operating a local National School. The patrons raised the necessary funds, and the new National School was opened in March 1850.[509] It would appear that the Clark children were all educated in the school.[510] For his own part, William remained a patron of the Wangaratta National School until 1858.[511]

The Victorian National Schools Board (the successor body in Victoria to the National Schools Board of New South Wales after Victoria's separation from New South Wales in 1851) and the Victorian Denominational Schools Board were amalgamated in 1862 pursuant to the *Common Schools Act 1862* (Vic) (No. 149) to form the Victorian Board of Education. Following this amalgamation, the Wangaratta National School was vested in the new Board of Education. In May 1868, the *Ovens and Murray Advertiser* noted that William Clark was one of three men appointed by the Board to be "members" of the Wangaratta Common School – clearly the in role of overseers.[512] In this capacity, William's active involvement in education likely continued until his death.

Other Community Activities

William Clark's church, municipal and educational activities did not exhaust his community commitments. On 4 April 1859, and at his *Commercial Hotel*, William was elected to the first

---

507 See Whittaker, *op. cit.*, p. 117.
508 *Ibid.*
509 *Ibid.* See also Murray, *op. cit.*, p. 50.
510 See the obituary for Charlotte Sophia Cusack (née Clark) in the *North Eastern Despatch*, Wednesday, 2 October 1912, p. 2.
511 See the *Sixth Report of the Commissioners of National Education for the Colony of Victoria for the Year 1858* (1859), pp. 58-59 (https://tinyurl.com/m8w5n9s) (at 7 April 2023).
512 See the *Ovens and Murray Advertiser*, Thursday, 28 May 1868, p. 2.

Committee of the newly-formed Ovens and Murray Agricultural and Horticultural Society.[513] He was also a trustee of the Wangaratta Cemetery Trust.[514] When a mailman carrying mail slipped off his horse and drowned while endeavouring to cross the Ovens River on 24 April 1844, William joined with others to rescue the mail and arrange for another rider to deliver it to its destination.[515]

In addition to his many other interests, William Clark was long associated with horse racing in Wangaratta. In the early days of the settlement, there were few sporting outlets for those living in the area. The first local race meeting was said to have been held in 1845 or 1847. It was apparently a well-attended and gala affair.[516] However, according to Robert Mason, who arrived in the region in the early 1850s, there was only about one race meeting a year held at Wangaratta at about the time of his arrival.[517]

In 1856, it was decided to give horse racing a permanent home in Wangaratta. In that year, the Wangaratta Racing Club was formed. A site on Three Mile Creek was chosen for the Wangaratta Racecourse, and William Clark was elected one of the trustees of the property.[518] William remained a trustee of the racecourse until his death.[519]

William Clark's Appearance and Character

There would seem to be only one extant photo of William Clark.[520] This shows a man with an apparently unlined face, a head of long and dark hair and a luxuriant white beard. Of William's beard, one of his great-grandsons, Albert ("Bert") Moore, joked that it was so luxuriant that small creatures could have lived in it.[521] It could be said that the photo shows William to have been a man with kindly, but nonetheless shrewd, eyes.

The evidence of his life would suggest that William Clark was indeed shrewd – and much more. He was clearly intelligent, ambitious, industrious and a canny businessman to boot. As can be seen above, he was also civic-minded and gregarious. As a publican, he probably enjoyed a drink or two.

No doubt drawing on family tradition, Bert Moore observed of his great-grandfather that William Clark was "unobtrusive, kind and obliging and had no enemies."[522] As was attested

---

513   See Whittaker, *op. cit.*, p. 127.
514   See *The Argus*, Saturday, 15 March 1856, p. 5.
515   See Whittaker, *op. cit.*, p. 47.
516   See Whittaker, *op. cit.*, p. 150.
517   See "Wangaratta Dispatch and North-Eastern Advertiser, Wednesday 26 June 1907 – Robert J. Mason" in *Kaye's Webpages*, p. 4.
518   See Whittaker, *op. cit.*, p. 150; and O'Callaghan, *op. cit.*, p. 19.
519   See the *Ovens and Murray Advertiser*, Thursday, 21 September 1871, p. 3.
520   See photo 33 below. A copy of this photo of William Clark is to be found in a corridor leading to the Vestry of Holy Trinity Cathedral in Wangaratta. It hangs beside a photo of William's wife, Elizabeth Clark; with their youngest son, George Arthur Clark, on her knee: see photo 34 below. George appears to have been only one or two years old when the photo was taken. As he was born shortly before 16 June 1859 (being his known baptismal date), this would mean that the photo of George and his mother was likely taken in the early 1860s. Assuming that the photo of William was taken at the same time, the later would then have been in his early 50s.
521   See *The Chronicle*, Friday, 24 March 1995, p. 14.
522   *Ibid.*

by the attendance of hundreds of persons at his funeral, William was clearly well-regarded in Wangaratta and its surrounds. His kindly nature was perhaps apparent when he gave character evidence on behalf of a former employee, James Bellew, when the latter was tried for embezzlement of monies from a subsequent employer, Thomas Cusack, before Judge Cope and a Jury at the Beechworth Court of General Sessions in February 1865. Bellew was in due course acquitted of the charge.[523]

William Clark's kindly disposition clearly extended to his wider family. It will be recalled that at some presently unknown point in the early to mid 1840s, William's parents moved to Wangaratta from John Clark Jnr's establishment at Seymour. What caused them to make that move is not now known. However, they presumably found the personalities and support of William Clark and his wife, Elizabeth Clark Jnr, agreeable. The two older Clarks died in Wangaratta in the late 1840's.[524]

Two of William Clark's younger brothers, Thomas and George Clark, also moved to Wangaratta in the 1840s.[525] In all probability, Thomas and George would in life have been the recipients of some measure of William's largesse. Thomas Clark certainly was; being bequeathed an annuity of £25 per annum by William in the first Codicil to the latter's Will.[526]

However, William Clark's concern for his extended family is most clearly evident from his vain efforts to assist the family of yet another brother, Richard Clark, after Richard's death in 1869.

As will be seen in more detail in the next section of this book, Richard Clark settled in 1839. on the Broken River at what was to become Benalla. There, he constructed a hotel known as the *Black Swan Inn*.[527] Like his elder brothers, John and William Clark, Richard became a squatter; holding first the *Hurdle Creek* run, and then later the *Junction* run adjacent to Benalla.[528] However, by the middle 1860s, he found himself heavily in debt and, in 1868, the defendant to an action in the Supreme Court of Victoria taken by the National Bank of Australasia to recover monies owing to it.[529] These proceedings were stayed, but on 20 January 1869, Richard died.[530]

Following Richard's death, William Clark paid £1,217 at a Sheriff's auction in an endeavour

---

523 See the *Ovens and Murray Advertiser*, Thursday, 23 February 1865, p. 2. The newspaper summarised William Clark's evidence thus:
"William Clark, formerly a publican at Wangaratta, but now a squatter, sworn: Have known defendant for the last 15 years. He had full charge of [my] business for about three and a half years. Had every confidence in his integrity. The defendant, since he left my service, had been to England, and on his return had entered Mr Cusack's employ.":
Ibid.

524 See footnotes 382, 383 and 384, and their accompanying texts above.

525 See footnotes 393, 394, 397, 399, 401, 402 and 403, and their accompanying texts, above.

526 See *Lorraine Key's manuscript*, p. 12; *Victoria Deaths Register: Thomas Clark* (1879) (No. 3289/1879); *William Clark's Will: First Codicil* (PROV, VPRS 28 P/o, Unit 103); and footnote 549 and its accompanying text below. George Clark pre-deceased his brother William; dying on 9 June 1854: see footnote 402 and its accompanying text above. It might be noted that it was Thomas Clark who formally identified his brother William's body after the latter's death on 24 April 1871: see *New South Wales Deaths Register: William Clark* (1871) (No. 2828/1872).

527 See A. J. Dunlop, *op. cit.*, pp. 30-32.

528 See Billis and Kenyon, *Pastoral Pioneers*, pp. 222 and 225; and Spreadborough and Anderson, *op. cit.*, pp. 53 and 54.

529 See *The Age*, Tuesday, 13 July 1869, p. 3.

530 *Ibid.*

to acquire title to 63 allotments of land then standing in Richard Clark's name. Shortly prior to Richard's death, his son-in-law, Michael Farrell, had successfully sued Richard in an undefended Supreme Court action for £2,034 (including legal costs) on a Bill of Exchange. The Sheriff's sale at which William Clark seemingly acquired the land was the product of Farrell's attempt to recover at least part of his judgment debt out of the proceeds of the sale. It seems very likely that William sought to purchase the 63 allotments so as to preserve them for Richard's children.

However, by a second action in the Supreme Court taken by the National Bank against William Clark in 1869, the Bank succeeded in establishing that it held a first mortgage from Richard Clark over all 63 allotments; and that accordingly it, rather than William was entitled under its mortgage to the land. The Bank then promptly foreclosed on that mortgage. Not only did Richard Clark's children lose the opportunity to gain the land in question, but William Clark found himself some £1,500 out of pocket.[531]

William might have been a kindly man, but it's not easy to accept Bert Moore's assertion that he had no enemies. Few persons as locally prominent as William Clark was could travel through life without stirring up some measure of enmity. The following Notice published in the *Ovens and Murray Advertiser* in April 1870 perhaps speaks for itself:

> "REWARD – On the night of Sunday, the 18th of February last, a horse belonging to William Clark was maliciously stabbed with some sharp instrument, probably the side of a pair of shears, at Three Mile Creek, Wangaratta, in the Benalla district; and on the night of the 25th of February and the 1st and 2nd of March last, two other horses belonging to the same owner were similarly injured, one of them fatally: and whereas Mr Clark offers a reward of twenty pounds for the detection of the person or persons guilty of these outrages, Notice is hereby given that a reward of twenty pounds (supplemental to that offered by Mr Clark) will be paid by the Government for such information as will lead to the conviction of the person or persons guilty of the outrages above described."[532]

Despite these rewards, there is nothing extant to suggest that the perpetrator or perpetrators of the stabbings was or were ever brought to justice.

Like many, if not most, squatters and overlanders, William Clark would have been a tough and agile young man. His toughness and agility were demonstrated in 1855 when a patron at his *Hope Inn* tried to pass two bogus bills of exchange, with a purported total value of £36, on to him. Judging the bills to be fakes, William sent a messenger to summon the police.

---

531 As mentioned above, the full circumstances surrounding William Clark's attempt to aid his brother Richard's children in this manner will be canvassed in some detail in the next section in this book. William borrowed a total of £1,500 from the Colonial Bank of Australasia to pay for Richard's allotments and associated costs, including legal costs. At William's death in 1871, this sum was still owing to the Colonial Bank, and was the largest single liability encumbering William's estate. It would seem that neither William nor his executors made any attempt to recover any part of the purchase monies paid by William for the 63 allotments from Michael Farrell.

532 See the *Ovens and Murray Advertiser*, Tuesday, 12 April 1870, p. 2.

However, before the latter could arrive, the fraudster attempted to make his escape. William gave chase, overtook the man, forcefully apprehended him and gave him over to the police.[533]

The Death of William Clark

Unfortunately, toughness proved to be no match for disease when, in the late 1860s, William Clark found himself overtaken by hepatitis and gall stones.[534]

It would appear that William had had his medical needs attended to over many years by Dr William Dobbyn. The latter commenced practice in Wangaratta in about 1852. He developed a close friendship with William Clark. According to David Whittaker, Dobbyn left Wangaratta in 1870, and for many years thereafter was the resident physician at the Beechworth Hospital.[535] Be that as it may, it is clear that in early 1871, Dobbyn was living and practising across the Murray River in Corowa. And it was to Corowa and to Dr Dobbyn that William ventured when his medical conditions worsened.[536]

It is not now known when in early 1870 William Clark arrived in Corowa. However, it seems likely that it was at some time between 11 March and 17 April.[537] In Corowa, he saw out his last days in Dobbyn's home. As he deteriorated, there was probably little that the latter could do for William apart from perhaps providing him with some measure of pain relief.

William Clark died on 24 April 1871 at the age of 61 years.[538] Following his death, his body was returned to Wangaratta and "lay in state" for a time in the *Commercial Hotel*.[539] On 26 April, he was buried in the Wangaratta Cemetery in his parents' grave.[540] In a brief report, the *Ovens and Murray Advertiser* described William's funeral in the following terms:

> "There was a large attendance at Mr Clark's funeral, not less than four hundred persons being present, together with sixty vehicles. The funeral Service was conducted by the Ven. Archdeacon Tucker, assisted by the Rev. Mr Cross. The meeting of the borough council was adjourned as a mark of respect."[541]

William Clark lived to see his four eldest daughters married. Of his remaining living

---

533   See the *Ovens and Murray Advertiser*, Saturday, 20 January 1855, p. 5.
534   See *New South Wales Deaths Register: William Clark* (1871) (No. 2828/1872).
535   See Whittaker, *op. cit.*, p. 139.
536   It seems likely that after departing Wangaratta in 1870, Dobbyn lived and practised for a short while in Corowa before moving to the Beechworth Hospital.
537   William Clark executed the first Codicil to his Will in Wangaratta on 11 March 1871, and the second Codicil to that Will in Corowa on 17 April 1871: see *William Clark's Will: First and Second Codicils* (PROV, *VPRS* 28/P0, Unit 103).
538   See *New South Wales Deaths Register: William Clark* (1871) (No. 2828/1872); *The Age*, Thursday, 27 April 1871, p. 2; and the *Ovens and Murray Advertiser*, Thursday, 18 May 1871, p. 3.
539   See Jones, *op. cit.*, p. 14.
540   See *New South Wales Deaths Register: William Clark* (1871) (No. 2828/1872); *The Argus*, Thursday, 27 April 1871, p. 5; and *The Australasian*, Saturday, 29 April 1871, p. 15. See also photo 35 below.
541   See the *Ovens and Murray Advertiser*, Thursday, 27 April 1871, p. 2.

children, his eldest son, William John Clark was 21 years old at the time of his father's death.[542] William's next child, Alice Rebecca Clark, was then 19 years old. Although unmarried when her father died, she had already borne a child to an unknown father. William's four youngest children ranged in age between 16 and 10 years.[543] His widow, Elizabeth Clark, was about 47 years old when her husband died.

William Clark's Will

William Clark died leaving a Will executed by him on 24 February 1871, together with two Codicils to that Will.[544] He almost certainly made his Will in the knowledge that his health was fast failing. The fact that he executed two Codicils to it suggests that the disposition of his estate after his death weighed heavily upon him.

By his Will, William Clark appointed three men to be his executors, the trustees of his estate and the guardians of his infant children: David Evans, Arthur Jennings Smith and James Willett (clauses 10, 34 and 35). Evans was one of William's close friends. Smith was a Wangaratta bank manager. Willett was one of William's sons-in-law, and a farming partner to boot.[545]

William's Will was lengthy and complex. By its provisions, he devised specified parcels of land to three named beneficiaries (clauses 1 to 9). He left the residue of his real and personal estate to be held in trust by his trustees for most, but not all, of his children (clauses 10 to 29).

In the first place, William Clark devised Allotments 1, 2 and 3, Section 12, Parish of South Wangaratta to James Willett for his use absolutely (clause 1). Secondly, to his daughter, Elizabeth Mary Moore (née Clark), the wife of John Moore Jnr, William devised that part of *Pre-Emptive Section E* marked by posts and lying between her husband's land and the Ovens River. He further left Elizabeth Moore Allotments 1 and 2, Section 40, Parish of Wangaratta North (clause 2).[546] Thirdly, William devised the unsold portion of Allotment 1, Section 1, Parish of Wangaratta North to his trustees to be held in trust for his grandchild, Elizabeth Ellen Clark (clauses 3 to 9). The latter was the child of William's eldest daughter, Sarah Ann Clark, and was born out of wedlock shortly prior to 9 August 1861. Sarah Ann Clark subsequently married George Davies in 1862, and then John Baker on 27 June 1864.[547]

Fourthly, and as mentioned above, William Clark left the residue of his estate to be held

---

542 An unverified family story has it that William John Clark had intended to enter the clergy of the Anglican Church but had been unable to attend Melbourne University for that purpose due to straightened family financial circumstances following his father's death. It has been said that instead, he commenced a carrier service between Wangaratta and Whitfield.

543 See footnote 449 and its accompanying text above.

544 See *William Clark's Will* (PROV, VPRS 28/P0, Unit 103).

545 James Willett had married William Clark's daughter, Emily Jane Clark, on 9 October 1862: see the *Moore Considine Family Website* (https://tinyurl.com/58ntx5sc) (at 10 April 2023). *See also* footnote 449 and its accompanying text above.

546 John Moore Jnr had married Elizabeth Mary Clark on 1 February 1864: see the *Moore Considine Family Website* (https://tinyurl.com/58ntx5sc) (at 10 April 2023). In 1866, William Clark had transferred land in the north-west of *Pre-Emptive Section E*, together with some adjacent land, to John Moore Jnr: see Faithfull and Lewis, *op. cit.*, p. 102.

547 See the *Moore Considine Family Website* (https://tinyurl.com/58ntx5sc) (at 10 April 2023).

in trust by his trustees (clause 10). They were directed to sell or otherwise convert this residuary estate into money (clause 11). The trustees were further directed to use this trust money to pay all of William's funeral, testamentary and other debts, together with the costs of administering his estate (clause 15), and then to divided the balance equally among his children and their issue per stirpes:

> "excepting my son George Arthur Clark and my daughter Florence Amelia Clark, both of whom are already fully provided for by me in my lifetime and who shall not take any interest under this my Will" (clause 16).[548]

As was usually the case with wills of this kind and times, William Clark's Will provided his trustees with wide powers and discretions with respect to their administration of the trust property; including the power to advance monies available to them at their discretion for the maintenance, education and advancement of William's children (clause 24).

The first Codicil to William's Will was executed by him on 11 March 1871. By it, William further devised Allotment 5, Section 8, Parish of Wangaratta North to his daughter, Emily Jane Willett. He went on to declare that the lands cumulatively devised to Emily and her husband, James Willett, were deemed to be valued in total at £500, and that Emily was to receive no further benefit from the residue of William's estate unless and until that sum had been paid by her or her husband into that estate. William further directed his trustees to "improve" the unsold portion of Section 42, Parish of Wangaratta North so that it produced and annual income of £25. This income was to be paid to William's brother, Thomas Clark, during his life, and after Thomas' death to the latter's wife during her life. Upon her death, the land was to pass to William's oldest surviving son, William John Clark, absolutely.[549]

William Clark executed the second Codicil to his Will on 17 April 1871 – a mere one week prior to his death. Its contents were short and to the point, providing that:

> "if any child or person taking any share or interest under my Will shall take any proceeding at law or in equity to dispute the acts of my trustees or the validity of any provision of my said Will, he or she shall forfeit and lose all such share or interest."

It is sad to think that William, so close to death, was troubled by the possibility, real or imagined, that one of his children or another beneficiary might seek to challenge his Will, or the actions of his trustees, in court. In the event, no such challenge seems to have eventuated.

There are a number of puzzling questions which arise in relation to William Clark's Will.

---

548 "Per stirpes" translates from Latin as "by root, stock or branch". It is a method of distribution of estate assets by the substitution of the children of a named beneficiary under a Will where the beneficiary has pre-deceased the testator: see *In re McInnes, deceased* [1925] VLR 496.

549 Thomas Clark married his wife, Elizabeth Clark (née Watson) in 1855. He died on 24 January 1859; his wife having predeceased him on 26 November 1873: see the *Moore Considine Family Website* (https://tinyurl.com/58ntx5sc) (at 10 April 2023). See also footnotes 399, 400 and 526, and their accompanying texts, above.

In the first place, the Will makes no provision for William's widow, Elizabeth Clark. It is hard to believe that he intended to leave her with nothing on his death; particularly given that their younger children were presumably in her care. It may be that William made an inter vivos settlement of property on Elizabeth prior to his death (as he may well have also done with respect to his two youngest children, George Arthur Clark and Florence Amelia Margaret Clark).[550] If so, the nature and extent of that property, and when and how it was settled on Elizabeth, are presently unknown.

Alternatively, there may have been some informal family arrangement concluded before William died by which it had been agreed that one of William's married daughters would house and provide for her mother and younger, unmarried siblings. If this had been the case, it would seem likely that the daughter in question would have been either Emily Jane Willett or Elizabeth Mary Moore.

In the second place, it might be thought strange that William Clark did not make any provision in his Will for an immediate gift of real estate to his eldest surviving son, William John Clark. He had, after all, not only devised land by the Will to his daughter, Elizabeth Mary Moore, but also to his son-in-law, James Willett. And by the first Codicil to his Will, William had also devised other real estate to a second daughter (and James Willett's wife), Emily Jane Willett. However, it may be that William made his testamentary dispositions in the manner that he did in the expectation that William John Clark would pursue a career as an Anglican cleric, and would accordingly not wish to work land or otherwise be encumbered by it.[551]

In the third place, William Clark left land by his Will in trust for a grand-daughter, Elizabeth Ellen Clark, the daughter of Sarah Ann Clark. Elizabeth Ellen Clark was illegitimate at birth. Although her mother did subsequently marry twice, it is by no means clear that either of her two husbands, George Davies and John Baker, was Elizabeth Ellen Clark's biological father.[552] Yet William had a second infant grand-daughter, Alice Rosetta Moore, who was also born illegitimate and for whom he made no specific provision in his Will. Alice Rosetta Moore was born shortly before 8 August 1869. Her mother, Alice Rebecca Clark, married William Moore on 1 May 1872.[553] Again, it is not clear that William Moore was Alice Rosetta Moore's biological father. It is not now known why William Clark thus distinguished between his two illegitimate grand-daughters.

Finally, William Clark declared in his Will that he had made no provision in it for his two youngest children, George Arthur Clark and Florence Amelia Clark, because he had already provided for them during his lifetime. However, it is not presently known how William so provided for the two children.

---

550 See footnote 598 and its accompanying text above.
551 See footnote 542 above. However, it would appear that William John Clark did, in fact, purchase land in the vicinity of Wangaratta following his father's death: see Faithfull and Lewis, *op. cit.*, pp. 101 and 107.
552 See the *Moore Considine Family Website* (https://tinyurl.com/58ntx5sc) (at 10 April 2023).
553 *Ibid.*

Estate Administration

Although by his Will, William Clark appointed three men to be the executors of it, only one of them, James Willett, initially moved to prove the Will and the two Codicils to it.[554] Of the remaining two appointees, David Evans renounced his right to apply for probate of the Will and Codicils on 10 July 1871. Earlier, on 29 May 1871, William's last appointee, Arthur Jennings Smith, also sought to renounce his right to apply for probate. However, it seems that on some presently unknown date between 29 May 1871 and 13 July 1871, Smith withdrew his renunciation.

On 13 July 1871, and on the motion of Mr George Kerferd of Counsel, probate of William Clark's Will and two Codicils was granted by Mr Justice Molesworth in the Supreme Court of Victoria to James Willett; with leave being reserved to Arthur Smith to come in and prove the Will and the Codicils.[555]

In an Inventory of Assets and Liabilities filed with the Court in support of his application for the grant of probate, Willett listed assets in William's estate with a total value estimated by Willett to amount to £7,752.[556] These assets included 49 discrete parcels of land held either as Freehold, under Crown leases or by licence. Willett valued this real estate in all at £5,605.

The largest single asset in the £2,147 worth of personal property which formed part of William Clark's estate consisted in £1,330 in unpaid monies payable to the estate by Daniel Hugh Evans for the purchase of William's interest in the *Victoria Flour Mills*.[557]

James Willett's Inventory of Assets and Liabilities went on to list estate debts totalling £3,008-17-11. Of these debts, far and away the largest were sums of £1,500 owing to the Colonial Bank of Australasia, Wangaratta on a bond and promissory note, and £1.225-6-2 owing to the Bank of New South Wales, Wangaratta. The amount of £1,500 owing to the Colonial Bank had originally been borrowed by William Clark in his attempt to acquire 63 allotments of land standing in the name of his late brother, Richard Clark, in an ultimately futile effort to prevent their forfeiture under a mortgage to the National Bank.[558] In all, Willett's estimates gave William Clark's net estate a value of £4,744-2-1.

At first blush, the estimated total value of £5,605 given by James Willett for his late father-in-law's extensive land holdings appears to be surprisingly low. It is possible (perhaps likely) that Willett provided deliberately low estimates for the values of the individual

---

554 See *William Clark's Will: Probate* (PROV, *VPRS* 28/P0, Unit 103).

555 *Ibid.* It is, perhaps, interesting to note that at the time that he moved the motion for probate, George Kerferd was the Member for Ovens in the Victorian Legislative Assembly. He was Premier of Victoria from 1874 until 1875, and later a judge of the Supreme Court from 1886 until his death in 1889: see Margot Beever, "Kerferd, George Briscoe (1831-1889)" in *Australian Dictionary of Biography* (https://tinyurl.com/mr2ewcz7) (at 10 April 2023).

556 See *William Clark's Will: Inventory of Assets and Liabilities* (PROV, *VPRS* 28/P0, Unit 103).

557 See footnote 472 and its accompanying text above.

558 See footnote 531 and its accompanying text above. See also **Appendix 3** below for an extracted table of assets and liabilities, taken from the Inventory of Assets and Liabilities filled by James Willett with the Supreme Court in support of his application for a grant of probate of William Clark's Will and Codicils.

parcels of land with a view to minimising the probate duty payable by the estate.[559] However, the main reason for the low figure is almost certainly that most of the parcels of land were undeveloped, and located within or around the bounds of what was then still a small Victorian country township. Had William Clark lived another 20 years or so, the position may have been very different.

Given the number of allotments of land falling into William's estate, and the complexities of his Will and first Codicil, administration of the estate under the Will and Codicil was always likely to be complex and time-consuming. During 1872 and 1873, James Willett placed a significant number of those allotments on the market, and many were duly sold at auction.[560] Then, on 2 April 1875, James Willett died.[561]

Without moving to obtain a grant of probate from the Supreme Court pursuant to the leave granted to him by Mr Justice Molesworth on 13 May 1871, it seems that Arthur Smith simply stepped into James Willett's shoes after the latter's death and began himself administering William Clark's estate. Thereafter, things clearly moved slowly. Then, some 26 years after the original grant of probate to Willett, Smith finally did exercise his leave and applied to the Court in 1897 for his own grant of probate.[562]

In an Affidavit sworn by him on 31 May 1897 in support of his application for his grant of probate from the Supreme Court, Arthur Smith deposed that:

> "I am advised that in order to perfect the title to certain land belonging to the estate sold since the date of death of the said James Willett by me as the surviving Trustee appointed by the said Will, it is necessary that I should take out probate to the said Will and Codicils in pursuance of the leave reserved."[563]

Probate of the Will and Codicils was duly granted to Smith by the Registrar of Probates on 19 August 1897.[564]

Notwithstanding this second grant of probate, and the passage of decades, there was still further delay in administering William Clark's estate. In 1900, Supreme Jemima Maria Kett (née Clark), William and Elizabeth Clark's second youngest daughter, on her own behalf and on behalf of all others interested in William's Will and Codicils, commenced a proceeding in the Supreme Court of Victoria at Melbourne against Arthur Smith in the latter's capacity as William's surviving executor and trustee.[565]

It is unclear precisely what relief Jemima Kett was seeking by her application to the

---

559 Probate duty was first introduced into Victoria in 1870 by the *An Act to Enforce and Collect Duties on the Estates of Deceased Persons 1870* (Vic) (34 Vict. No. 388) (https://tinyurl.com/2yaf42r6) (at 10 April 2023).
560 See the *Ovens and Murray Advertiser*, Friday, 17 May 1872, p. 2; the *Ovens and Murray Advertiser*, Tuesday, 21 May 1872, p. 2; and the *Ovens and Murray Advertiser*, Wednesday, 26 February 1873, p. 2.
561 See the *Moore Considine Family Website* (https://tinyurl.com/58ntx5sc) (at 10 April 2023).
562 *William Clark's Will: Grant of Probate to Arthur Smith* (PROV, *VPRS* 28/P2, Unit 2).
563 *Ibid.*
564 *Ibid.*
565 See *Jemima Kett v Arthur Smith* (PROV, *VPRS* 7591/P2, Unit 3).

Court. It may have been directions from the Court to Smith for a speedy conclusion to the administration, or perhaps she was merely seeking information from an executor and trustee reluctant to provide it. In any event, it would appear that Smith was able to give some measure of satisfaction to Jemima Kett because the latter seemingly discontinued her proceeding. At some presently undefined time after 1900, William Clark's estate must have been finally wound up.

William Clark is commemorated in Wangaratta by a street bearing his surname. His name is also inscribed on a stone monument dedicated to "The First Pioneers Of Wangaratta District" and located on Ryley Street adjacent to Merriwa Park.[566] However, the most personal of the memorials are two windows in the porch in Holy Trinity Cathedral, Wangaratta which were installed in 1910 and which are dedicated jointly to William and his wife, Elizabeth Clark.[567]

The Death of Elizabeth Clark

Elizabeth Clark seemingly lived quietly for the balance of her life after the death of her husband. She died unexpectedly on 29 September 1888. She was around 64 years old when she died. Her death record noted that the causes of her death were "hamophysis" and "exhaustion".[568] Elizabeth was buried in her own grave in the Wangaratta Cemetery on 1 October 1888.[569]

Elizabeth Clark may have lived quietly with members of her family until her death, but she nonetheless appears to have been active until the end. In an obituary published in the *Wangaratta Chronicle* on 2 October 1888, it was said of her that"

> "Having been married when not more than 15, she lived to bring up a large family, and could count up to 54 grandchildren and 4 great grandchildren in addition to her sons and daughters. The deceased lady, who at the time of her death was sixty four years of age, had always enjoyed good health until about a year ago, when she began to fail. She was in her usual way, however, up to the last, and attended the Church of England Tea Meeting a few days before her death, which came unexpectedly through the bursting of a blood vessel."[570]

---

566 See photo 36 below.
567 See photo 37 below; and the *Albury Banner and Wodonga Express*, Friday, 7 January 1910, p. 2.
568 See *Victoria Deaths Register: Elizabeth Clark* (1888) (No. 16158/1888). "Hamophysis", more normally spelled as "haemophysis" or "haemoptysis", is a haemorrhage; most often occurring in the lungs or the bronchial passages, and frequently caused by tuberculosis or another chronic pulmonary disease: see Health Direct, *Haemoptysis (coughing up blood)* (https://tinyurl.com/tjxdddsc) (at 10 April 2023).
569 See Ancestry: *Jonathan Harris Family Tree – Elizabeth Harris* (https://tinyurl.com/y4dc6h3h) (at 10 April 2023); and photo 38 below.
570 See the *Wangaratta Chronicle*, Tuesday, 2 October 1888, p. 3.

Interestingly, it would seem that Elizabeth died somewhere in Ely Street, Wangaratta.[571] Whether she was living in a house in that street at the time of her death or was visiting a relative or friend is presently unknown.

A further testimonial, which speaks of Elizabeth Clark's kind nature and place in the history of Wangaratta and North Eastern Victoria, along side William Clark's place in that history, is to be found in the following obituary by an anonymous author published in the *Ovens and Murray Advertiser* on 13 October 1888. This states that:

> "I confess I was surprised that so little had been said in any of the district papers about the curious history and services of Mrs Clarke, of Wangaratta, recently deceased, widow of the late William Clarke, more familiarly and generally known as 'Old Bill Clarke' in the early days. Mrs Clarke, who was born in England, and came to Australia in her earliest youth, arrived in Wangaratta with her husband as far back as 1839, she being then little more than 15 years of age....
>
> Mr Clarke, between the punt and the public house, figuratively speaking, coined money, which he invested in property, and in building – after the bridge was finished – the Commercial Hotel, in Murphy-street, which is now a much more pretentious establishment. The writer of this was in those golden days a cadet in the police force – the troopers, as they were then called – and as the gold and prisoners' escorts always stopped at Mrs Clark's, he had plenty of opportunities of knowing that lady and her kindly ways, and of hearing from others of the earliest part of her career in the district. It is of this latter I desire to chiefly speak. When Mrs Clarke settled in Wangaratta, there was not another woman in any direction within twenty miles; but she used to travel that distance on horseback on occasions, to comfort the sick or help to bring little native Australians into the world, her own first child – she had twelve altogether – being the first ever born in Wangaratta. All this was authenticated to me at a later date, although few now remain who witnessed it. But there are very many still living who stand to her almost in the light of foster children, owing to her kind and charitable attention to their mothers in their need. I can speak personally of Mrs Clarke's friendly and pleasant ways when her family was growing more and more numerous, and I know that she made us fellows feel not only comfortable, but as if we were at home again. I write this because Mrs Clarke's many good qualities and great services – when such services were invaluable, and indeed, but for her, unprocurable – seem to be either unknown or forgotten."[572]

---

571 See *Victoria Deaths Register: Elizabeth Clark* (1888) (No. 16158/1888).
572 See the *Ovens and Murray Advertiser*, Saturday, 13 October 1888, p. 6.

24. Rattray's store and punt, 1839.

25. History plaque at the site of William Clark's first wheat crop in what is now the King George V Memorial Gardens, Wangaratta.

26. A model of William Clark's second punt, W. H Edwards Museum Wangaratta.

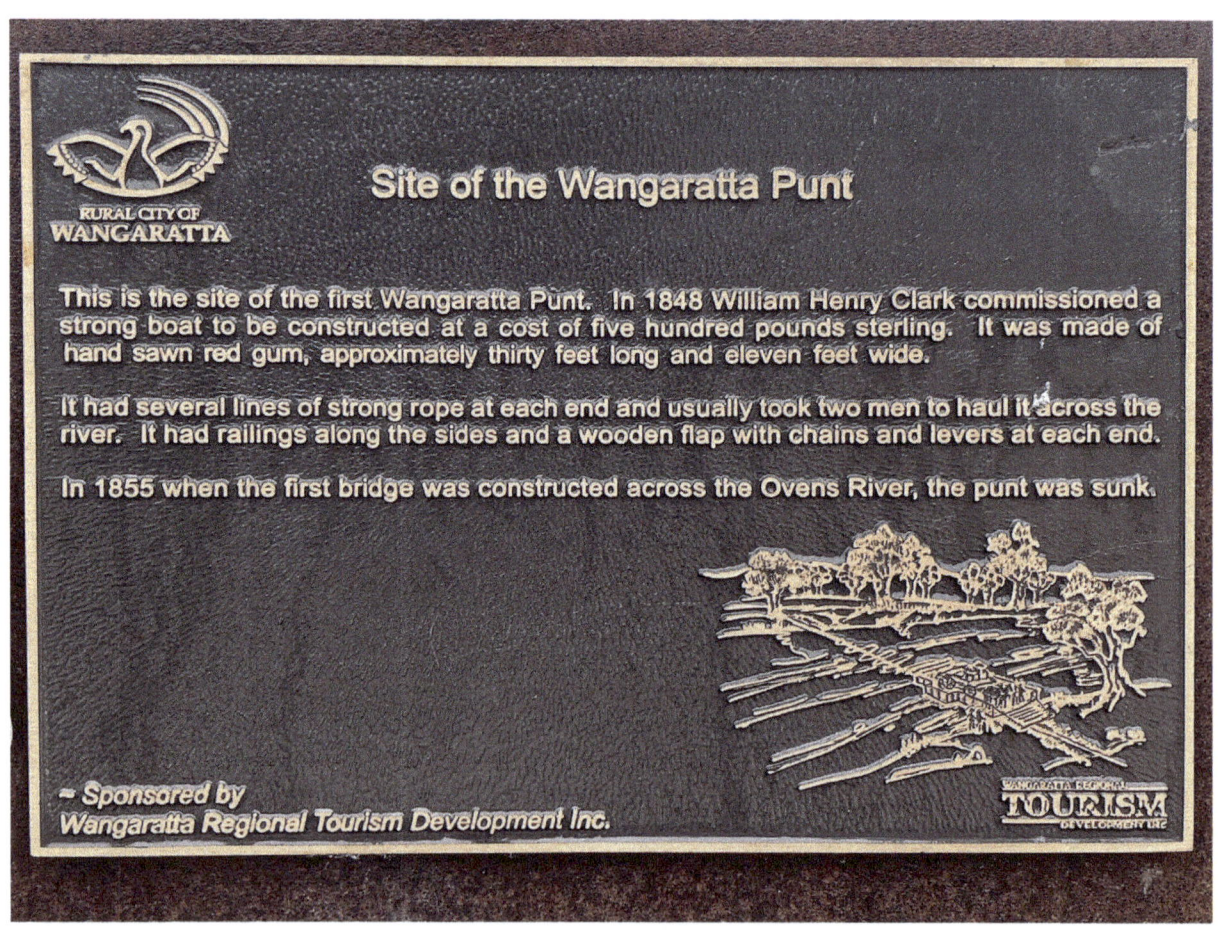

27. History plaque located near the site of William Clark's punt.

28. A close-up view of the Commercial Hotel, Wangaratta.

29. The Commercial Hotel, looking north-east along Murphy Street towards the Ovens River.

30. The Sydney Hotel; built by William Clark on the site of the Hope Inn following the latter's destruction by fire in 1859.

31. The remaining wall of the Wangaratta Brewing and Malting Company's warehouse (at the centre rear of the photo).

32. The remains of an exposed side of the Kneebone Gold Mining Company's main shaft, Eldorado.

33. William Clark's photo in Holy Trinity Cathedral, Wangaratta.

34. Elizabeth Clark (née Harris)'s photo in Holy Trinity Cathedral, Wangaratta; with George Arthur Clark on her knee.

Elizabeth Clark (1824-88) and her youngest son, George, who shared with her husband, W.H. Clark, in a generous gift of land to the Church.

35. William Clark's grave in the Wangaratta Cemetery.

36. The monument to the pioneers of Wangaratta.

37. Two windows dedicated to the memory of William and Elizabeth Clark in the porch of Holy Trinity Cathedral, Wangaratta.

38. Elizabeth Clark (née Harris)'s grave in the Wangaratta Cemetery.

RICHARD CLARK

Missing Years

Whilst John and William Clark moved directly overland from the Yass Plains to the Port Phillip District in the late 1830s, the circumstances surrounding the arrival of their younger brother, Richard Clark, in that District in around 1939 have been obscured by the passage of time.

As was observed in the second section of this book, very little is currently known of Richard Clark's movements between his likely arrival in Sydney in around 1833 and his next recorded appearance, in the Port Phillip District, in about 1839. Based on the scant available records, it seems possible that during much of this period, he worked as a sailor on a coastal trading vessel, rather than on the land like his older brothers, and that he travelled as a sailor to ports in New South Wales, Van Diemen's Land and the Port Phillip District. Alternatively, he could have found work on a fishing boat. If that fishing boat had been a whaler, he could well have hunted whales in the waters surrounding Van Diemen's Land, including Bass Strait. In any event, it would be but a short journey across that Strait from Van Diemen's Land to the Port Phillip District.[573]

Richard Clark's Move to the Port Phillip District

The earliest mention of Richard Clark's presence in the Port Phillip District is to be found in a somewhat cryptic entry in the diary of Lady Jane Franklin.

On their way north during her intrepid overland trip from Melbourne to Sydney in 1839, Lady Franklin and her party spent the nights of 10 and 11 April of that year on the bank of the Goulburn River in close proximity to John and Martha Clark.[574] On 12 April 1839, they crossed the Goulburn River and made their way to the north-east; reaching William Clark's hut on the left bank of the Ovens River on 16 April 1839.[575] However, before reaching

---

573 See *Victoria Deaths Register: Richard Clark* (1869) (No. 514/ 1869); and the *Benalla Standard*, Tuesday, 31 July 1934, p. 3. See generally here footnote 54 and its accompanying text above.

574 See footnotes 129 and 130, and their accompanying texts, above.

575 See footnote 364 and its accompanying text above.

the Ovens River, Lady Franklin was necessarily required to cross the intervening Broken River. This she did on 14 April 1839. Of her arrival at the latter River, Lady Franklin wrote in her diary:

> "Saw some split boards placed as [a] tent on [the] [left] b[ank] to be intended for [the] brother of Clark's who was going to keep a tavern here, but was frightened away by accounts of the natives."[576]

Lady Franklin then approached a partly built police station nearby. The station was manned by a corporal and four other soldiers acting as policemen. Lady Franklin and some of the more senior members of her party were invited to dine that evening with the corporal and the soldiers in the station. It was stormy weather. One of the members of the Franklin party, Dr Edmund Hobson, described the dinner in the following terms:

> "[S]carsely had we pitched our tents when it began to rain, thunder and lightning in a most fearful manner. We were politely invited to dine in a hut that was in progress of building belonging to the mounted police – the only room that was at all roofed was covered with an old tarpaulin in which there was not a foot without a hole. Under this shower bath our dinner table was laid. It rained in a perfect torrent all the time we were at dinner….The floor of our dining room was knee deep in water."[577]

Given his later known history, there can be little doubt that the "brother of Clark's" referred to by Lady Franklin in her diary was Richard Clark.

The observation by Lady Franklin in her diary that the "brother of Clark's" had been "frightened away by accounts of the natives" invites comment. There is no suggestion in the diary that Lady Franklin ever spoke to Richard Clark. In all probability, she learned that he had apparently been "frightened away" from the Broken River "by accounts of the natives" from the soldiers manning the new police station at the River.

The Broken River police station was established as part of the New South Wales Colonial Government's response to the *Faithfull Massacre* and other incidents involving Aborigines and Europeans along Major Mitchell's return track between Melbourne and Sydney.[578] In a letter to Captain William Lonsdale, the Police Magistrate and Commandant for the Port Phillip District in Melbourne dated 29 June 1838, Edward Deas Thomson, the New South Wales Colonial Secretary, wrote:

---

576 See *Lady Franklin's Diaries*, pp. 29, 35 and 42. See also Russell, *op. cit.*, pp.43-45.
577 See Harry Speechly Parris, "From Melbourne to the Murray. Extracts from the Diary of a Pioneer Naturalist, Dr. Edmund Charles Hobson" ("*From Melbourne to the Murray*") in (1950) 66 *Victorian Naturalist* 183, p. 204.
578 As to the *Faithfull Massacre*, see footnotes 114, 115, 116, 117, 118, 119 and 120, and their accompanying texts, above.

"The Colonel commanding Her Majesty's troops has been requested to co-operate in the establishment of military posts on the road, and it has been suggested to him that the following forces may be necessary at each station:-

Mounted Police Infantry

Murray..................... 3 9

Ovens........................ 5

Violet Creek............... 5

Goulburn................... 3 9

16 18...."[579]

In the event, the New South Wales Colonial Government decided to move its planned police station from Violet Creek to the Broken River; and it was the partially constructed station on the latter River where Lady Franklin dined on the stormy evening of 14 April 1839.[580]

It seems unlikely that Richard Clark would have been "frightened away" from the Broken River "by accounts of the natives" after the arrival of soldiers sent to establish the police station. Presumably, he would have been greatly reassured by their presence had he been at the River at the time of their arrival. Although it is possible that the soldiers met and spoke with Richard on their way to establish the station, it seems more likely that they learned of his earlier presence at the Broken River, of his intention to establish an inn and of his departure from some third party or parties.

It also seem likely that Richard Clark first reached the Broken River after the *Faithfull Massacre*. There is no mention of his presence there in any of the contemporaneous accounts of that event or of its aftermath.[581]

Given the above, it is highly probable that Richard Clark initially arrived at the Broken River at some point in time between the occurrence of the *Faithfull Massacre* in April 1838 and the arrival of the soldiers sent to build and man the police station in early 1839. Having amassed and stacked "split boards" intended for the construction of his "tavern", it also seems probable that he temporarily left the area prior to the soldiers' arrival. He may, indeed, have been frightened off by a fear of Aboriginal violence, as suggested by Lady Franklin. Alternatively, he may have left the Broken River for some other reason, such as to journey to Melbourne to obtain more building materials, or simply to spend some time with his older brother and his family on the Goulburn River.[582]

---

579   See letter from Edward Deas Thomson to William Lonsdale dated 29 June 1838, cited in Parris, *Early Mitchellstown*, p. 134. See also Despatch No. 115 from the Governor of New South Wales, Sir George Gipps, to the Secretary of the Colonies, Lord Glenelg, dated 21 July 1838 in *Robertson*, Ser. 1, Vol. 19, pp. 526-528; and Dunlop, *op. cit.*, p. 30.

580   See Dunlop, *op. cit.*, pp. 30-31; and George Edwards, *op. cit.*, p. 10. The cost of constructing the Broken River police station apparently amounted to £117.15.0: see the *Sydney Herald*, Tuesday, 8 June 1841, p. 2.

581   See, in particular, footnote 117 and its accompanying text above; and **Appendix 2** below.

582   Cf. footnotes 155, 156, 160, 161, 162 and 163, and their accompanying texts, above.

The Construction of the First Black Swan Inn

In any event, what is certain is that William Clark did return to the Broken River to resume the construction of his Inn. Whilst it is possible that he returned late in 1839, it appears more likely that he arrived back at the River in 1840. It would seem at least that the Inn was not in operation in January 1840. During that month, Edward Bell and James Watson crossed the Broken River with cattle they were overlanding from a property on the Tumut River to Melbourne. At the crossing, they were "entertained", at a price, not by Richard at his Inn, but by the soldiers at the police station. In a letter dated 12 August 1853, to Lieutenant Governor Latrobe, Bell observed:

> "A party of mounted police was stationed at the Broken River, who entertained us, as they appeared to do all travellers, for a consideration."[583]

The Inn built and opened by Richard Clark in 1840 was almost certainly a simple structure. It would have been constructed using split logs (Lady Franklin's "split boards") for the walls and sheets of bark for the roofing. It probably closely resembled to first inns constructed by Richard's older brothers, John and William Clark.[584] It has been asserted that the greater part of the construction work was effected by "a young man who was one of the party that escaped….from the pursuit of the blacks, being one of Faithfull's party."[585] However, this assertion was unsourced and remains unverified. The building was located along side of Major Mitchell's track, near to what is now the north-east corner of Arundel Street and Lakeview Close, and close to the site of the *Faithfull Massacre* on the left bank of the Broken River.[586] Richard named his premises the *Black Swan Inn*.[587]

On 24 April 1841, a General Innkeepers Licence was granted to one James Lawler with respect to the *Black Swan Inn*. However, it is likely that the Inn had been trading for the better part of a year before this licence was granted.[588] The identity of James Lawler is not presently known, but he could well have been employed by Richard Clark as a barman. In the words of Edward Robertson:

---

[583] See Bride, *op. cit.*, p. 202. See also Edward Robertson, *Discovery and Settlement of the Murray District of Port Phillip, Part 2* ("*Discovery and Settlement*"), p. 8 (University of Melbourne Archives, manuscript, 1985.0068 Robertson, E., 1855-1953, Box 1). Edward Robertson was born in Benalla in 1870. He qualified in Scotland as a medical practitioner in 1896 and spent almost all of the rest of his working life in the Victorian Public Service. He was the permanent head of the Victorian Health Department from 1919 until 1937. Robertson took a keen interest in Victorian history, and particularly in the history of his home town. He died in 1969: see E. M. Robertson, "Robertson, Edward (1870-1969)" in *Australian Dictionary of Biography* (https://tinyurl.com/y9h8mdug) (at 16 April 2023).

[584] See footnotes 105 and 377, and their accompanying texts, above.

[585] See Anon, "Recollections of Benalla" in the *North Eastern Ensign*, Friday, 23 June 1893, p. 3. See also the *Benalla Standard*, Tuesday, 4 December 1923, p. 4,

[586] See Dunlop, *op. cit.*, p. 32. See also the 1851 Benalla Plan and photo 39 below.

[587] See Robertson, *Discovery and Settlement*, pp. 9 and 27; and Dunlop, *op. cit.*, p. 31.

[588] *Ibid.* See also the *Port Phillip Gazette*, Wednesday, 26 April 1843, p. 2.

"At this time it was the custom for the owner of a licensed house to nominate his manager or head barman as the licensee."[589]

On 26 April 1844, the licence was transferred from Lawler to an Angus McKenzie.[590] Later in that year, on 3 September 1844, it was finally transferred from McKenzie into the hands of Richard Clark.[591]

The Establishment, Naming and Growth of Benalla

Richard Clark was the first permanent European settlor in what was to become the town of Benalla.[592]. However, he was not the first European to settle in the wider Benalla district. In about May 1839, William McKellar and William Black established the *Lima* squatting run to the south of what was to become Benalla. Shortly afterwards, in about December of that year, John Binney and Alexander Anderson acquired the *Warrenbayne* run to the south-west of the site of Benalla. Also in 1839, the brothers William and Albert Brodribb settled on the *Broken River* or *Junction* run. Others followed in 1840; most notably Alexander and Peter Cheyne on the *Hollands Creek* run and Edward Grimes on the *Benalta* run.[593]

In time, a small hamlet grew up around the *Black Swan Inn* and the nearby crossing place over the Broken River. In July 1848, Thomas Wedge surveyed the little settlement. The squatter then in occupation of the *Benalta* run, Edward Grimes, had earlier been appointed to be the Commissioner of Crown Lands for the Western Port District in October 1846. In that capacity, he apparently became friendly with the then-Superintendent Latrobe in Melbourne.[594] In a gesture designed to honour his friend, Latrobe chose the name "Benalta", after the name of Grimes' squatting run, for the newly-surveyed settlement. However, although the settlement was officially gazetted as "Benalta", it would seem that a government clerk took the "t" in Benalta for an "l" and incorporated his error in the official lithographed plan. This led to the settlement in due course receiving the name "Benalla".[595]

The growth of Benalla was slow for over a decade. On 29 April 1849, Mrs Fanny Perry visited the settlement in company with her husband, Charles Perry, the Anglican Bishop of Melbourne. She was not particularly impressed with what she saw; writing at the time in her diary:

---

589 See Edward Robertson, *Correspondence and Notes compiled by Edward Robertson concerning the history of the Benalla district* ("*Correspondence and Notes*"), p. 1 (State Library of Victoria, manuscript, MSB 277-280A).

590 See Dunlop, *op. cit.*, p. 31.

591 See the *Port Phillip Gazette*, Wednesday, 3 September 1844, p. 2.

592 See Robertson, *Correspondence and Notes*, p. 1. The soldiers who erected and manned the police station on the bank of the Broken River were, of course, likely to have been in occupation at the River earlier than Richard Clark: see footnote 582 and its accompanying text above. However, their occupation was, of its nature, transient.

593 See Dunlop, *op. cit.*, pp. 20 and 23.

594 See Dunlop, *op. cit.*, p. 23.

595 See *Supplement to the Port Phillip Government Gazette* (No. 20), Thursday, 2 May 1849, p. 291; Robertson, *Discovery and Settlement*, pp. 18-19; Robertson, *Correspondence and Notes*, p. 2; and Dunlop, *op. cit.*, pp. 33-34.

"The township on the Broken River is called Benalla, and contains at present a rude court-house and lock up, small barracks, an inn, and half-a-dozen of the rudest bark-huts we have yet seen. When the ground is put up for sale, which will be the case in a few days, the owners of these will purchase, and build more decent dwellings. It is not an ugly site, the ground being prettily broken, and the trees slightly superior, being near the river."[596]

In its earliest years, the *Black Swan Inn* would likely have catered in the main for travellers passing up and down the Sydney to Melbourne track. In all probability, this would not initially have produced many customers. During this early period of his life in the little township, Richard Clark was probably left with quite a measure of free time. The details of his use of such free time are now lost. However, it seems highly likely that he would have spent some of it visiting Melbourne, his parents and brother John on the Goulburn River and his brother William on the Ovens River.

Marriage to Mary Sparrow

The year 1844 was a significant one in Richard Clark's life. On 10 February 1844, he married his first wife, Mary Sparrow, in the Wesleyan Methodist Church in Melbourne. The marriage was solemnised by the Church's minister, the Reverend William Schofield; with the witnesses to the marriage being William C. Sparrow and Henry Frencham, both said to be from Melbourne.[597] Save to say that she was apparently born in Ireland in about 1816, Mary's origins, and her circumstances prior to her marriage to Richard, are presently unknown.[598] Nor is it currently known where and how the two first met. However, it does appear that a William C. Sparrow, who may have been Mary's father or a brother, was apparently living in 1856 on his freehold land at Whittlesea in Victoria.[599]

1844 also saw the birth in Melbourne of Richard and Mary Clark's first child, a son they named Alfred Clark. Unfortunately, the infant boy died in the year of his birth.[600]

On 20 March 1844, the first allotments in the newly-surveyed township of Seymour were offered for sale in Melbourne by the New South Wales Government. As has been seen above, John Clark Jnr purchased a number of the allotments on offer. Interestingly, Richard Clark also purchased one of the allotments – Allotment 3, Section 2, located between Ballandella Place and Emily Street, and bounded on either side by allotments purchased by his brother

---

596 Mrs Perry published her diary under the pseudonym "Richard Perry": see Richard Perry, *Contributions to an Amateur Magazine in Prose and Verse* (1857), pp. 121-122. See also Dunlop, *op. cit.*, p. 33; and "Benalla" in the *Australian Handbook* (1903), cited in *Victorian Place – Benalla* (https://tinyurl.com/ycwl4ml3) (at 16 April 2023).

597 See *Wesleyan Methodist Church: Melbourne, Port Phillip District, New South Wales – Marriages 1841-1844* (No. 31) (https://tinyurl.com/y6ufvupa) (at 17 April 2023).

598 See Rootsweb: Wermore: *From Whence We Came For Family Ties To Gaele Arnott Nee Moore – Mary Sparrow* (https://tinyurl.com/3a7n8us3) (at 17 April 2023).

599 See Ancestry: *Australian Electoral Rolls for 1856 – William C. Sparrow* (https://tinyurl.com/yaa72oak) (17 April 2023).

600 See the *Moore Considine Family Website* (https://tinyurl.com/58ntx5sc) (at 17 April 2023).

John.[601] Richard's purchase of his allotment provides unambiguous evidence of his close relationship with John at this time.

Squatting at Hurdle Creek

The allotment in Seymour was not the only acquisition of land made by Richard Clark in 1844. He also acquired a licence for the *Hurdle Creek* run from a Roderick Mackay in that year. This run, occupying around 25,000 acres, was located between Carboor and Merriang to the east of Benalla and to the west of Myrtleford. It was assessed as being capable of carrying up to 300 head of cattle or 6,000 sheep.[602]

The following year, in 1845, Richard's brother, William Clark, acquired the *Whitfield* run to the west of the *Hurdle Creek* run, and separated from it only by the *Edi* run.[603] The two brothers would almost certainly have been aware of each other's acquisitions. Indeed, they could conceivably have acquired their respective runs in concert with one another.

Postmaster

Also in 1844, Richard Clark was appointed as Postmaster at "Broken River". The *Port Phillip Government Gazette* of 3 December 1844 published notice of his appointment; with the notice reading in part:

> " **New Post Office**
>
> **Notice** is hereby given, that under sanction of His Excellency the Governor, and from 1st December next, a Post Office will be established as follows, viz:-
>
> At BROKEN RIVER, on the Sydney Road; Richard Clark to be Postmaster.
>
> The delivery from this office will embrace, beside the neighbourhood of the Broken River, the district of the Devil's River.
>
> This mail will be received at, and despatched from, Melbourne with the Sydney mail....
>
> **HENRY D. KEMP**
>
> Postmaster
>
> Post Office, Melbourne,
>
> 21st November, 1844."[604]

---

601 See Martindale, *op. cit.*, p. 34 and Plate 4 on the page following p. 36. See also the *Melbourne Weekly Courier*, Saturday, 23 March 1844, p. 2; Parris, *Early Mitchellstown*, pp. 152-153; and footnotes 162 and 199, and their accompanying texts, above.

602 See Billis and Kenyon, *Pastoral Pioneers*, p. 222; and Spreadborough and Anderson, *op. cit.*, p. 53. See also Squatting Runs Map 7 below.

603 See footnotes 389, 390 and 391, and their accompanying texts, above.

604 See the *Port Phillip Government Gazette* ((No. 49), Tuesday, 3 December 1844, p. 219. See also the *Port Phillip Herald*, Tuesday, 29 November 1944.

Richard Clark almost certainly conducted this first Post Office on the Broken River from his *Black Swan Inn*. His postal district was very large, extending northwards to the Murray River and southwards to cover the Devil's River area.[605] It is highly unlikely that other than on rare occasions, Richard himself ever delivered or collected mail across his far-flung district. He may have employed a postman or postmen to perform that task. However, in all probability, most of the district's inbound and outbound mail would have been collected from, or posted at, the *Black Swan Inn*.

On 1 January 1845, Richard and Mary Clark's second child, a girl, was born at the Broken River settlement. She was christened on 26 October 1845 and given the name Sarah Jane Clark.[606] Sarah became the first white child born in what was soon to become Benalla to survive infancy.

The Black Swan Inn and the Early Benalla Community

As the 1840s progressed, Richard Clark no doubt extended, upgraded and modernised his original *Black Swan Inn*. Over time, it became the social hub, both of the little settlement on the Broken River and of the wider pastoral district surrounding it. In an article published in the *North Eastern Ensign* on 23 June 1893, an anonymous contributor (described in the paper to be "an old resident") wrote in part:

> "The Black Swan was Benalla. 'Twas here all the fast young occupants of Crown lands met, and often these meetings would last from two to three weeks, during which a fight for love, or a horse race for a gallon of rum, formed part of the daily proceedings. Generally speaking, the liquors were of the vilest kind. I have frequently seen men – stout stalwart fellows – sleep for two days after imbibing a couple of glasses of rum. I have known others to turn temporarily mad after drinking for a day or two. But these direful effects were by no means attributable to the inn-keeper, as there can be no doubt but that he sold it as the genuine thing, having paid the highest price in the market for it. As a proof, I have known bullock drivers to steal grog that performed part of the loading consigned to this very inn-keeper, and to have been half cranky for weeks on the road in consequence. The landlord and landlady were obliging to an extreme; the house and everything appertaining were of an air of comfort and cleanliness. The host and hostess were young and appeared to be determined to do everything in their power to accommodate their customers satisfactorily, and by doing

---

605 "Devil's River" was an early colonial name given to the area surrounding the junction of the Delatite River and Brankeet Creek, and broadly lying between what are now the towns of Mansfield and Bonnie Doon. In 1839, George Watson and Alexander Hunter established the first squatting run in this area, which they called *Wappan*: see *The Australasian*, Saturday, 4 April 1931, p. 4; Mansfield Historical Society, *History of Mansfield* (https://tinyurl.com/ya8urd6l) (at 17 April 2023); and footnote 378 and its accompanying text above.

606 See *Victoria Births Register: Sarah Jane Clark* (1845) (No. 14485/1845).

so, to do something for themselves, which they did; for within 10 years afterwards they were reputed to be worth £20,000."[607]

These recollections should be viewed with some caution. In the first place, the article as a whole contains a number of obvious errors. In the second place, the "landlord" and "landlady" referred to in it may not have been Richard and Mary Clark, but rather a subsequent lessee and/or licensee and his wife.

Disposing of the Hurdle Creek Run

In January 1846, Richard Clark disposed of his licence to occupy the *Hurdle Creek* squatting run to James Templeton.[608] It is not currently known what, if any, consideration Richard received from Templeton upon the transfer. Nor is it now known why Richard disposed of the property. Perhaps he needed money. Alternatively, he may not have had the wherewithal to properly operate the run. Most likely, he found the property too difficult of regular access from the Broken River.

Crossing the Broken River

There have been some reports to the effect that Richard Clark emulated his two oldest brothers by constructing and operating a punt across the Broken River.[609] John Clark certainly operated a punt on the Goulburn River, and William Clark a punt on the Ovens River. However, there is no strong evidence suggesting that Richard ever operated a punt on the Broken River.

When Major Mitchell crossed what would later become known as the Broken River on 13 April 1836, he named it the "Swampy River", as it appeared to him to be little more that a chain of swamps. Of the River, Mitchell wrote more descriptively:

> "[We] came to a river of very irregular width and which, as I found on further examination, spread into broad lagoons and swamps bordered with reeds. Where we first approached it the bank was high and firm, the water forming a broad reach evidently very deep. But both above and below that point the stream, actually flowing, seemed fordable and we tried it in various places but the bottom was everywhere soft and swampy."[610]

---

607 See the *North Eastern Ensign*, Friday, 23 June 1893, p. 3.
608 See Billis and Kenyon, *Pastoral Pioneers*, p. 222; and Spreadborough and Anderson, *op. cit.*, p. 53.
609 See the *Benalla Standard*, Tuesday, 10 July 1923, p. 4; and Anon, *Benalla Past and Present: Illustrated History of the Town and District 1838 to 1929* ("*Benalla Past and Present*") (1929), pp. 12 and 16.
610 See Thomas Mitchell, *Three Expeditions Into The Interior Of Eastern Australia* (1838), Vol. 2, p. 194.

Almost exactly three years later, on 14 April 1839, Lady Franklin's companion on her overland journey from Melbourne to Sydney, Dr Edmund Hobson, observed that:

"The Broken River is not at present running but merely consists of a chain of ponds."[611]

In an article published in the *Ovens and Murray Advertiser* on 31 July 1875, and anonymous correspondent was more dismissive; observing that:

"The Broken River at Benalla, is a fraud, being a muddy, sluggish stream full of unsightly snags, and unrelieved by foliage. A few dismal-looking trees fringe its banks, but save in winter time when the floods are up, it looks a mere ditch."[612]

In his *Discovery and Settlement*, Edward Robertson noted that:

"The first crossing place over the River was that in line with Major Mitchell's track…. It was a U shaped affair. Doubtless it was marked by stakes or some other devices, for these would have been necessary when the River was in flood. John Conway Bourke, when crossing the River a few days after the Faithfull affray, remarked that the crossing was zig-zag and consequentially impeded his way.

Later, the crossing was shifted higher up the River close to where the bridge now is….Doubtless both crossings were used for cattle according to convenience. No evidence is available as to when the new crossing was first used. It was used even when the bridge was built, for tolls were then charged and people were no more keen on paying tolls then than now."[613]

An advertisement seeking tenders for the construction of the bridge referred to by Robertson was published in the *Port Phillip Government Gazette* on 3 March 1847.[614] The bridge was probably completed during the same year, and was one of the earliest built in the Port Phillip District. Constructed of timber, the bridge, together with adjacent river embankment works, was built at a total cost of £350.[615]

There would appear to be no contemporaneous record of a punt being available for the use of travellers crossing the Broken River prior to the construction of the bridge in 1847. Robertson's notes, although not conclusive, are strongly suggestive that there was no such punt, let alone one operated commercially by Richard Clark.

---

611 See Parris, *From Melbourne to the Murray*, p. 204.
612 See the *Ovens and Murray Advertiser*, Saturday, 31 July 1875, p. 5. Cf. Mrs Fanny Perry's impressions of the environs of the Broken River: see footnote 596 and its accompanying text above.
613 See Robertson, *Discovery and Settlement*, p. 16.
614 See the *Port Phillip Government Gazette* (No. 9), Wednesday, 3 March 1847, p. 74.
615 See the *Port Phillip Government Gazette* (No. 49), Wednesday, 20 November 1850, p. 984. See also Dunlop, *op. cit.*, p. 16.

On 21 October 1847, Richard and Mary Clark's third child and only surviving son, John Robert Clark, was born. He was baptised on 1 May 1849.[616] According to an obituary for him following his death on 28 July 1934 and published in the *Benalla Standard* on 31 July 1934: "John was born in a two-roomed cottage almost opposite the old 'Black Swan' in Arundel-st."[617]

This obituary would appear to contain the only reference to the "two-roomed cottage" housing the Clark family presently extant. When it was built, and for how long it was occupied by the Clarks, are questions now probably lost in time. In any event, John Robert Clark has been said to have been the first white male child born in Benalla.[618]

Squatting on the Junction Run

Having surrendered his licence to occupy the *Hurdle Creek* squatting run in January 1846, Richard Clark acquired the *Junction* or *Broken River* run from Robert and George Benson in November 1848. Located immediately to the south-west of Benalla, the *Junction* run extended over some 8,640 acres. It was deemed to be capable of supporting around 2,500 sheep.[619]

The *Junction* run was first occupied by William and Albert Brodribb in 1839. They used it to fatten stock before overlanding them to Melbourne. The Brodribbs relinquished the run the following year to Alexander and Peter Cheyne. In 1844, Henry Galway acquired the property from the Cheynes. It was transferred by him to Robert and George Benson in February 1846.[620] Whereas his European predecessors only occupied the *Junction* run for short periods, Richard Clark was to hold it for almost 13 years.

Whilst the *Hurdle Creek* run would not have been easy of access for Richard, the *Junction* run was almost literally on his doorstep. It would therefore have been much easier for him to manage. The *Junction* run also had the advantage of having the Broken River as its eastern boundary. In contrast, the *Hurdle Creek* run was dependent for stock water on three small streams which often ran dry: Hurdle, Whorouly and Mayday Creeks. So, despite its smaller size, the *Junction* run would almost certainly have been the better and more valuable of the two properties from Richard's perspective.

The year 1849 also saw the birth in Benalla of Richard and Mary Clark's fourth and last child, Mary Elizabeth Clark. She was christened on 29 April 1849.[621] Unfortunately, it would seem that she died soon after her birth in the same year.

---

616   See *Victoria Births Register: John Robert Clark* (1849) (No. 16234/1849).
617   See the *Benalla Standard*, Tuesday, 31 July 1934, p. 3.
618   *Ibid.* See also *The Age*, Wednesday, 1 August 1834, p. 13; *Benalla Past and Present*, pp. 22 and 78; and Dunlop, *op. cit.*, p. 99.
619   See Billis and Kenyon, *Pastoral Pioneers*, p. 225; Spreadborough and Anderson, *op. cit.*, p. 54; Victorian Legislative Council, *Occupants of Crown Lands, Victoria, 13 September 1853*, p. 9 (https://tinyurl.com/y9epv29d) (at 19 April 2023); and Squatting Runs Map 7 below.
620   See Billis and Kenyon, *Pastoral Pioneers*, p. 225; and Dunlop, *op. cit.*, pp. 20 and 23. See also footnote 593 and its accompanying text above.
621   See *Victoria Births Register: Mary Elizabeth Clark* (1849) (No. 16259/1849).

Property Purchases

As mentioned above, Richard Clark purchased an allotment on 20 March 1844 in the first sale of allotments in the newly-surveyed township of Seymour. This Seymour allotment was situated between two allotments also purchased that day by his older brother, John Clark.[622] Richard went on to purchase a great deal more property in the North East of Victoria.

Following Thomas Wedge's 1848 survey of the site for what was shortly to become Benalla, both urban and rural allotments in the surveyed site were soon offered for sale by the New South Wales Government. The first auction of Benalla urban allotments took place in Melbourne in 1849. At that auction, Richard Clark purchased four allotments; being Allotments 1 to 4, Section 1.[623]

On 11 November 1855, Richard purchased a number of allotments fronting Arundel Street in Benalla.[624] In a subsequent land sale in 1856, he purchased allotments on Deas Street.[625] It is possible that he constructed a home for himself and his family on one of the latter allotments.[626] Again, in 1858, Richard purchased 11 acres of rural land in the Parish of Benalla.[627]

Not all of the land purchased by Richard Clark was situated in Benalla or in its immediate surrounds. In 1857, he was recorded as owning a property of 120 acres known as *Duck Ponds* in conjunction with a family friend, James Campbell Grassie.[628] The property, comprising the land to be found in Allotment 11 in the Parish of Balmattum, was located between Euroa and Violet Town and was acquired by Richard and Grassie by way of a Crown Grant. It would seem that Richard also purchased Allotment 2 in Section 1 in the township of Merton.[629]

Further, at time of his death, Richard Clark was the owner of an allotment or allotments in Portion 34, Parish of Moorabbin.[630] He could well have purchased this land in around 1852 from a Melbourne property developer, Josiah Holloway.[631] The land was situated in

---

622 See footnote 601 and its accompanying text above.
623 See Dunlop, *op. cit.*, p. 167.
624 See *Benalla Past and Present*, pp. 11-12.
625 See *Benalla Past and Present*, p. 12.
626 See the *Benalla Standard*, Tuesday, 31 July 1934, p. 3. See also *Benalla Past and Present*, p. 12.
627 See Dunlop, *op. cit.*, pp. 41-42.
628 See *Ownership of "Duck Ponds"* (PROV, *VPRS* 267/P7, Unit 66, Item 1864/2537). James Campbell Grassie was a squatter who had settled on the *Poon Poon* run north of Swan Hill. His precise relationship with the wider Clark family is unclear. However, it is noteworthy that on 18 January 1862, Grassie was appointed with Richard Clark as replacement trustees of the *Gooparl* trust; a trust designed to protect the interest of Martha McIntosh (who was the widow of John Clark Jnr, and Richard Clark's sister-in-law) in the *Gooparl* property. On 21 May 1862, Richard Clark and Grassie secured an order from the Victorian Supreme Court evicting Martha's estranged second husband, William McIntosh, from *Gooparl*: see footnotes 303 and 305, and their accompanying texts, above. Further, on 6 January 1868, Martha appointed Grassie to be one of the two executors of her Will. Richard Clark was appointed as the second executor. Following Martha's death, Grassie renounced probate of the Will on 14 April 1868: see *James Grassie's Renunciation of Probate* (PROV, *VPRS* 7591/P0001, Unit 28B) and (PROV, *VPRS* 28/0000, Unit 73); and the *Illustrated Australian News for Home Readers*, Saturday, 21 May 1870, p. 102. See also footnotes 311 and 312, and their accompanying texts, above.
629 See the *Ovens and Murray Advertiser*, Tuesday, 9 February 1869, p. 4.
630 *Ibid.*
631 See City of Kingston, *Kingston Local History: Josiah Morris Holloway – Pioneering Land Developer* (https://tinyurl.com/3hdtj6sx) (at 19 April 2023). Interestingly, it would appear that Josiah Holloway purchased four allotments in Benalla in 1852.

Black Rock, close to where the Royal Melbourne Golf Club is now located. It may be that it was purchased by Richard with an expectation that he would ultimately retire to a house he would construct on the site. Alternatively, the land may simply have been purchased as an investment.

In any event, by the time of his death in 1869, Richard Clark was the owner of at least 63 properties.[632]

A Suggested Fifth Child

According to the *Moore Considine Family Website*, Richard and Mary Clark had a fifth child, Amelia Elizabeth Clark, who was born at Collingwood in 1850. The Website has Amelia dying as an infant in 1851.[633] However, it seems almost certain that the Amelia Elizabeth Clark who was born in Collingwood in 1850 was not the child of Richard and Mary Clark.

The *Victoria Deaths Register* indeed lists an Amelia Elizabeth Clark as having died in Collingwood on 14 January 1850 at the age of 10 months. That Amelia's father is stated in the Register to have been a Richard Clark, with her mother said to be "unknown". But the father's occupation is given as "Printer".[634] Sadly, it would seem that "Richard Clark – Printer" of Collingwood lost another child in 1851. That child was named Mary Anne Clark, and was said to have been 5 years old when she died on 27 May 1851.[635]

Thus, Richard Clark, the printer from Collingwood, would appear to have been a different man than Richard Clark, the innkeeper and squatter from Benalla.

The Trial of Thomas Kelly

It would appear that Richard Clark may have come close to violently losing his life in 1850. On Tuesday, 19 November 1850, one Thomas Kelly stood trial in the Supreme Court at Melbourne before Mr Justice A'Beckett and a Jury of 12 men. Kelly was charged with the attempted murder of a John Brunt, and further with assaulting Brunt with intent to cause grievous bodily harm.

The evidence adduced by Richard Clark and a number of other witnesses called at Kelly's trial was to the effect that Kelly had been drinking at the bar of the *Black Swan Inn* on 9 July 1850. He revealed himself over time to be troublesome and probably drunk. When he endeavoured to move without permission into the rear part of the Inn, Richard apparently took him by the collar and brought him back to the bar. Kelly subsequently struck unsuccessfully at Richard with a knife before stabbing another patron in the arm. When

---

632 See the *Ovens and Murray Advertiser*, Tuesday, 9 February 1869, p. 4.
633 See the *Moore Considine Family Website* (https://tinyurl.com/58ntx5sc) (at 19 April).
634 See *Victoria Deaths Register: Amelia Elizabeth Clark* (1851) (No. 4953/1851).
635 See *Victoria Deaths Register: Mary Anne Clark* (1851) (No. 28427/1851). See also footnote 646 and its accompanying text below.

Brunt then attempted to intervene, he was stabbed in the chest by Kelly. The stab wound sustained by Brunt was a very serious one. Brunt nearly died from loss of blood. After Kelly had been subdued, Richard found a clasp knife in his waistcoat pocket.

After a short trial, the July acquitted Kelly of the charge of attempted murder, but convicted him of the second charge of assault with intent to cause grievous bodily harm.[636] On Wednesday, 20 November 1850, Mr Justice A'Beckett sentenced Kelly to a term of eight months imprisonment with hard labour.[637]

The Construction of the Second Black Swan Inn

The *Black Swan Inn* was the first hostelry to be constructed in Benalla. However, it was far from being the last. In early 1851, work commenced on the building of the *Benalla Hotel* on the corner of Bridge and Nunn Streets, to the east of the Broken River and in line with the wooden bridge over that River constructed in 1847. The 1851 building works for the *Benalla Hotel*, and the anticipated competition from the latter when completed, prompted Richard Clark to commission the erection of a new and grander *Black Swan Inn* on the opposite side of Lakeview Close to his original Inn.[638] Both the *Benalla Hotel* and the new *Black Swan Inn* opened prior to the end of 1851.

Of the construction of the new *Black Swan Inn*, the *Benalla Ensign and Farmer's and Squatter's Journal* wrote on 13 January 1872:

> "[I]t was thought that if [Richard Clark] did not build a new and larger house that some one might build one in opposition. Consequently, [Richard Clark] decided upon the building of Black Swan No. 2. No sooner said than done. The making of the bricks was commenced at once, and by the time the bricks were ready for building purposes, the plans had been prepared and the contract entered into for the whole of the building, including labour and materials, which was to be completed in 12 months from the time of contract. The successful tenderers were two young men, who were just completing a similar undertaking at Seymour."[639]

The second *Black Swan Inn* was a substantial two-storied structure. It contained a bar, a dining room, a kitchen, a sitting room, a sun room, a cellar, family bedrooms, a "woman's apartment" and visitors' rooms. Ancillary buildings included stabling for more than 12 horses,

---

636 See the *Port Phillip Gazette and Settler's Journal*, Thursday, 21 November 1850, p. 2; the *Melbourne Daily News*, Wednesday, 20 November 1850, p. 2; and the *Geelong Advertiser*, Monday, 25 November 1850, p. 2.
637 See the *Melbourne Daily News*, Thursday, 21 November 1850, p. 2.
638 See Dunlop, *op. cit.*, p. 36. See also photo 40 below
639 See the *Benalla Ensign and Farmer's and Squatter's Journal*, Saturday, 13 January 1872, p. 2. It seems that the bricklayer employed in building both the *Benalla Hotel* and the new *Black Swan Inn* was a John Smith: see *Benalla Past and Present*, p. 11.

a gig shed, a harness room and a storehouse. The Inn also had a cooperage courtyard and a skittle alley. A large orchard and garden were subsequently developed on the site.[640]

For some time after its construction, the new *Black Swan Inn* continued in the steps of its predecessor to be a focal point for social life in Benalla. Coaches used both the old and later the new Inn as changing stops. After the establishment of Cobb and Co. in 1853, that company maintained its Benalla coaching office at the new Inn.[641]

On 3 June 1853, Richard Clark seconded the nomination of Matthew Hervey as a candidate for election to the Victorian Legislative Council for the Pastoral District of Murray. No other nominations being received by the Returning Officer, Hervey was declared by the latter to be duly elected. He subsequently celebrated his election by entertaining a party of his friends to dinner at the new *Black Swan Inn*.[642]

The Death of Mary Clark

On 9 June 1853,, only six days after Richard Clark's nomination of Matthew Hervey as a candidate for election to the Victorian Legislative Council, Richard's wife, Mary Clark, died in Benalla.[643] Like almost all other details of Mary's life, the circumstances surrounding her death are not presently known. That death left Richard with two small children to care for on his own: Sarah Jane Clark, then aged 8 years old; and John Robert Clark, who was only 5 years of age.

Shortly after, Mary's death, Richard resigned as Benalla's Postmaster. He was succeeded in that office on 1 August 1853 by a James Sim.[644]

Whether dictated by his changed personal circumstances following Mary's death or not, Richard Clark leased the *Black Swan Inn* on 10 November 1853 to the brothers William and David Standring for a term of five years.[645] Although he likely retained title to the property on which the Inn was located for some presently undetermined time, this lease effectively severed Richard's involvement in the operation of the Inn itself.

Marriage to Sarah Maddock

On 28 February 1854, Richard Clark married his second wife, Sarah Maddock, in St. Peter's Anglican Church in Melbourne. At the time of this marriage, Richard was 37 years old. His

---

640 See Robert Cole, *Index of Victorian Hotels – Country, A to Car* (State Library of Victoria, manuscript MS 7592), p. 184(a).
641 See the *Benalla Standard*, Tuesday, 10 July 1923, p. 4; and *Victorian Places – Benalla* (https://tinyurl.com/ycwl4ml3) (at 20 April 2023).
642 See *The Argus*, Tuesday, 7 June 1853, p. 7. See also the *Ovens and Murray Advertiser*, Tuesday, 4 December 1866, p. 2; and Dunlop, *op. cit.*, p. 36.
643 See the *Moore Considine Family Website* (https://tinyurl.com/58ntx5sc) (at 20 April 2023).
644 See David Baker, *One Hundred And Twenty-Four Years Of P.M.G. Service At Benalla* (1968), (copy manuscript, National Trust of Australia (Victoria) Files), p. 3.
645 See Edward Robertson, *Lease of the Black Swan Inn, 10 November 1853* (University of Melbourne Archives, manuscript, 1985.0068, Robertson, E. 1855-1953, Box 2).

bride was 19 years of age. A spinster, she had been born in Ireland in the County of Wexford and had apparently emigrated from there to Melbourne shortly prior to her marriage to Richard.[646] There was to be no issue from this marriage.

Sarah's mother's maiden name was given as Mary Ann Sparrow on Sarah and Richard Clark's Marriage Certificate. This strongly suggests that both Sarah and her mother Mary were related to Richard's first wife, Mary Clark (née Sparrow).[647] Perhaps Mary Ann Sparrow was Mary Clark's aunt or cousin? Perhaps Mary Clark was also born in Wexford? Further, it is interesting to note that Sarah's father, Patrick Maddock, was said on the Marriage Certificate to be a "Mariner". Perhaps Richard Clark first became acquainted with the Sparrow family in consequence of meeting Patrick Maddock while both were serving as sailors?[648]

Benalla may have been surveyed as a town by Thomas Wedge in 1848 but, in the words of *The Australian Handbook* of 1903, it was:

> "of small account until 1854, when it sprang into importance as the centre of a district admirably suited to the growth of grain, and most of the fruits of the temperate zone."[649]

No doubt the movement of people and goods to the various Victorian Goldfields in the early 1850s gave a fillip to the small settlement, but it was the rapid expansion of agriculture in the district which was the principal driver of the expansion and development of the town.[650]

The Decline of the Second Black Swan Inn

Both the first and the second *Black Swan Inns* were constructed close to where the track created by Major Mitchell forded across the Broken River. That track, of course, became the original Sydney – Melbourne road. Travellers on it were the primary patrons of Richard Clark's original Inn.

The construction of the timber bridge upstream across the Broken River in 1847 altered the course taken by traffic passing through Benalla. Thereafter, in the words of Edward Robertson, for most travellers heading in the direction of Sydney:

> "Mitchell's track was used as far as the Black Swan. Instead of using the old crossing, traffic [then] proceeded in a south-easterly direction across the present Recreation Grounds until it reached the new Crossing and the bridge."[651]

---

646 See *Victoria Marriages Register: Richard Clark and Sarah Maddock* (1854) (No. 796/1854). It is interesting to note that on the Marriage Certificate, Richard Clark is said to be a widower, with two living and two dead children: see footnotes 633, 634 and 636, and their accompanying texts, above.
647 See footnote 598 and its accompanying text above.
648 *Ibid.*
649 See "Benalla" in *The Australian Handbook* (1903), cited in *Victorian Places – Benalla* (https://tinyurl.com/ycwl4ml3) (at 20 April 2023).
650 See Dunlop, *op. cit.*, p. 36.
651 See Robertson, *Discovery and Settlement*, p. 27.

Most travellers heading in the opposite direction towards Melbourne used the same route in reverse.

Whilst this new route remained convenient for those patronising the first *Black Swan Inn*, which was Benalla's only hostelry prior to 1851, it was inevitable that some travellers would "cut the corner" on their ways to and from the bridge. As Edward Robertson put it:

> "It was inevitable that traffic having no business at the Black Swan would make direct for the bridge. As long as the Black Swan was the only hostelry, travellers were compelled to use it. However, it only needed the establishment of a suitable hotel near the bridge to cause a decline in the patronage of the Black Swan. When the Benalla Hotel was opened [in 1851], traffic by-passed the Black Swan."[652]

The year 1856 saw two further blows inflicted on the business of the *Black Swan Inn*. In the first place, the route taken by the original Sydney to Melbourne road was realigned at the direction of a Victorian Government surveyor, John Wilmot, so that it by-passed Richard Clark's Inn and led more directly to and from the bridge, following the route now taken by Bridge Street West.[653]

1856 also saw the construction and opening of Benalla's third hotel, the *Commercial Hotel*, which was built on the south side of Bridge Street East almost opposite the *Benalla Hotel*. The new hotel further diminished the *Black Swan Inn's* trade. In the words of Alan Dunlop:

> "The business of the Black Swan began to decline. It could handle the rivalry of one hotel but not two, particularly as it was no longer on the main route through the town."[654]

In 1862, a James Stewart acquired the licence to the *Black Swan Inn*. By this time, there were no less than five hotels trading in Benalla.[655] Stewart was succeeded as licensee by a Frederick Ridgway in 1864.[656] Further, it would appear that for some years prior to 1864, a Joseph Hatwell operated a brewery from the Inn.[657]

Notwithstanding these developments, the *Black Swan Inn's* trade continued to decline. In 1868, its liquor licence was not renewed. However, the Inn continued to operate as an accommodation house serving meals.[658] It received another setback in 1878 with the abolition of tolls imposed on those crossing on the bridge over the Broken River. This meant that

---

652 *Ibid.*
653 See Dunlop, *op. cit.*, p. 38.
654 *Ibid.*
655 See the *Ovens and Murray Advertiser*, Saturday, 31 May 1862, p. 2.
656 See Cole, *op. cit.*, p. 184(a).
657 See the *Benalla Standard*, Friday, 23 February 1906, p. 2. See also the *Benalla Standard*, Tuesday, 10 July 1923, p. 4.
658 See Dunlop, *op. cit.*, p. 38. See also Robertson, *Discovery and Settlement*, p. 29; and *Benalla Past and Present*, p. 16.

persons who had previously avoided the tolls by continuing to use the old ford close to the *Black Swan Inn* had no further cause to do so. As Alan Dunlop put it, this meant that: "the old inn was still more in a back-water. It had once been the centre of everything."[659]

Although Richard Clark had ceased to operate the *Black Swan Inn* by 1853 at the latest, it is presently unclear whether he continued to own the title to the property, and derived any further income from it, up until the time of his death in 1869.[660] The property does not appear to have been mortgaged, and it may have been inherited by Richard's children after his death.

Whatever was the case, it is at least clear that by 1871, the *Black Swan Inn* was perceived to have little value. On 3 October of that year, the *Ovens and Murray Advertiser* reported as follows:

> "Boger and Watts offered for sale on Saturday, at the Royal Hotel, Benalla, the Black Swan Hotel; there was no purchaser, only one bid being given, and that was for the munificent sum of £50, and this for a property that the original owner, the late Mr Richard Clarke, refused at one time the sum of £4500 for. There is attached to the building about three acres of good land, and the building itself is one of the most substantial in the township, but unfortunately it is situated in a very inaccessible spot, and no one is anxious to have it. Before the police barracks were built here, the Government offered Mr Clarke £4500 for it, but Mr Clarke was inexorable. It is reported that he wanted £7000 for it; and in the course of a comparatively short time its value has so extraordinarily depreciated that only the insignificant amount of £50 was offered for it. The auctioneers, of course, could not let it go for this trifling figure, and Mr Boger said there would be no sale. It is almost incredible how this once valuable property could have decreased so much in value. Its erection and completion must have cost Mr Clark over £2000."[661]

In 1889, the former *Black Swan Inn* gained a new lease of life when it was acquired by Thomas McCristal. McCristal enlarged the structure and converted it into a school which was initially called *Benalla College* but was later re-named the *North-Eastern College*. Run on Christian, but strictly "unsectarian principles", the school offered classes which included those in bookkeeping, writing and arithmetic, as well as evening preparatory classes for

---

659 See Dunlop, *op. cit.*, p. 38.
660 See footnote 645 and its accompanying text above.
661 See the *Ovens and Murray Advertiser*, Tuesday, 3 October 1871, p. 2. A different, and perhaps less reliable, account of negotiations for the sale of the *Black Swan Inn* by Richard Clark to the Victorian Government appeared in the *Benalla Standard* on March 1902. This account alleged that in or shortly after 1855, the Government sought to buy the building and convert it into a dedicated post and telegraph office. The account went on to assert that:
"Officers from the department in Melbourne were sent up to inspect and report, and after two or three visits had been paid, Mr Clark, the owner of the Black Swan, was offered the sum of £8,000, but he allowed himself to be persuaded by the then district surveyor, Mr Wilmot, to intimate that he would not accept less than £10,000. The result of this was that negotiations were broken off...."
See the *Benalla Standard*, Tuesday, 11 May 1902, p. 2.

matriculation.⁶⁶². In 1896, McCristal was succeeded as principal of the *North-Eastern College* by the Reverend John Coutie. In turn, the latter was succeeded by John Russell Crowther in 1902.⁶⁶³ On Crowther's return to Melbourne in mid 1909, the *North-Eastern College* closed.⁶⁶⁴

The *North-Eastern College* produced at least two distinguished alumni, who occupied different ends of the political spectrum. The first, Michael Savage, was born at Tatong to the south-east of Benalla in 1872. He later went on to serve as the Labour Party Prime Minister of New Zealand from 1935 until his death in 1940.⁶⁶⁵ The second distinguished alumnus, Sir Leslie McConnan, was born in 1887. He became the Chief Manager of the National Bank of Australasia and, as Chairman of the Associated Banks of Victoria, was a leader in the fight by the Australian banks against the Chifley Government's bank nationalisation legislation of the late 1840s.⁶⁶⁶

After a number of unsuccessful attempts to sell the *North-Eastern College*, Crowther ultimately disposed of it to a Mr and Mrs Laird.⁶⁶⁷ The building was later converted into several apartments before being demolished in the 1970s.⁶⁶⁸

Richard Clark's Other Economic Pursuits

The *Black Swan Inn* probably turned out to be a financial disappointment for Richard Clark. However, it is clear that by 1859, he had a number of other financial irons in the fire.

As mentions above, grain growing was developing apace around Benalla as the 1850s progressed.⁶⁶⁹ By 1872, upwards of 70,000 acres were said to be under cultivation.⁶⁷⁰ The grain so grown would in the main have been wheat. It seems highly likely that Richard Clark would not have been slow in commencing cultivation of at least part of his *Junction* run. It is, perhaps, significant that at a Benalla Agricultural Society "ploughing match" held in "Mr Clark's paddock on the banks of the Broken river" on 6 June 1867, one Samuel Baker, described as a "ploughman for Mr Richard Clark", won first prize in the swing plough division of the competition.⁶⁷¹ No doubt, Richard also continued to raise and sell stock on and from the run.

---

662 See Baker, *op. cit.*, p. 2. See also Barry Gustafson, "Employment in Benalla" in *The Early Years of Michael Joseph Savage* (https://tinyurl.com/2rfct98t) (at 22 April 2023); *The Advocate*, Wednesday, 28 March 1945, p. 14; and photo 41 below.

663 See *The Age*, Monday, 6 February 1922, p. 8.

664 See the *Benalla Standard*, Tuesday, 11 May 1909, p. 3.

665 See Gustafson, *op. cit.*; and Barry Gustafson, "Savage, Michael Joseph (Mick) (1872-1940)" in *Australian Dictionary of Biography* (https://tinyurl.com/39we39h4) (at 22 April 2023).

666 See D T Merrett, "McConnan, Sir Leslie James (1887-1954)" in *Australian Dictionary of Biography* (https://tinyurl.com/55u4cy8y) (at 22 April 2023); and the *Benalla Ensign*, Thursday, 23 December 1954, p. 1.

667 See the *Benalla Standard*, Tuesday, 17 August 1915, p. 3.

668 See Bulleid Family History: *Bulleid News* (No. 37, 2 December 2009) (https://tinyurl.com/y9thkhkr) (at 22 April 2023); and photos 42 and 43 below.

669 See footnotes 649 and 650, and their accompanying texts, above.

670 See "Benalla" in the *Australian Handbook* (1875), cited in *Victorian Places – Benalla* (https://tinyurl.com/ycwl4ml3) (at 22 April 2023).

671 See the *Ovens and Murray Advertiser*, Saturday, 8 June 1867, p. 3. Cf. footnotes 164 and 408, and their accompanying texts, above.

Apparently not content with simply growing wheat, Richard turned to grinding it. In 1855, he commissioned the construction of a flour mill in Benalla.[672] Built of brick, the mill was located on the left bank of the Broken River to the south-east of the bridge, and close to what is the northern end of Maud Street.[673] It was seemingly a grand structure. According to the anonymous author of *Benalla Past and Present*, the mill became:

> "the Mecca for wheat traffic from places as remote as Yarrawonga and Mansfield. Later on, Geo. Sharpe and the Reilly Bros. built mills, but for a long time, Clark's had no rival nearer than Wangaratta 25 miles on the north side."[674]

That flour milling was central to Richard Clark's business life after 1855 is perhaps attested by the fact that he was described as a "Miller" on his Death Certificate.[675]

Following Richard's death in 1869, it would seem that his mill was acquired by a William Magennis. The latter continued to operate it until his own death in the early 1880s.[676] Magennis apparently used his own punt, worked by a rope and pole, to convey his flour to the Benalla Railway Station across the Broken River. The journey from mill to station was completed faster in this manner than by way of the bridge.[677] It is not presently known whether this punt was in use for transporting flour during Richard Clark's time as the owner of the mill. The mill itself was apparently demolished soon after Magennis' death.[678]

In addition to his pastoral, agricultural and flour milling pursuits, it would seem that by 1859, Richard Clark was also acting as the Benalla agent for the Melbourne Fire Insurance Company.[679]

The Cancellation of Richard Clark's Junction Run Squatting Licence.

On 24 September 1861, Richard Clark's licence to occupy his *Junction* run was cancelled by the Victorian Government and the land, or what remained of it by then, was thereafter sold.[680] Richard probable purchased freehold title to part or parts of the property at this

---

672 See *The Argus*, Friday, 30 November 1855, p. 5.
673 See Edward Robertson's Benalla Plan and photo 44 below.
674 See *Benalla Past and Present*, p. 12. It is interesting to note that perhaps the largest of Wangaratta's flour mills, known as *Victoria Flour Mills*, was constructed on land owned by William Clark, and was for a time partly owned by the latter: see footnotes 468, 469 and 470, and their accompanying texts, above. See also footnote 244 and its accompanying text above.
675 See *Victoria Deaths Register: Richard Clark* (1869) (No. 514/1869).
676 See Dunlop, *op. cit.*, p. 38.
677 See Robertson, *Correspondence and Notes*, p. 5; and Robertson, *Discovery and Settlement*, p. 2.
678 See Robertson, *Correspondence and Notes*, p. 5.
679 See *The Argus*, Wednesday, 23 March 1859, p. 7(2).
680 See Spreadborough and Anderson, *op. cit.*, p. 54. See also Billis and Kenyon, *Pastoral Pioneers*, p. 46; and Dunlop, *op. cit.*, p. 165.

time. Indeed, at some point in time after August 1852 and prior to September 1861, he could very well have already exercised his pre-emptive right to purchase the 640 acre "homestead" block on the run.[681] This freehold land could then have formed the nucleus of what later became known as "*Clark's Farm*".[682]

The Marriage of Sarah Jane Clark

On 16 April 1866, Richard Clark's daughter, Sarah Jane Clark, married Michael Farrell in St. Thomas' Anglican Church, Essendon. At the time of the marriage, the bride was 21 years old and the groom 24 years of age. Born in Melbourne, Michael, like Sarah, was a resident of Benalla when they married.[683] In his *Correspondence and Notes*, Edward Robertson observed that he thought that Michael Farrell had been employed as Richard Clark's secretary and bookkeeper; adding disparagingly:

"I never knew him to do any work but suppose that he must have done something."[684]

Richard Clark's Financial Decline

Over the course of the 1860s Richard Clark's financial position deteriorated to the point of insolvency. The reasons for this financial decay can only be surmised. Richard's loss of revenue after the decline and then closure of the *Black Swan Inn* could well have played a part. Local flour milling competition as time went on would also have reduced his income. Unprofitable investments, particularly in parcels of land, may have substantially contributed to the financial deterioration.[685] Finally, Richard's health was likely declining in the latter part of the decade, and this decline could have played its part.

During the first half of the 1860s, Richard Clark did take steps to address financial difficulties he faced. In particular, he initiated a number of court actions to recover monies and property. Thus, on 23 June 1863, he secured a judgment for £38.8.0 against Donald Cumming, a carrier from Big River Junction near Jamieson, on a dishonoured Bill of

---

681 See footnote 406 and its accompanying text above.

682 By the time of Richard Clark's death in 1869, *Clark's Farm* was said to contain around 400 acres of land. Some of *Clark's Farm* may have been sold by him prior to his death: see letter from James Cooper Stewart, Solicitor, to the National Bank of Australasia dated 20 February 1871 in *National Bank of Australasia v William Clark* (PROV, *VPRS* 267/P7, Unit 193, Item 1869/2652).

683 See *Victoria Marriages Register: Michael Farrell and Sarah Jane Clark* (1866) (No. 1157/1866). Michael Farrell's father, Henry Charles Farrell, had been the proprietor of a hotel at Mia Mia in the Port Phillip District before acquiring the *Pier Hotel* at Sandridge (now Port Melbourne) in 1851. Henry Farrell was elected as an Alderman for the Macarthur Ward on the Melbourne City Council in October 1856, but died the following year on 10 August 1857: see *The Farrell Family* (Section 4, Version 7a, January 2022), pp. 50-54 (https://tinyurl.com/ydes6374) (at 22 April 2023).

684 See Robertson, *Correspondence and Notes*, p. 5.

685 Alan Dunlop noted that:
"As the fortune of the Black Swan Inn began to decline, Clark bought a large number of town blocks."
See Dunlop, *op, cit.*, p. 42. See also footnotes 100 to 108, and their accompanying texts, above.

Exchange.[686] Again, on 28 October 1865, Richard obtained a judgment against Stephen Stephens, of Queen Street, Melbourne, for £24.4.0 on a dishonoured cheque.[687] It is not now known whether Richard ultimately recovered either of these judgment debts from the judgment debtor concerned.

On 11 October, 1864, Richard Clark and James Grassie secured a court order for the ejectment of a St John Oakshott from the *Duck Ponds* rural property jointly owned by Richard and Grassie at Balmattum. Whether Oakshott had originally occupied *Duck Ponds* as a licensee or as a trespasser is unknown.[688]

Richard also resorted to selling assets. On 23 October 1866, he sold a number of his stud horses at auction. The *Ovens and Murray Advertiser* somewhat dismissively described the sale in the following terms:

> "Mr A. C. Bayly sold today, at the Black Swan Hotel, a portion of the stud of horses of Mr Richard Clarke. The majority off them were of an inferior kind, and they sold at an average of about six guineas. The highest was purchased by Mr James McKellar for £14 10s, and the lowest went at fifteen shillings. There was a tolerably large crowd, but there seemed to be little anxiety to purchase."[689]

However, legal actions such as those taken against Cumming, Stephens and Oakshott referred to above, together with horse sales, ultimately did little to halt Richard Clark's economic decline.

In the event, Richard's financial deterioration led to two actions taken by the National Bank of Australasia in the Victorian Supreme Court at Melbourne. In the first action, the Bank sued Richard.[690] In the second, the Defendant was his older brother, William Clark.[691] The Bank was ultimately successful in the second of these suits. It is from the court documents in the two actions, together with contemporaneous newspaper reports, that one is able to trace significant steps taken in consequence of Richard Clark's financial decline.[692] The court documents and newspaper reports also serve to illuminate the ultimately futile steps taken by Michael Farrell and by William Clark in an apparent attempt to save at least some of Richard's real estate for the latter's daughter and son.

It would seem that in 1860, Richard Clark opened an overdraft account with the National

---

686 See *National Bank of Australasia v Richard Clark* (PROV, *VPRS* 267/P7, Unit 38, Item 1863/1074).
687 See *National Bank of Australasia v Richard Clark* (PROV, *VPRS* 267/P7, Unit 90, Item 1865/3054).
688 See *National Bank of Australasia v Richard Clark* (PROV, *VPRS* 267/P7, Unit 66, Item 1864/2537). See also footnote 628 and its accompanying text above.
689 See the *Ovens and Murray Advertiser*, Tuesday, 23 October 1866, p. 3.
690 See *National Bank of Australasia v Richard Clark* (PROV, *VPRS* 267/P7, Unit 176, Item 1868/1224).
691 See *National Bank of Australasia v William Clark* (PROV, *VPRS* 259/P1, Unit 111, Item 1151). See also footnotes 529, 530 and 531, and their accompanying texts, above.
692 As to the relevant newspaper reports, see *The Age*, Tuesday, 13 July 1869, p. 3; *The Argus*, Friday, 23 July 1869, pp. 2 and 4; the *Benalla Ensign and Farmer's and Squatter's Journal*, Friday, 5 November 1869, p. 2; and *The Advocate*, Saturday, 12 February 1870, p. 9.

Bank at its Benalla branch office. At the same time, he deposited the title deeds to some of the parcels of land owned by him with the Bank for safe keeping. By 1862, Richard's account with the Bank was overdrawn. In February of that year, he executed a legal mortgage over some of his properties in and in the vicinity of Benalla in favour of the Bank to secure £3,000 of the overdraft debt he then owed to the latter

Richard's overdraft debt to the National Bank continued to increase as the 1860s progressed. This left the Bank exposed, with an unsecured debt over and above the amount secured by its mortgage from Richard.

On 26 March 1868, Richard Clark was called to a meeting with Frederick Wright, the General Manager of the National Bank, at the latter's office in Melbourne. In evidence which was subsequently accepted by a Supreme Court Jury in Melbourne, Wright deposed that during this meeting, Richard agreed that the remainder of his title deeds held for safe keeping by the Bank should thereafter be held by it as security for the balance of the overdraft monies owed by Richard to the Bank.

Richard Clark was called to a further meeting with Wright in Melbourne on 8 April 1868. At that meeting, he was presented with, and asked to sign, a Conveyance to the Bank, in trust for sale, of the lands the title deeds to which he had agreed on 26 March 1868 were to be held by the Bank as security for the balance of his overdraft debt ("the *Remaining Lands*"). Once in possession of the signed Conveyance, the Bank no doubt intended to sell the *Remaining Lands* so conveyed, together with Richard's lands earlier mortgaged by him to the Bank, in order to recover some or all of the outstanding overdraft debt. In the event, Richard refused to sign the conveyance there and then. However, he took the document away from the meeting with him; stating that he wished to discuss it with a friend, a Mr Carter.

Later in 1868, Richard advised Wright that he was endeavouring to borrow monies to pay off his overdraft debt to the Bank. He further advised that if he failed in his bid to borrow the necessary monies, he would either execute the Conveyance the Bank had presented to him or execute a legal mortgage of the *Remaining Lands* in favour of the Bank.

As matters turned out, Richard Clark was unable to borrow the monies he apparently sought. Further, it seems that he found himself unable to pay off any of his overdraft debt to the Bank from his own resources. Finally, he took no steps to execute either the Bank's Conveyance or a legal mortgage of the *Remaining Lands*.

The Death of Sarah Clark

Richard Clark's woes were compounded when, on 30 June 1868, his second wife, Sarah Clark, died in West Melbourne aged 33 years old. Her causes of death were given on her Death Certificate as hepatitis and gastritis of three years duration.[693] It appears likely that she was receiving medical care in Melbourne at the time of her death. Sarah was buried

---

693 See *Victoria Deaths Register: Sarah Clark* (1868) (No. 6931/1868).

on 2 July 1868 in the burial plot of her husband's brother, John Clark, in the Melbourne General Cemetery.[694]

The National Bank's First Legal Action

On 13 October 1868, the National Bank issued a Writ out of the Supreme Court of Victoria to recover a total of £5,538.16.4 from Richard Clark. The latter entered an appearance to the Writ on 6 November 1868. His first responses to the Writ were apparently to deny being served with the particulars of the Bank's demand, and to dispute the Bank's calculation of the monies said to be owed to it by Richard.

Subsequently, Richard advised the Bank that his Solicitor, Henry Hedderwick, of Palmer Hedderwick in Melbourne, had prepared a new Conveyance in trust for sale with respect to the *Remaining Lands*. Richard further advised that he would "forthwith" execute the new Conveyance, see that the *Remaining Lands* were sold and pay his debt to the Bank out of the proceeds of sale. On this basis, the Bank agreed to stay its Supreme Court action.

In December 1868, and whilst the national Bank's action against him had been stayed by the Bank, Richard Clark was sued by his son-in-law, Michael Farrell, on a Bill of Exchange for £2,000 which allegedly dated from 1866. Richard did not defend the suit and, on 23 December 1868, Farrell obtained judgment against him in the Victorian Supreme Court in the sum of £2, 034 (inclusive of legal costs). Immediately after obtaining his judgment, Farrell invoked the Court's execution processes to require the Sheriff at Beechworth to seize and sell the *Remaining Lands*, together with other lands owned by Richard the title deeds to which had never been lodged by him with the National Bank, to satisfy Farrell's judgment debt.

The Death of Richard Clark

Prior to the Sheriff's sale of the *Remaining Lands*, together with other lands belonging to Richard Clark, in satisfaction of Michael Farrell's judgment debt, Richard died in Benalla on 20 January 1869. He was 52 years old when he died. On his Death Certificate, his cause of death was said to have been "inflammation of the liver." The duration of this disease was not given on the Certificate.[695]

It is likely that the "inflammation of the liver" which cost Richard Clark his life was caused by hepatitis. Not only did that disease result in the death of Richard's second wife, Sarah Clark, but it also probably was to kill his older brother, William Clark, in 1871.[696]

Alternatively, Richard's liver inflammation may have been caused by some disease

---

694 The burial plot is located at the Melbourne General Cemetery in Church of England Compartment F, Grave 201.
695 See *Victoria Deaths Register: Richard Clark* (1869) (No. 514/1869).
696 See footnotes 534, 538 and 693, and their accompanying texts, above.

associated with alcohol consumption such as cirrhosis of the liver. In this regard it might be recalled that Richard's younger brother, George Clark, apparently had an excessive fondness for alcohol; dying in 1854 from "exhaustion consequent of delirium tremens".[697] Again, Richard's eldest brother, John Clark, died in 1857 of hydrothorax and heart disease.[698] Hydrothorax, a form of pleural effusion, can develop in consequence of cirrhosis of the liver. Accordingly, it may be of significance that Richard, like his brothers John and William, was a publican over the course of many years.

On 21 January 1869, Richard Clark was buried in the Benalla Cemetery following a Church of England funeral service conducted by the Reverend John Sheldon.[699]

It sadly appears to be the case that Richard Clark's death was not marked by the contemporaneous publication in any local newspaper of an obituary for the man who was to all intents and purposes the founder of the township of Benalla. It seems likely that this lack of an obituary was one outcome of Richard's precipitous economic decline and fall. Shortly prior to his death, an anonymous Benalla correspondent wrote this in the *Ovens and Murray Advertiser* on 7 January 1869 of that decline and fall:

> "The sudden and unexpected change in the fortunes of Mr. Richard Clarke, so long a resident of this township, has staggered the belief of many. Mr. Clarke was always looked upon as the safest man in the township, as the phrase goes."[700]

Later newspaper articles were kinder to Richard. By way of example, on 12 August 1875, the *Ovens and Murray Advertiser* described him as "the real founder" of Benalla.[701]

The Purported Sale of Richard Clark's Lands to William Clark

In a notice published in the *Ovens and Murray Advertiser* on 9 February 1869, the Sheriff at Beechworth advertised that he proposed to sell Richard Clark's interest in a total of 63 allotments of land by a public auction to be held at noon that day at the *Royal Victoria Hotel* in Wangaratta. A total of 61 of these allotments were located in and around Benalla. One was to be found in the township of Merton, and the last allotment was situated in the Parish of Moorabbin.[702]

At the auction on 9 February 1869, Richard's brother, William Clark, purchased all of the parcels of land on sale for a total consideration of £1,217. It seems that few other persons bid at the auction for any of the properties.

---

697 See footnote 402 and its accompanying text above.
698 See footnotes 292 and 293, and their accompanying texts, above.
699 See *Victoria Deaths Register: Richard Clark* (1869) (No. 514/1869). See also photo 45 below.
700 See the *Ovens and Murray Advertiser*, Thursday, 7 January 1869, p. 3.
701 See the *Ovens and Murray Advertiser*, Thursday, 12 August 1875, p. 3.
702 See the *Ovens and Murray Advertiser*, Tuesday, 9 February 1869, p. 4. See also footnotes 629, 630, 631 and 632, and their accompanying texts, above.

The circumstances surrounding the sale of Richard Clark's lands to his brother William generated controversy at the time. One unnamed correspondent wrote the following in the *Ovens and Murray Advertiser* on 13 February 1869:

"That very important sale of the late Richard Clarke's property, at the suit of his son-in-law, Mr Michael Farrell, came off today at Wangaratta, but decidedly it was a misnomer to call it a sale; these writs of fieri facias are more property swindles than genuine sales. Nearly all this valuable property which Mr. E. G. Nethercott was deputed to sell to-day was under mortgage to the National Bank of Australasia for the sum of £3,500 and interest thereon, so that the Bank is absolute owner of the property, as they hold the deeds and all the title. The sale, however, took place and all the property was put up in two lots. The town property went at, I think, £215, and the other at £1012, or something near that. It is very evident that the real intrinsic value of the first was beyond £1000, and to go at £215 plainly shows that the public had no confidence in the sale, and looked upon it as a fallacy from beginning to end; the second portion, which comprises a farm of 550 acres and some scores of valuable allotments, went at £1012 or thereabouts. No person, unless a member of Clarke's family, would of course attempt to go in for any of this ground, because the seller could produce no title. It was only at the sale it was announced that all was in the hands of the Bank; so that those Benalla men who went up to get allotments were entirely disappointed."[703]

However, in the same edition of the *Ovens and Murray Advertiser*, the newspaper's editor took strong issue with this unnamed correspondent, stating that:

"Our correspondent is so entirely at fault as to his facts that it is no wonder he is entirely wrong as to the conclusions at which he arrives. The following are the real facts of the case:- The sheriff's bailiff at first offered for sale the allotments upon which there was no claim whatsoever, and announced them as such; but all were offered subject to any possible legal claim. These allotments were afterwards put up separately, and no offer being made, all these unencumbered lots were put up together. Mr. Nethercott [the sheriff's bailiff] announced that he did not consider the last bid for this, namely £190, at all sufficient; and without knocking them down, passed on to the sale of the property, concerning which the National Bank of Australasia had given notice that they had filed a bill in Equity, and this was also announced at the sale by the clerk of the Bank's solicitors. The Bank, no doubt, hold the deeds of this portion of the property as collateral security, but the Bank can in no sense be considered as the owner of the property; and to show that there was something to sell outside the claims of

---

703   See the *Ovens and Murray Advertiser*, Saturday, 13 February 1869, p. 4.

the Bank, this was knocked down to Mr. Wm. Clarke, who must be in possession of all the circumstances, for £1015. Then the unencumbered property was again put up in one lot, and finally knocked down to the same buyer for £202."[704]

William Clark borrowed a total of £1,500 from the Colonial Bank of Australasia on a bond and promissory note to pay for his brother Richard's auctioned allotments and associated costs, including legal costs. At William's death on 24 April 1871, this debt was still owing to the Colonial Bank and constituted the largest single liability encumbering William's estate.[705]

Michael Farrell's judgment against Richard Clark, the latter's death and William Clark's acquisition of the *Remaining Lands* were setbacks for the National Bank in its quest to recover all of the monies which Richard owed to it. Although the Bank was still able to foreclose on the legal mortgage Richard had executed in its favour over some of his lands in February 1862, and then sell such mortgaged lands, it was unable to continue its Supreme Court action against Richard by reason of his death.

The Bank took the view that Michael Farrell's undefended action against Richard Clark, and William Clark's consequential purchase of Richard's auctioned lands, were coordinated artifices solely designed to deny the Bank an entitlement to sell those properties after it had obtained a judgment against Richard. It would seem that the Bank's apprehensions here were probably well-founded.

The circumstances surrounding Richard Clark's alleged debt of £2000 to Farrell on an 1866 Bill of Exchange are now lost in time. However, it seems most odd that Richard would have incurred a debt of such magnitude on a Bill of Exchange he allegedly provided to his son-in-law and employee.[706] And why did around two years elapse between the provision of that Bill of Exchange and Farrell's suit against Richard? The possibility that Richard in fact executed the Bill in 1868 and pre-dated it to 1866 cannot readily be excluded.

It is conceivable that in purchasing the auctioned lands for a total of £1,217 at the Sheriff's auction on 9 February 1869, William Clark was simply seeking to acquire the properties at a bargain price for his own enrichment. However, it would appear to be more likely that he purchased the properties to deny them to the Bank; and, moreover, with a view to ultimately making them available to his late brother's surviving children, Sarah Jane Farrell and John Robert Clark.

After deduction of the Sheriff's auction costs, the balance of the £1,217 paid by William Clark to acquire the auctioned lands went to Michael Farrell; Sarah Farrell's husband. Further, it is clear that William maintained a close relationship with his nephew, John Robert Clark, after William had purchased the properties. Richard Clark died intestate. On 8 July 1869, John Robert Clark was granted Letters of Administration of his late father's estate

---

704 *Ibid.*
705 See *William Clark's Will; Inventory of Assets and Liabilities* (PROV, *VPRS* 28/P0, Unit 103). See also footnote 558 and its accompanying text and **Appendix 3**, both below,
706 See footnote 684 and its accompanying text above.

by the Supreme Court of Victoria.[707] In order to assist his nephew in acquiring that grant, William provided the Court with an administration bond; being a sworn assurance and monetary guarantee that John Robert Clark would properly administer Richard's estate.[708]

It may be that William Clark was a party to an agreement whereby the Farrells and John Robert Clark would share the balance of the £1,217 William had paid for his late brother's auctioned lands. It may also be that William intended to convey the properties to his nephew and niece (or the latter's husband) in return for the repayment by Michael Farrell of the monies paid by William for those properties. Whatever had been the plan, it was circumvented by the National Bank.

The National Bank's Second Legal Action

In March 1869, the National Bank commenced its action against William Clark. By this suit, it sought an order from the Victorian Supreme Court in essence rendering William's title to the *Remaining Lands* void. The central arguments of the Bank were that:

(a) Richard Clark had agreed at his meeting with the Bank's General Manager on 26 March 1868 that the title deeds to the *Remaining Lands* which were then held by the Bank for safe keeping would thenceforth be held by it as security for the balance of Richard's overdraft debt.

(b) By that agreement, Richard had created a valid equitable (or unwritten) mortgage of the *Remaining Lands* in favour of the Bank.

(c) William Clark had purchased the *Remaining Lands* in full knowledge of his brother Richard's agreement with the bank, and of the Bank's consequent equitable mortgage.

(d) The Bank was entitled to foreclose on its equitable mortgage and to sell the *Remaining Lands* to satisfy at least part of the balance of the overdraft debt owed to it.

In defending the Bank's action against him, William Clark denied that Richard had ever agreed to the Bank holding the title deeds to the *Remaining Lands* as security for the balance of his overdraft debt. William asserted that the Bank's General Manager had misconstrued the substance of the conversation he had had with Richard on 26 March 1868. William contended that the Bank had only ever held the title deeds in question in safe custody for

---

707 See *Letter of Administration of Richard Clark's Estate* (PROV, *VPRS* 28/P1, Unit 20, Item 7/639). See also the *Ovens and Murray Advertiser*, Tuesday, 9 February 1869, p. 4.
708 See *Richard Clark's Estate: William Clark's Administration Bond* (PROV, *VPRS* 28/P0, Unit 84, Item 7/639).

Richard. Accordingly, it had never acquired an equitable mortgage over the *Remaining Lands*, and was therefore unable to challenge William's own title to the properties.

On 22 July 1869, Mr Justice Molesworth in the Victorian Supreme Court ordered that the issue of whether or not Richard Clark had left the title deeds to the *Remaining Lands* with the National Bank for safe keeping or as security for his debt be tried before a Judge and a Jury of 12 men. On 5 November 1869, and following a hearing on this issue conducted before Chief Justice Stawell, the Jury returned a verdict in favour of the Bank; affirming that Richard had in fact agreed to the Bank holding the title deeds in question as security for the balance of his overdraft debt. Judgment was accordingly entered by the Court for the Bank.

Following further evidence taken before the Supreme Court with respect to the amount of the residue of Richard Clark's overdraft debt, the latter's estate was found on 14 February 1870 to owe a total of £2,870.15.6. The National Bank was given liberty to sell the *Remaining Lands* to recover this amount.

Subsequently, the Sheriff provided the Bank with the following particulars regarding a number of the properties to be sold by him from the *Remaining Lands* in consequence of the Supreme Court's order of 14 February 1870:

"(a) Lot 1: Farm at Benalla containing four hundred acres and known as 'Clark's Farm'.
(b) Lot 2: Cottage at Arundel Street, Benalla and land containing about three acres.
(c) Lot 3: Store at corner of Arundel and Thomas Streets known as 'Munro's Store and land.
(d) Lots 4 & 5: Two paddocks near Benalla containing about one hundred acres.
(e) Lot 6: Cottage and one acre of land situate in Bridge Street, Benalla.
(f) Lot 7: Half an acre of land at Benalla being Allotment 4, Section X, Bridge Street."

These would appear to have been the more important and valuable of Richard Clark's properties, and one can readily see why he would have done his utmost to avoid providing the National Bank with any interest in them. One can also see why William Clark would have done his best to resist the Bank's action to secure the Supreme Court's recognition of its equitable mortgage over them, and over the balance of the *Remaining Lands*.

It is not now known what amounts were realised by the National Bank from the sale of the *Remaining Lands*, or from the sale of the lands originally mortgaged to it by Richard Clark in February 1862. Nor is it now known what other debts may have encumbered Richard's estate. However, it seems unlikely that there would have been much, if anything, left over to be shared between Sarah Farrell and John Robert Clark.

The Fates of Richard Clark's Surviving Children

Sarah Farrell died on 23 July 1920 in Orbost of pneumonia. She was 75 years of age when she died and was buried in Orbost. Her husband, Michael Farrell, had died in Benalla in 1906. Sarah was survived by three daughters and one son. She was very likely living with one of her daughters and the latter's husband when she died.[709]

John Robert Clark received his early schooling in Benalla, as probably did his older sister.[710] In an obituary for him, it was said in the *Benalla Standard* on 31 July 1934 that he finished his education at Brighton Grammar School.[711] However, this seems highly unlikely as that school was not founded until 14 February 1882, when John would have been 33 or 34 years old.[712] It may be that he did attend one of a number of small, somewhat ephemeral private schools located in Brighton in the 1860s.[713] If so, he would, of course, have had to board somewhere in Brighton in proximity to the school.

In any event, after completing school, John evidently returned to Benalla and worked for a time in a mill. The mill in question might well have be the flour mill founded by his father.[714] He was later appointed as the Shire of Benalla's rate collector; and then later still as the rate collector for the Benalla Waterworks Trust. He remained working in those positions until his retirement in 1917.[715]

John was apparently very keen on sport. He was a particularly good cricketer, at one point playing in a Victorian cricket team in Benalla against a team from England.[716] It is interesting to note that in September 1859, his father had been appointed by the Victorian Government as one of four trustees:

> "of the ground set apart at Benalla as a site for cricketing, and other purposes of public recreation."[717]

It seems likely that father and son shared a passion for cricket.

On 28 May 1884, John Robert Clark married Sarah Hindes at Christ Church Anglican Church, St Kilda; with the Reverend John Low officiating. John's bride was the daughter of a Benalla blacksmith, Jabez Hindes, and the latter's wife, Janet Hindes. Like her husband,

---

709 See *Victoria Deaths Register: Sarah Farrell* (1920) (No. 11837/1920).
710 See the *Benalla Standard*, Tuesday, 31 July 1934, p. 3.
711 *Ibid.*
712 See *Wikipedia – Brighton Grammar School* (https://tinyurl.com/2s4chn38) (at 24 April 2023).
713 See Weston Bate, *A History of Brighton* (1983, 2nd ed.), pp. 321-327.
714 See footnote 672 and its accompanying text above.
715 See the *Benalla Standard*, Tuesday, 31 July 1934, p. 3; and Dunlop, *op. cit.*, p. 99.
716 See the *Benalla Standard*, Tuesday, 31 July 1934, p. 3.
717 See *The Argus,* Wednesday, 14 September 1859, p. 5.

Sarah was born in Benalla.[718] The marriage produced three sons: Charles Richard Clark, John Clark Jnr and Russell Clark.[719]

Sarah Clark (née Hindes) died at Benalla on 18 December 1906 at the age of 54 years. On her Death Certificate, her causes of death were said to be "capillary bronchitis and apnoea". She was buried in the Benalla Cemetery on 19 December 1906.[720]

John Robert Clark himself died of heart failure on 28 July 1934 in Benalla. He was 86 years old and was survived by his two younger sons. He was buried in the Benalla Cemetery the following day, 29 July 1934.[721] In 1929, the anonymous author of *Benalla Past and Present*, observed of John Robert Clark, some five years before the latter's death, that:

> "He recalls many scenes of the early days, notably the great corroborees held by the blacks on the river bank opposite his old home....His earliest recollection of Benalla is when there were six houses in it.[722]

---

[718] See *Victoria Marriages Register: John Robert Clark and Sarah Hindes* (1884) (No. 2077/1884).

[719] See the *North Eastern Ensign*, Friday, 3 August 1934, p. 3.

[720] See *Victoria Deaths Register: Sarah Clark* (1906) (No. 11848/1906).

[721] See *Victoria Deaths Register: John Robert Clark* (1934) (No. 15699/1934). See also the *Benalla Standard*, Tuesday, 31 July 1934, p. 3; the *North Eastern Ensign*, Friday, 3 August 1934, p. 3; and *The Age*, Wednesday, 1 August 1934, p. 13. John Robert Clark lies buried in the same plot in the Benalla Cemetery as do his wife, Sarah Clark, and their oldest son, Charles Richard Clark; both of whom predeceased him. The grave marker over the plot asserts with respect to both Sarah and John Robert Clark that they were the "first white people born in Benalla". While this assertion would seem to be correct with respect to John Robert Clark, it is not correct so far as his wife, Sarah Clark, is concerned. The inscription would appear to confuse the latter with John Robert Clark's older sister, Sarah Jane Farrell (née Clark), who lies buried in Orbost: see footnotes 606 and 720, and their accompanying texts, above.

[722] See *Benalla Past and Present*, p. 22.

39. The site of the first Black Swan Inn, Broken River.

40. The site of the second Black Swan Inn, Benalla.

41. An early photo of the North-Eastern College, occupying the building which was formerly the second Black Swan Inn.

42. The second Black Swan Inn building after its conversion into apartments.

43. The second Black Swan Inn building in ruins prior to its demolition in the 1970s.

44. The approximate site of Richard Clark's flour mill on the left bank of the Broken River, Benalla.

45. *The grave of Richard Clark and his first wife, Mary Clark (née Sparrow), in the Benalla Cemetery.*

CONCLUSION

In his expansive work, *The World: A Family History*, Simon Sebag Montefiore wrote:

> "The first rule of history is to realise how little we know about people in the past, how they thought, how their families worked."[723]

Whilst this is undoubtedly true as a generality, it is also true that much can nonetheless be gleaned regarding the Clark family from both primary and secondary sources.

The last surviving of the three Clark brothers who together constitute the principal subjects of this book, William Clark, died more than 150 years ago. Yet the story of his life, and the lives of his brothers, John and Richard Clark, can be traced in considerable detail. That level of detail substantially illuminates the character and motivations of each of them.

John Clark was, of course, much more than a grandfather of Sir Stanley Argyle. He was both a pioneer and an entrepreneur. Over the course of a short life, he travelled a long way, both literally and figuratively, from his origins in the Medway River valley of Kent to *Gooparl* on the banks of the Saltwater River near Melbourne. He overlanded from New South Wales to become one of the earliest European settlers in Victoria; founding both Mitchellstown and Seymour on the Goulburn River. Rising from humble beginnings, he used his wits and initiative to amass considerable wealth in Victoria and new South Wales prior to his early death. Throughout his life, he displayed a fierce determination to succeed.

In life, John was fortunate to have in Martha Clark a wife of courage and determination equal to his own – a wife who was no doubt exposed to dangers and hardships and yet was able to rise to the difficult circumstances which often confronted her; a wife who was able to successfully raise a family of seven children in a frontier environment.

An anonymous author summed John Clark up with some licence in the *North Eastern Ensign* thus:

> "[T]his gentleman was the founder of Seymour. He built a punt for crossing the Goulburn river, sufficiently large for all requirements. Commencing in a very small way he, by his indomitable perseverance, affability and civility, rapidly became the

---

723 See Simon Sebag Montefiore, *The World: A Family History* (2022), p. xxxix.

favourite of all who travelled that way – the man whose opinion was solicited on all sides; and at the same time he assisted and befriended many a person who deserved it, and many a one who did not deserve it! During this time his wealth increased as rapidly as his popularity. He was the first to occupy the country known now as the Goulburn Valley, and by breeding and grazing on such an unlimited area of fertile country made money fast....Thus a good man leaves a good name, and such was Mr. John Clark, the founder of Seymour."[724]

Whatever else one might say about William Clark, he lived an extraordinary life – a life which took him from rural poverty in England to extensive landholdings in Victoria. If he didn't die possessed of great wealth, it wasn't for want of effort on his part. But he was also a man who gave much to his church, his community and his family. He was respected and well-regarded. He was also a man who, like his brothers John and Richard Clark, was acknowledged in his lifetime and afterwards for the part he played in the early European occupation and settlement of Victoria.[725]

In Elizabeth Clark, William was also blessed with a wife who lived her life well. From an exceedingly difficult childhood, an early marriage and the rigours of a frontier existence in the formative years of the Port Phillip District, she was of pleasant disposition, raised a large family and rendered considerable assistance to those – particularly expectant mothers – in her community in need.

The following obituary, published in the *Ovens and Murray Advertiser* on 27 April 1871, if not entirely accurate in its detail, captured much of the essence of William Clark's life and character:

"It is with regret we record the death of Mr Wm. Clark, one of the oldest – if not the very oldest – residents of Wangaratta, which occurred at the residence of Dr Dobbyn, Corowa, on Monday. Mr Clark had been a resident of the Wangaratta neighbourhood for over thirty years, having at an early period taken up the Ovens Crossing run, on part of which now stands the borough of Wangaratta; he was also the first to establish a punt on the river, near to where the town has since been erected. Mr Clark always took a great interest in the progress of the town with which he was so closely identified; for over four years he occupied a seat at the local borough council table, and during his whole career he was held in general esteem, owing to his many good qualities. The funeral of the deceased took place yesterday, and was one of the largest ever witnessed at Wangaratta, upwards of four hundred persons taking part in the procession."[726]

It is difficult at this juncture to fully gauge the character and personality of Richard Clark.

---

724 See "Recollections of Benalla" in the *North Eastern Ensign*, Friday, 30 June 1893, p. 3.
725 See footnote 14 and its accompanying texts above.
726 See the *Ovens and Murray Advertiser*, Thursday, 27 April 1871, p. 2.

Like his older brothers, John and William, he was clearly entrepreneurial. His life took him from settled England to the frontiers of colonial Australia; and from a nautical career to innkeeping, squatting, farming and grazing, flour milling and property speculation. As a hotelier, he was probably gregarious; and it is likely that he was fond of more than the occasional alcoholic drink.

It would also seem that Richard enjoyed good relations with his brothers, John and William Clark, and their families. He appears to have maintained a particularly warm relationship with Martha Clark, the wife of his brother John. This is evidenced by the substance and tone of his letter to Martha of 1 December 1865, by the fact that Martha appointed Richard to be both a replacement trustee of the *Gooparl* trust and an executor of her Will, and by the further fact that Richard's second wife, Sarah Clark, was interred after her death in John Clark's burial plot in the Melbourne General Cemetery on 2 July 1868.[727]

The depth and strength of Richard Clark's fraternal relations can also be inferred from the lengths to which his brother, William Clark, went to in an apparent and ultimately unsuccessful attempt to save a substantial portion of Richard's lands from the clutches of the National Bank for Richard's surviving children.

Of the three Clark brothers, only Richard died insolvent. There were probably many reasons for his insolvency; including, among others, imprudent investments in freehold land. However, perhaps the biggest cause of Richard Clark's financial decline was likely the impact of the movement of the Sydney to Melbourne road around 600 m upstream away from the *Black Swan Inn* to join up with the bridge constructed over the Broken River.[728] Over time, this greatly diminished the value of the Inn and no doubt adversely affected Richard's finances.

It is perhaps interesting to note that both John and William Clark were also confronted by the movement of the Sydney to Melbourne road away from their respective Inns. In John's case, the road was shifted for the convenience of travellers to a crossing some 20 km upstream on the Goulburn River from his *Travellers Rest Inn*. In William's case, the road was moved around 300 m to the south-east of his *Hope Inn* to align with the first bridge constructed over the Ovens River.

In John Clark's case, the movement of the road saw him moving his establishment to the new crossing place, and his construction there of the *Robert Burns Inn*.[729] With the re-alignment of the road in Wangaratta, William Clark moved quickly to construct his new *Commercial Hotel* adjacent to the re-aligned road.[730] Clearly, John and William each saw his respective move as being both necessary and financially prudent.

However, in Richard Clark's case, the re-alignment of the Sydney to Melbourne road did not see him move his Inn to front the newly-aligned road. This resulted in the *Black Swan Inn* languishing in a relative backwater as an asset of diminishing value.

---

727 See footnotes 16, 40, 303, 311 and 694, and their accompanying texts, above.
728 See footnotes 614 and 638, and their accompanying texts, above.
729 See footnotes 148 and 149, and their accompanying texts, above.
730 See footnotes 437 and 441, and their accompanying texts, above.

One can only guess why Richard Clark did not emulate his two eldest brothers and move to construct a new inn on the re-aligned Sydney to Melbourne road. Perhaps his mind was focussed on other investments. Perhaps he could not secure a suitable site on the newly-aligned road. Perhaps he lacked some of the business acumen of his two brothers.

Richard might have died insolvent, but there seems little doubt that he was nevertheless held in high regard by his fellow citizens in the Benalla district during the early years of its European occupation. The esteem in which they held him may be seen from the following remarks published on 30 June 1893 in the *North Eastern Ensign*:

> "Although the owner of the Black Swan cannot be said to have been the founder of Benalla, it might be truly said that he was the Father of Benalla. Everyone applied to him for assistance; everyone got what he or she wanted at the Swan – squatters and stockmen, splitters and shepherds. Although the population was not very numerous, there was not one who did not owe a debt of gratitude to the master and mistress of the Black Swan."[731]

In tracing the lives of John, William and Richard Clark, it should not be forgotten that the lands in the Port Phillip District on which they settled were lands which had been occupied and husbanded by Aboriginal tribes and clans for thousands of years. The Clarks may have built their lives and fortunes on those lands, but their settlements undoubtedly contributed to the dispossession, and perhaps decimation, of the original inhabitants.

That said, it should also be recognised that John, William and Richard Clark were each significant figures in the earliest days of European settlement of the localities in which they settled; and, as a family, in the whole of the North East of what ultimately became Victoria.

In this regard, it is perhaps worth repeating the words of the anonymous author of the article published in the *North Eastern Ensign* on 30 June 1893 and referred to in the Introduction to this book:

> "This trio of brothers, whose names are almost unknown to the present generation, are deserving of a monument to their memory in each of the respective towns in which they resided, and so liberally assisted to establish as centres in the north-eastern part of Victoria."[732]

Garry Moore
Melbourne
25 April 2023.

---

731 See the *North Eastern Ensign*, Friday, 30 June 1893, p. 3. Contrary to the assertion here that Richard Clark was not the founder of Benalla, it can be plausibly argued that Richard did indeed found Benalla. Although the military party which established the police station on the Goulburn River were seemingly stationed at that River before Richard moved into his first Inn, the soldiers concerned were only present there for short periods as individuals. Richard Clark was beyond doubt the first European to settle at the site.

732 *Ibid.*

APPENDIX 1

Extracts from the diary of John Conway Bourke

"Mrs Clarke & a friend of hers called to see me. She is the relict of the late John Clarke of Salt Water River. I have known her for 21 years &, if I am spared to write a memoir of my own life, she will be very prominent in my early adventures in this Colony.

Her husband & her were the first white persons that settled on the Goulburn River. They arrived there from the Murrumbidgee Country in January 1838. Their place was about 10 miles below Seymour, & the country opposite that township in them days was their cattle station.

When Mr Joseph Hawdon contracted with Sir Richard Bourke's Government to convey the mails to Port Phillip (now the Colony of Victoria), Mr Clarke sub-contracted with him to take the mail from the Goulburn to Melbourne. This was in the year 1838, & the first time an overland mail was established between Melbourne & Sydney.

In reference to Mrs Clarke, perhaps I may as well mention at once the story I have alluded to at page 12 [above in Bourke's diary]. About the commencement of February 1838, her husband had occasion to go to Melbourne. At that time there was at his place on the Goulburn only myself, & his wife & two children, his stockman & a man named Dudley residing, as he [John Clarke] had been there only a month. He had not time to erect his necessary improvements. In fact, there was only the frame of a hut without the roof for the convenience of himself & family. I & the other two men slept under a tarpaulin tent about a furlong from his place & close to the River bank.

On morning, about 11 o'clock, the dogs barked furiously &, on looking out (I & her being then in her hut), [we] perceived about 100 of the Aborigines marching towards us. They had no women with them, which in them days was always considered suspicious. We had a large dog chained at the door who at first seemed inclined to devour the first of them that came near him. But they yelled so savagely & brandished their tomahawks at him that he became absolutely cowered.

A little ill-looking dwarf of a fellow was the first that came to the door & commenced making unmistakable signs of their ultimate intentions towards her. I took one of her children in my arms & stood in the doorway with the intention of Blocking it up [to] try to prevent them reaching there if possible.

Mrs Clark was in her bedroom with her other child, & I told her to load the firearms as I was determined to sell my life as dear as possible. She commenced doing so & I must here remark that I never knew a man or woman display more determined coolness & indomitable courage than she did on that momentous occasion, because from their gestures she could easily perceive that their intention was to carry her away with them after they had murdered me & her two children.

As I stated before, they silenced the dog, & then a tall old man rushed thro the doorway in spite of my attempt at blocking it up with one of her children in my arms. He rushed past me yelling something in his own language. I then expected every second a general rush. This old fellow had a tomahawk & walked around the hut. But I altered my position at the doorway by standing sideways so that I could watch his movements, as well as the others outside.

By this time, the ill-looking dwarf before alluded to advanced to Mrs Clarke's bedroom door, & continued making signs that they intended to take her in the bush, & other signs too indelicate to mention here. I was just about sprinting into her room, as she then had two guns & a pistol loaded, & the fellows outside were getting impatient, as the tall wretch in the hut or room with me (thro fear I suppose, as I never took my eyes off him) had not dispatched me. I knew that if my eye was off him for ½ a second, his treacherous tomahawk would be buried in my skull.

Well, as stated before, as I was about going into her room, the fellows outside were just about coming in bodily to execute their work when a loud yell was heard, of so demoniac a character as would tamper with the nerves of the stoutest heart living. But, however, instead of advancing as they intended a second before, they ran away towards the River.

This gave us breathing time, altho we could not conjecture the cause of it. I then examined the firearms & told her when they returned for her to use the pistol at the first rush they made, & by which means we would be certain to floor two of them at once. And then, while I held the third piece, she could be reloading the two pieces we had already discharged. Such was our tactics of war, & she entered into the spirit of things in the most determined manner.

But that Providence that we should all trust in came to our aid at the critical moment when a catastrophe would have taken place similar & as barbarous as had ever taken place in the lonesome & unsettled parts of Australia often before.

When their yells subsided, we soon ascertained the cause of it. We heard the welcome galloping of a horse, & soon both horse and rider came into view. In fact, it was Mr Clarke's stockman. He happened (luckily for us) to be on the opposite side of the River that day, looking for stray cattle, & when within about 5 miles from home, he bore down to the road then leading towards Melbourne & perceived the tracks of the blacks bearing towards the homestead.

Knowing how unprotected we were, he galloped towards us as fast as the horse could carry him. This was the cause of their running from the hut, to learn where the noise proceeded from. When he came to us, his horse was covered with foam, & indeed no wonder for I suppose he was never put to the utmost of his speed so much before or since. When he dismounted, he took one of our guns & went to a tree close by & brought down a crow, which seemed to paralyse the would-be murderers.

The man Dudley was at work some distance from the hut, & had been watching the movements of the blacks all this time & was afraid to come & try to render us any assistance as he was without firearms. But, on perceiving the stockman, he immediately came towards us. This was another cause of mortification to them as we were then four strong, including Mrs Clarke who, as I have already proved, was a brave woman.

Dudley provided himself with an axe as Mrs Clarke would not give up her pistol, stating she was ready to use it then if occasion required as she was a few minutes before when we were not troubled by the honour of his presence; a taunt he did not seem to relish. But to hear him talk then, he was praying for them to commence until he could shew us his dexterity in cutting of a few of their heads to hang upon poles so that he would be the means of striking terror into the hearts of the Goulburn blacks for ever afterwards.

Such is the description of the vain braggadocios that be generally met with in this life. They are brave in comparative security, but when real danger is near, they play the craven.

As she justly observed to this man Dudley that he must have seen the blacks long before they approached the hut, & if he had immediately come over to us, what a world of suspense it would have saved us, because if they had seen two men instead of one man & woman, the fellows would not have been so bold – of which we had convincing proof when the stockman had so timely come to our assistance.

Altho they mustered about 100, our small number now prevented them from carrying their original intentions into execution. Such cowards do they generally prove when they have no chance of success. They seemed to alter their conduct altogether now, & wished to know the names of everything they saw – particularly the guns. We, however, kept inside the hut & continually kept possession of the firearms in our hands. They stayed about the place until evening but never attempted to come into the hut, altho they used to go around it & peep between the slabs to make sure of how we were occupied.

They at last withdrew & camped about ½ a mile away, as we supposed, for we heard them late that night shouting their corroboree – very likely singing their then disappointment at not having Mrs Clarke to make a Sable queen of their children, & her children & myself for supper.

They hovered about the place the next day until about one o'clock, when Mr Clarke came home accompanied by two men he had engaged to assist him in erecting his improvements. When they found we were so strongly reinforced, they took their departure.

Mr Clarke was surprised, but at the same time very much pleased, when he heard all the circumstances. And indeed no wonder, for if the stockman had not arrived at the opportune moment he did, there is nothing more certain than that he would have found his children murdered [and] his wife far away in the mountains with those savages. And as a matter of course, I would have been spared the opportunity of giving a description of this marvellous & at the same time providential escape, because to a moral certainty I would be the first object of their attention & the poor children afterwards. But thank God, as I ever should do, their scheme, which at one moment seemed to be on the threshold of consummation, was miraculously thwarted, & I & those concerned preserved to tell the tale

The tale that I have in the back pages of this Diary taken some pains to note down may perhaps in these civilised times be thought little of, but most certainly at the time of the occurrence, Mrs Clarke's escape from the degradation she would have been subjected to caused quite a sensation & was in the mouth of every person at the time. Some of the overland travellers in them days must have communicated the circumstances to some person in connection with the Press in Sydney, for it appeared in one of the broadsheets of that City. And like every other tale that travels any distance, it did not lose its interest for want of embellishment. For amongst other fibs, it was stated Mrs Clarke was taken by them to the Snowy Mountains, & that an adventurous band of picked bushmen after a search of ten days came on the sable captors, fought hard with them & at last, by their undaunted bravery, recovered the lady & slaughtered the greater part of the savage gentlemen that had behaved so rudely.

This tale is now, I think, about fairly told, & as it is only one of the many adventures with the blacks of this country in which I have figured, I will, as space admits, refer to them in this book.

I have already stated that Mr Clarke felt happy when he was made aware of the fortunate escape of his wife & family. Having help now, the first thing he done was to roof his own hut & make solid improvements for himself & servants; always taking the precaution to have plenty of men about his establishment for the double purpose of protection & improving his homestead; altho I never knew or heard of their molesting any of his people afterwards; he as a matter of course staying about home as much as possible for fear they may come again, take a fancy to his better half & make her the Queen of the Goulburn mountains.

That one tribe afterwards proved a scourge to distant settlers & travellers, which I will in due course record, God willing."

John Conway Bourke's Diary; Entry for 7 May 1858
(Royal Historical Society of Victoria, Box 38-l, MS 4652).

APPENDIX 2

Extracts from John Conway Bourke's Autobiographical Notes for Mr. Edward Wilson

"The third morning after this occurrence [the "Faithfull Massacre" of 11 April 1838], I was at the Goulburn River and, while bringing my horse up to Clarke's hut (who had himself just located on that River at what I now called the Old Crossing Place, some 12 miles below Seymour), I was accosted by a female who told me there was three men inside the hut who represented that they were the only survivors of a large party that had been killed at the Broken River by the blacks.

This lady told the tale with such a sneer that it was easy to perceive that she did not believe a word of it.

When I entered the hut, I could also note that Clarke gave the men but little heed, for he took them to be bolters or bushrangers from the Sydney Country. But I soon undeceived him, for I knew the men to be of Faithful's party, and amongst them was James Crossley, the overseer of the men who had just been murdered. He is now a butcher in Kilmore.

I shall never forget the sudden change in Mr Clarke's countenance when he found out that these men had told the truth, or something like it, for indeed they honestly thought from the overwhelming number of blacks, and the persevering manner in which they had been followed by them, that they were the only men that had escaped the slaughter.

Clarke at that time had for his nearest neighbour Mr Hamilton of the Sugar Loaf, in the direction of Melbourne, and none whatever nearer than the Murray in the opposite direction.

Having heard from these men the extraordinary number of blacks they had seen at the Broken River at once proved to him that the Goulburn blacks must be with them, as he had not seen one on his run, or about it, for a fortnight least. So that when they returned from the scene of slaughter, he would have to look out as his party consisted of himself & two men at his homestead, & only a stockman & hutkeeper on his out-station, which is the country opposite what is now called Seymour.

When he found that I recognised the men, he lost no time in procuring his very best horse for Mr Crossley and dispatched him to Melbourne for the purpose of reporting the particulars to Captain Lonsdale; who was then, as you are aware, known as the Commandant of Port Phillip."

[Notwithstanding the risk of encountering the Aboriginal participants in the Faithfull Massacre at or near to the Broken River, Bourke then announced his intention to continue on from the Goulburn River to the Murray River with the mail.]

"Crossley, before he started for Melbourne to see Capt Lonsdale, begged me not to attempt the journey until he returned, as he felt certain that the Captain would send some police with him to where the men had been murdered, & that I could then with safety go on with the mail. Clarke was silent all this time, neither urging me to go or stay, nor yet did he make an offer to send a man with me."

John Conway Bourke: Autobiographical Notes for Mr. Edward Wilson
(Royal Historical Society of Victoria, Box 38-f, MS 4117).

APPENDIX 3

Estate of the late William Henry Clark

Assets

Real Estate	**Estimated Value (£)**
(a) Part of Wangandary Section A (*Pre-Emptive Section A*):	835
(b) Allotments 1 and 2, Section 1, Parish of South Wangaratta:	400
(c) Allotment 2 and part of Allotment 1, Section 16 Parish of South Wangaratta:	320

(d) <u>Suburban Lands, Parish of Wangaratta North</u>

(i)	Allotments 1, 2, 9, 11 and 12, Section 3:	100
(ii)	Section 8:	200
(iii)	Allotments 1, 2, 3 and 3, Section 9:	100

(e) <u>Town Lands, Parish of Wangaratta North</u>

(i)	Part of Allotment 1, Section 1:	500
(ii)	Allotments 6, 7 and 8, Section 1:	400
(iii)	Allotment 5, Section 8:	100
(iv)	Allotments 1, 2, 3, 18 and part of Allotment 7, Section 11:	850
(v)	Allotment 5, Section 17:	150
(vi)	Allotment 7 and part of Allotment 6, Section 24:	200
(vii)	Allotments 1, 2 and 3, Section 27:	200
(viii)	Allotments 9, 10, 11, 12 and 13, Section 39:	600
(ix)	Allotments 1 and 2, Section 40:	120
(x)	Part of Section 42:	200

(f) <u>Suburban Lands, Benalla</u>
Allotments 3, 4 and 7, Section 5 ; and Allotments 2 and 14, Section 6: 75

(g) <u>Town Lands, Bundalong</u>
Allotments 5 and 6, Section 7: 10

(h) <u>Crown Leases (Conditional Freehold Land, Parish of South Wangaratta</u>
   (i) Lands adjoining Section 8 and in Section 16: 145
   (ii) Lands in Section 25: 120
   Total estimated value of real estate: £5,605

Personal Estate

(a) 22 shares in the *Kneebone Gold Mining Company*: 70
(b) 20 shares in the *National Insurance Company*: 5
(c) 4 shares in the *Wangaratta Brewing and Malting Company*: 321
(d) Balance due from *Evans and Company* on an account stated: 186
(e) Half share of farm stock and implements owned jointly with James Willett: 235
(f) Unpaid monies payable by David Hugh Evans on the sale of William Clark's interest in the *Victoria Flour Mills* and lands: 1,330
   Total estimated value of personal estate: £2,147
   Total estimated value of real and personal estate: £7,752

Liabilities

(a) Camille Reay, Wahgunyah, for wines, etc.: 12-8-0
(b) Thomas Sales, Wangaratta, blacksmith: 13-19-3
(c) William Murdoch, Wangaratta, hotel expenses: 14-9-6
(d) J B Woodhead, Wangaratta, tailoring: 11-6
(e) Samuel Norton, Wangaratta, wine: 10-0
(f) James Dixon, Wangaratta, groceries: 1-6-6
(g) Andrew Jones, Wangaratta, bread: 1-11-3
(h) William Bickerton, Wangaratta, stationery: 1-6-7
(i) James Pratt, Wangaratta, stabling: 2-10-3
(j) A Swan, Wangaratta, blacksmith's work: 1-0-0
(k) John Joseph Tucker, Wangaratta, school fees: 4-14-6

(l)	A M Gibson, Wangaratta, groceries:	13-8
(m)	T G Bullivant, Wangaratta, saddler's work:	21-11-0
(n)	David Dewar, Wangaratta, cabinet maker:	3-4-0
(o)	C A Rundle, Wangaratta, medicines:	11-0-6
(p)	William Painter, Wangaratta, inn bill:	8-5-6
(q)	Otto Martin, Wangaratta, tinware:	7-0
(r)	Dispatch newspaper subscription:	12-0
(s)	Borough of Wangaratta, rates:	1-0-6
(t)	John Lamont, Wangaratta, law costs:	6-8-6
(u)	William Augustus Dobbyn, Corowa, medical services:	66-10-6
(v)	Benjamin Clay Hutchinson, Wangaratta, medical services:	19-10-0
(w)	Robert Dunlop, Wangaratta, stores:	1-5-0
(x)	The Bank of New South Wales at Wangaratta, money paid:	1,225-6-2
(y)	C A Rundle, Wangaratta, bill of exchange:	26-6-0
(z)	Lucas and Thomas, Wangaratta, bill of exchange:	62-2-3
(aa)	The Colonial Bank of Australasia, money payable on bond and promissory note:	1,500-0-0
	Total estate debts:	£3,008-17-11

Total estimated net value of estate: £4,744-2-1

William Clark's Will: Inventory of Assets and Liabilities
(PROV, *VPRS* 28/P0, Unit 103).

GENEALOGICAL CHARTS

Proximate Family Tree of John Clark Senior and Elizabeth Jenkins

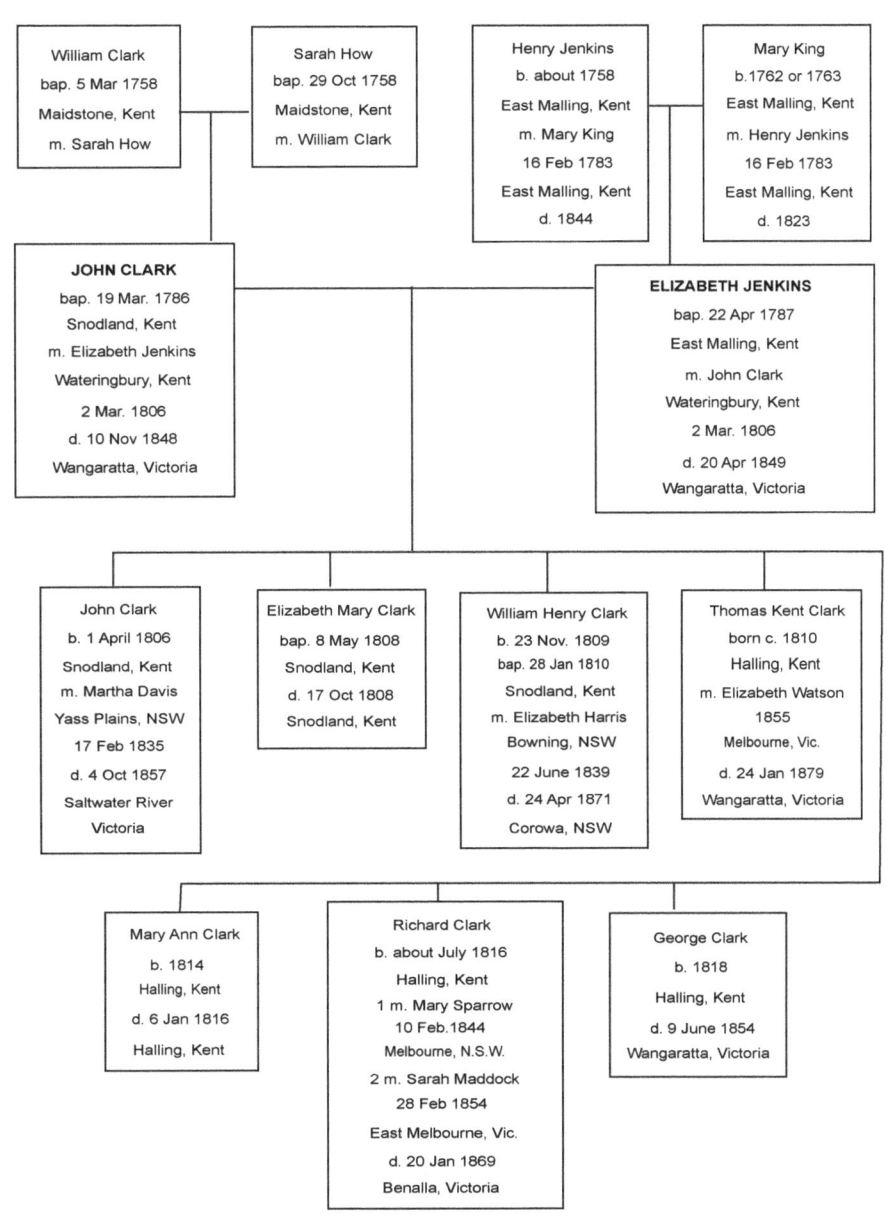

Proximate Family Tree of John Clark Junior

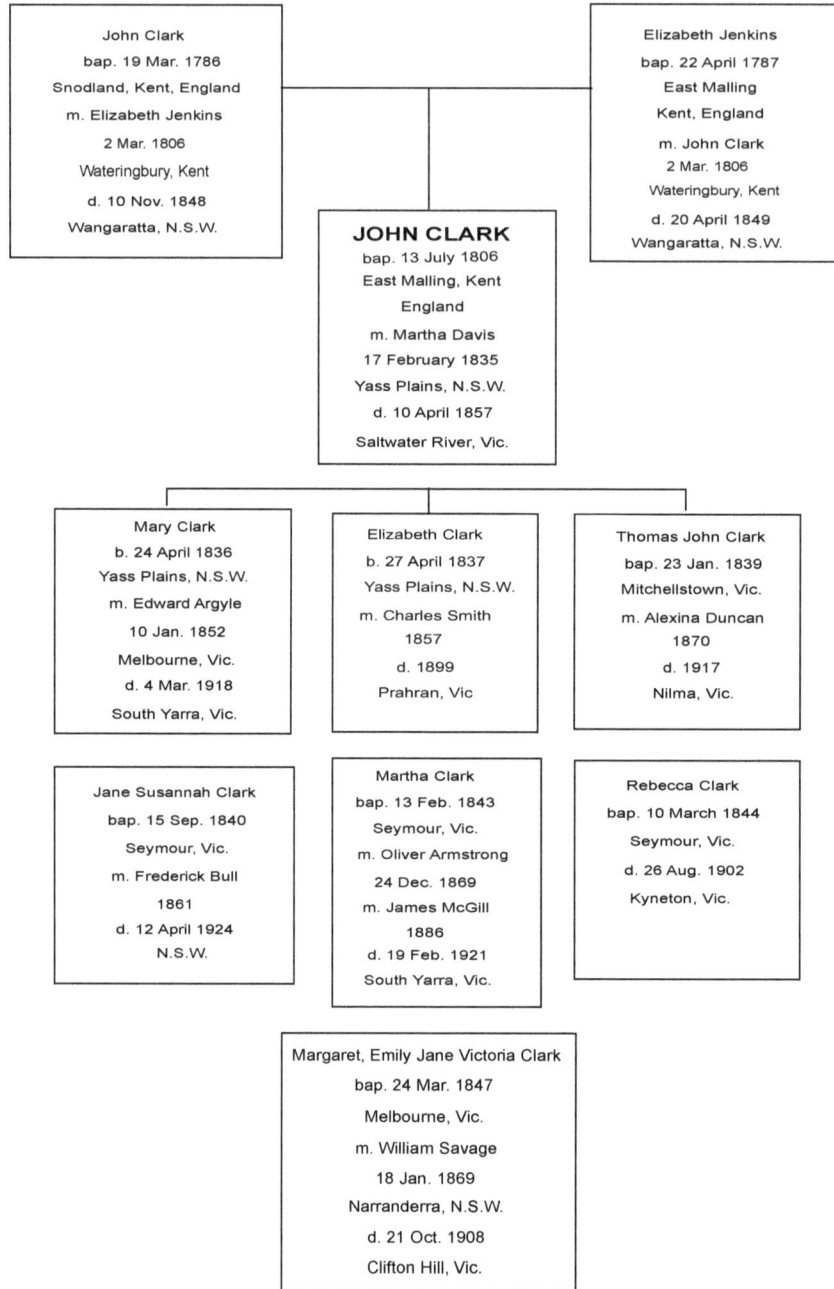

JOHN CLARK JUNIOR'S PROXIMATE FAMILY TREE

Genealogical Charts

Proximate Family Tree of William Henry Clark

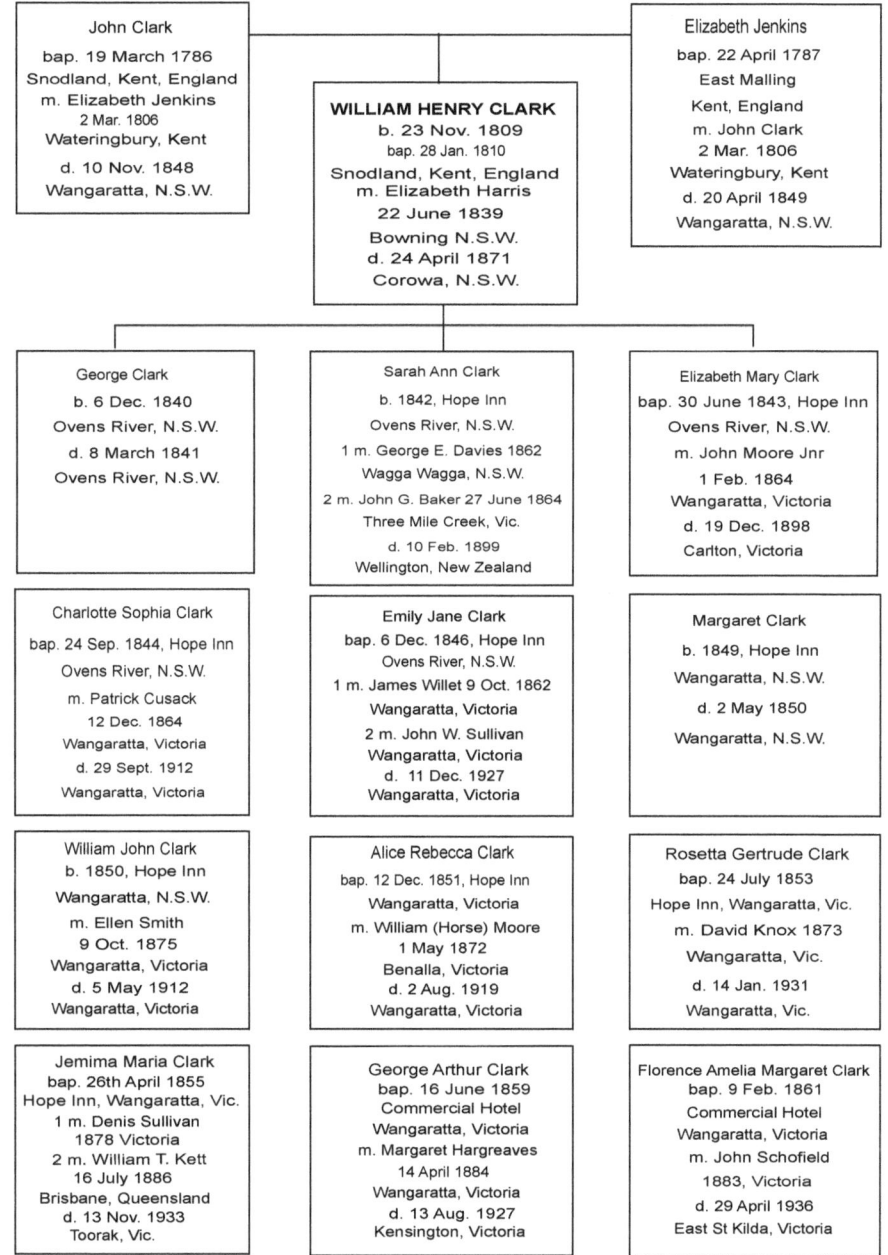

WILLIAM HENRY CLARK'S PROXIMATE FAMILY TREE

Proximate Family Tree of Richard Clark

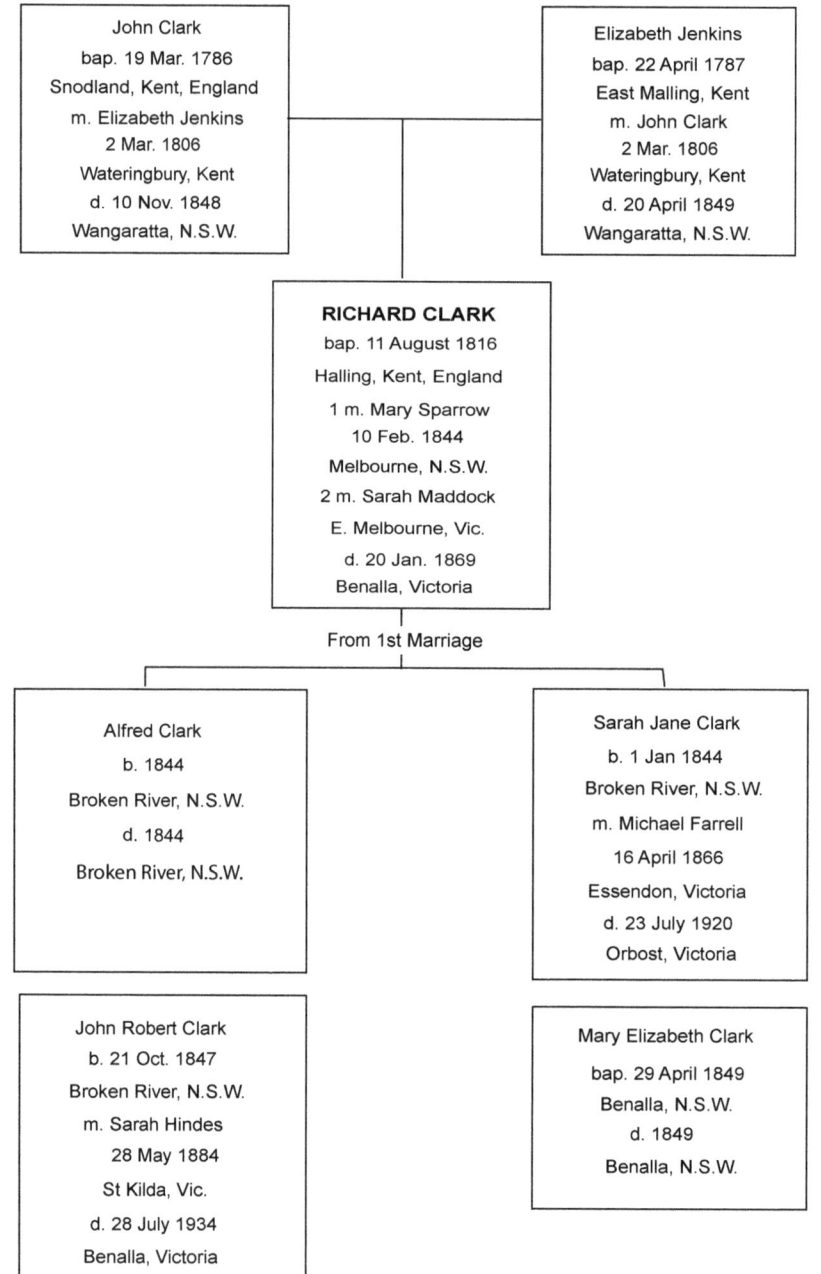

RICHARD CLARK'S PROXIMATE FAMILY TREE

MAPS AND PLANS

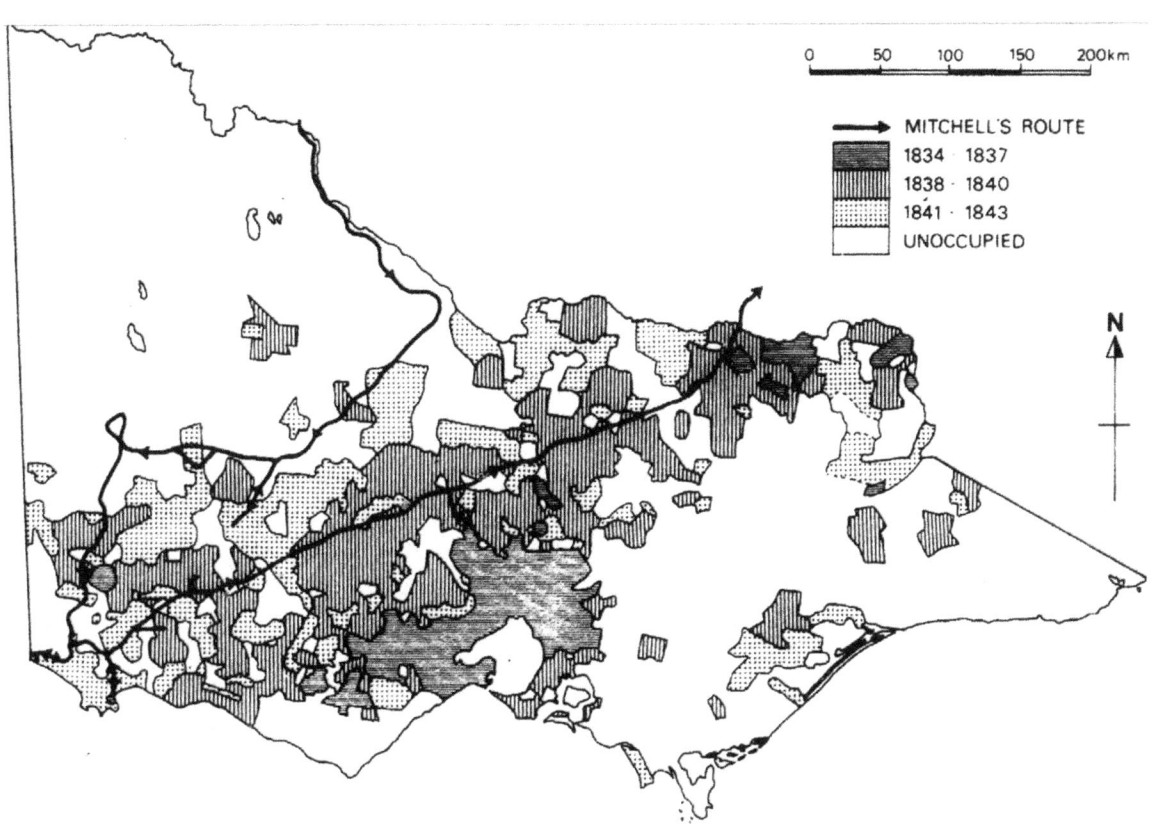

Port Phillip Pastoral Expansion Map

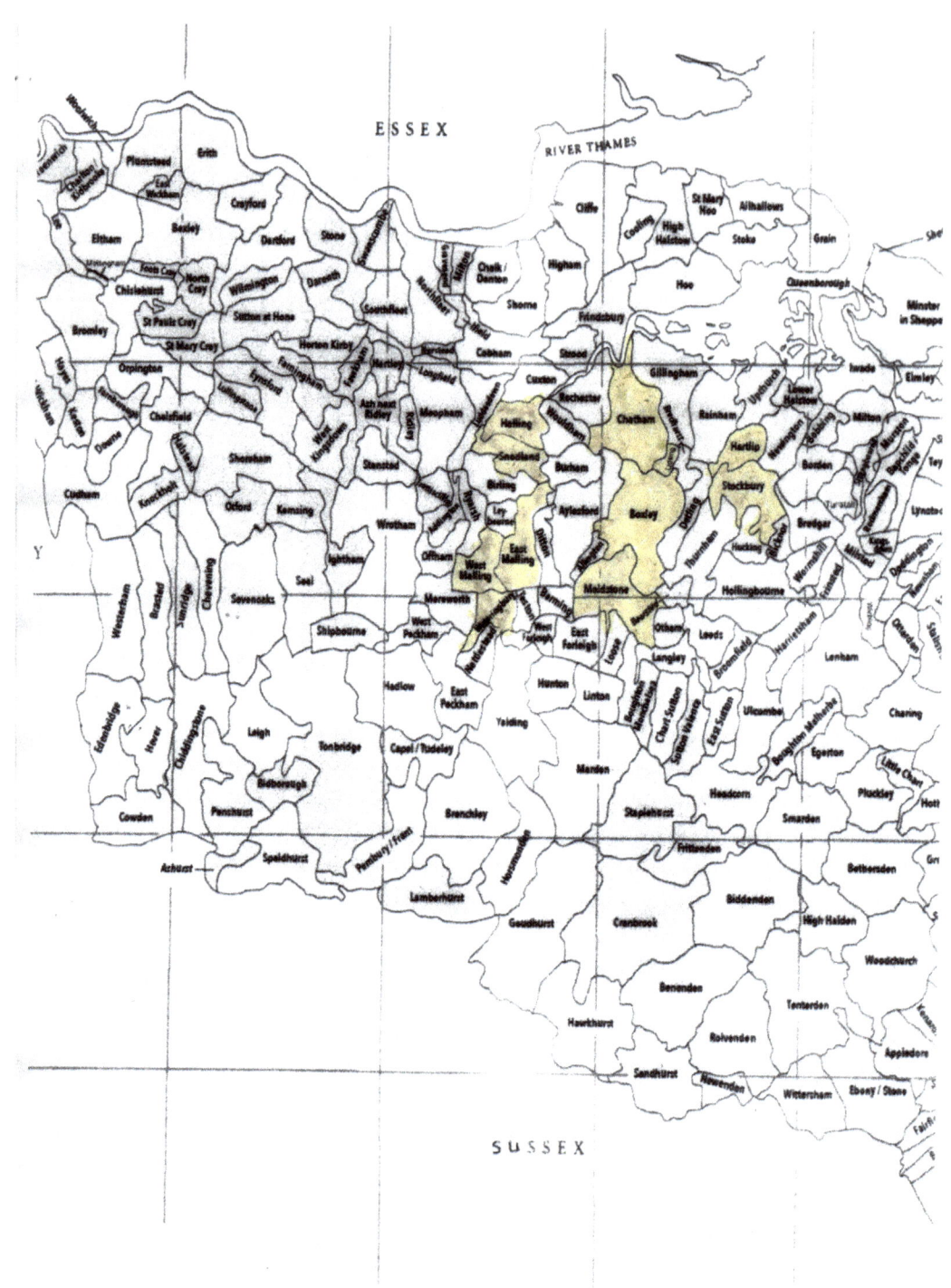

West Kent Parishes Map

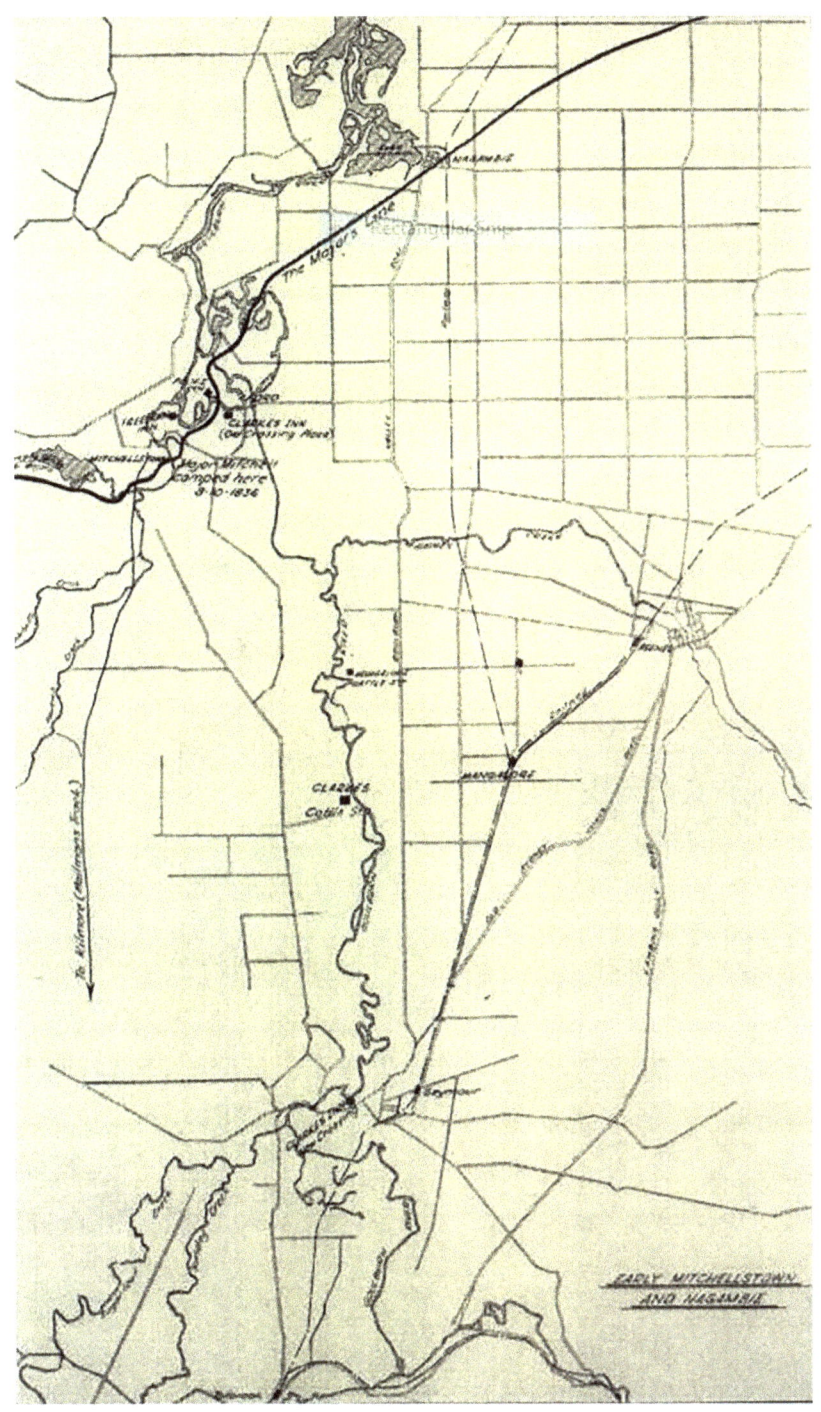

Mitchelton Map

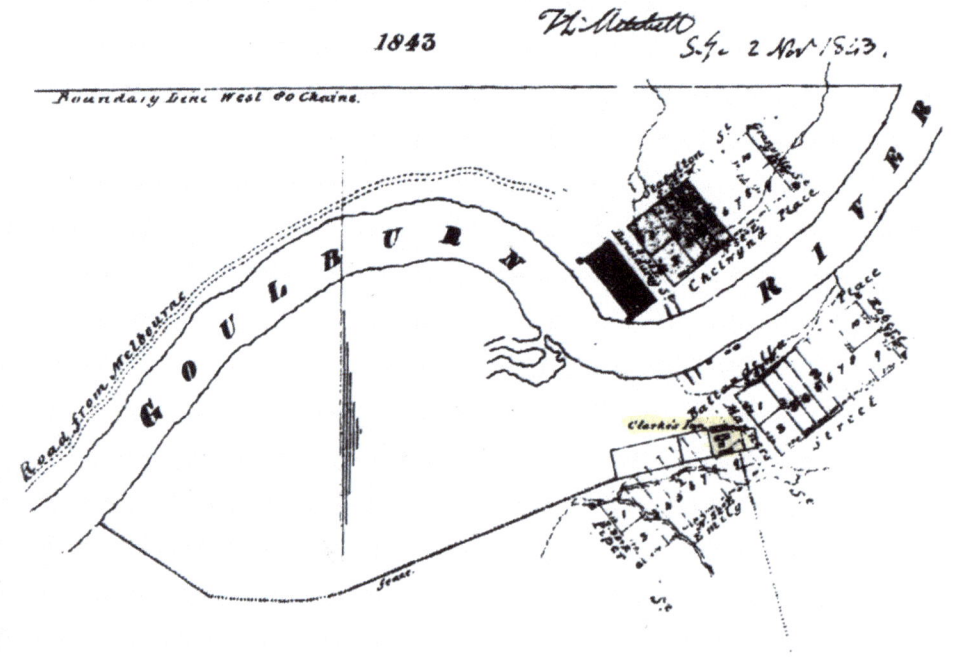

Squatting Runs Map 1 - Northwood

Seymour Village Plan (a)

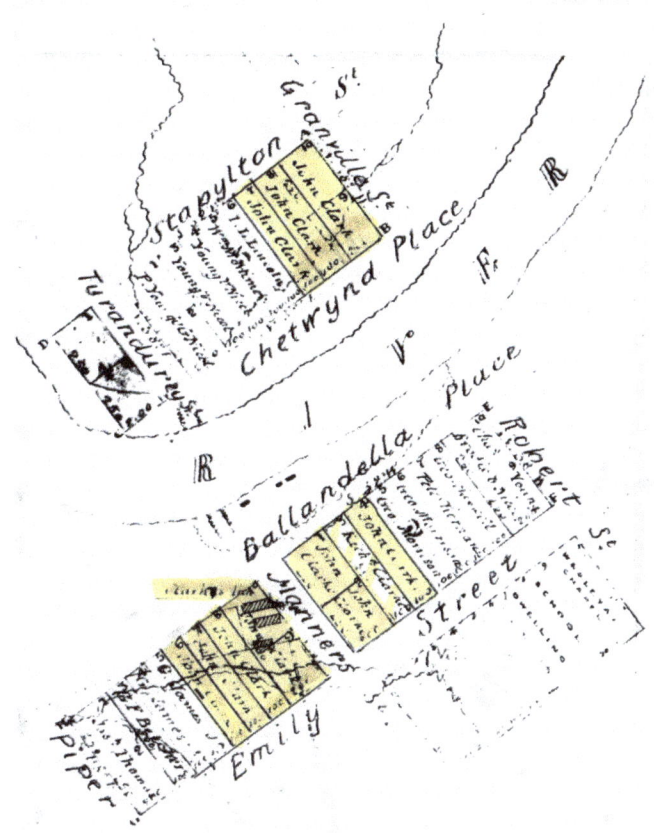

Seymour Village Plan (b)

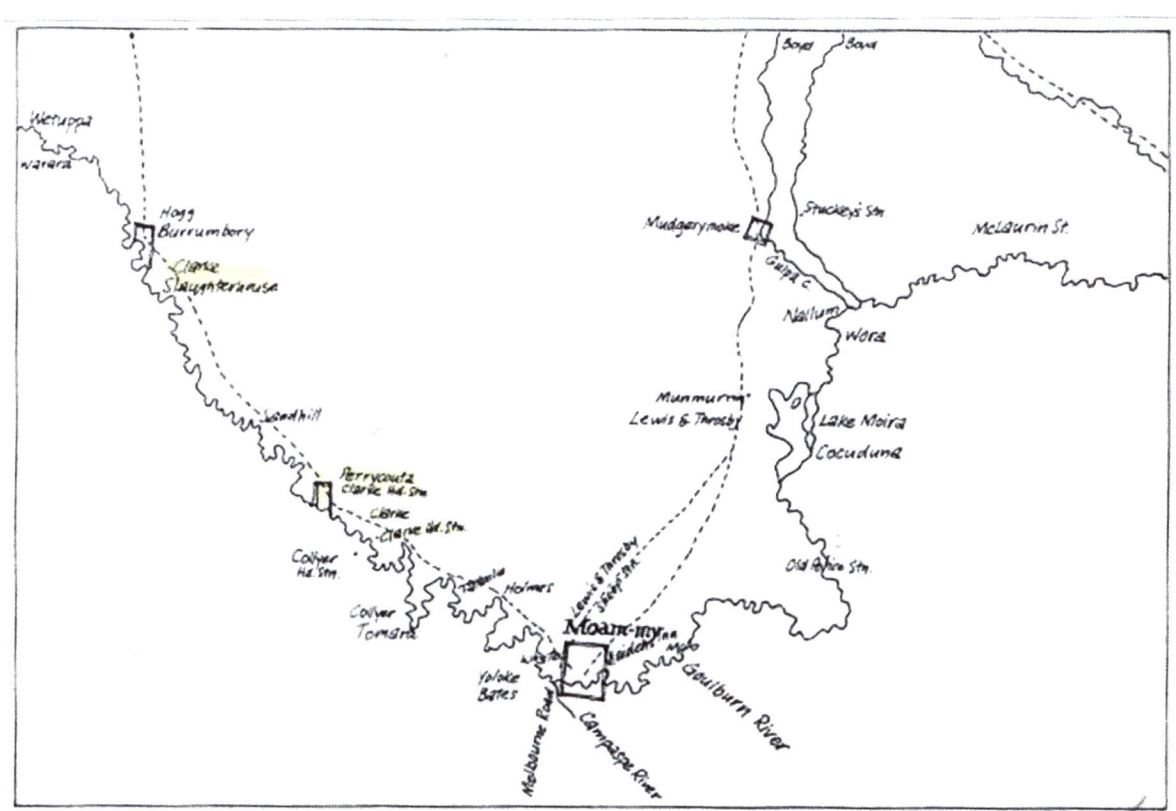

Squatting Runs Map 2(a) – Perricoota (Small Scale)

Squatting Runs Map 2(b) – Perricoota (Large Scale)

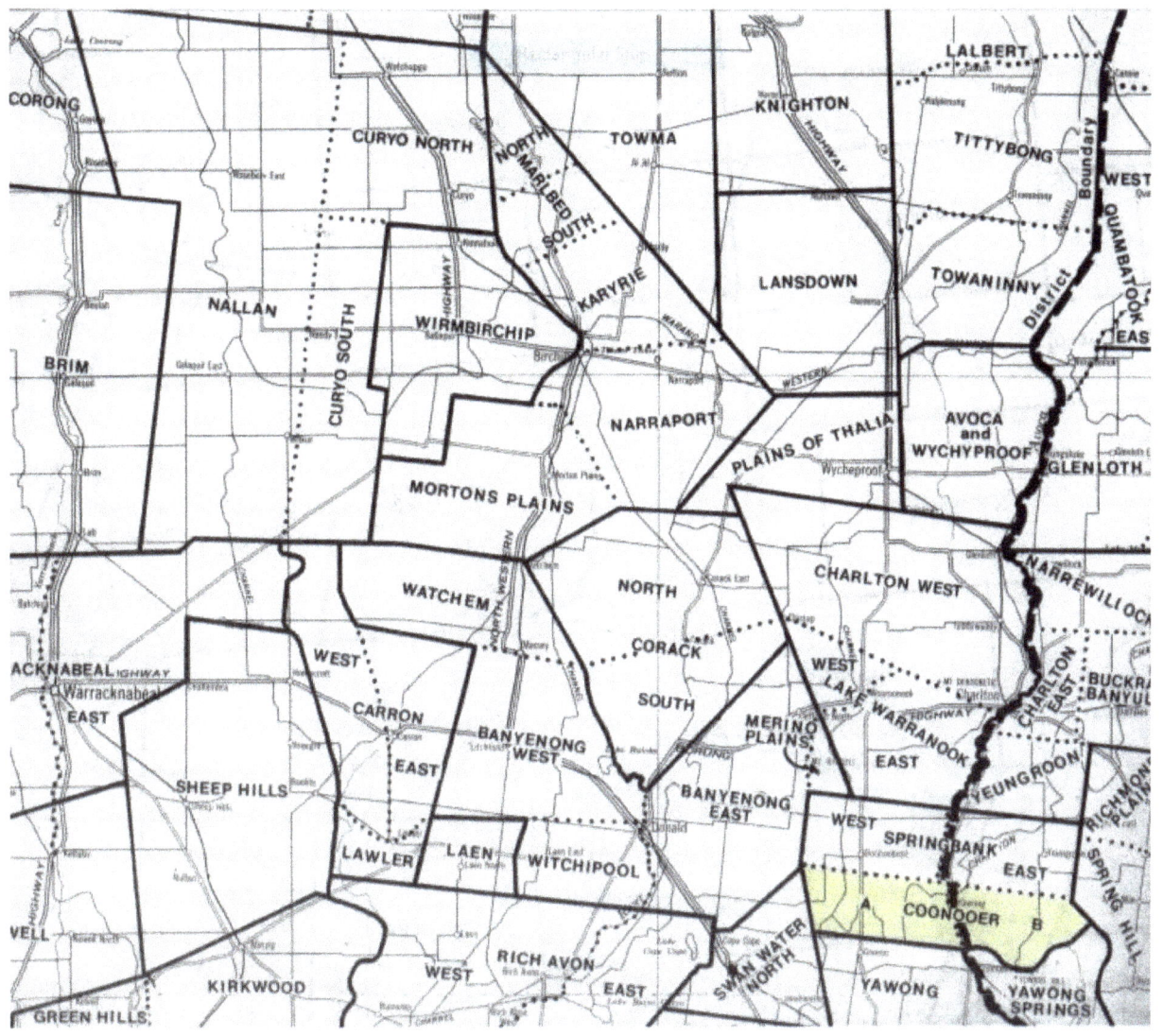

Squatting Runs Map 3 – Coonooer

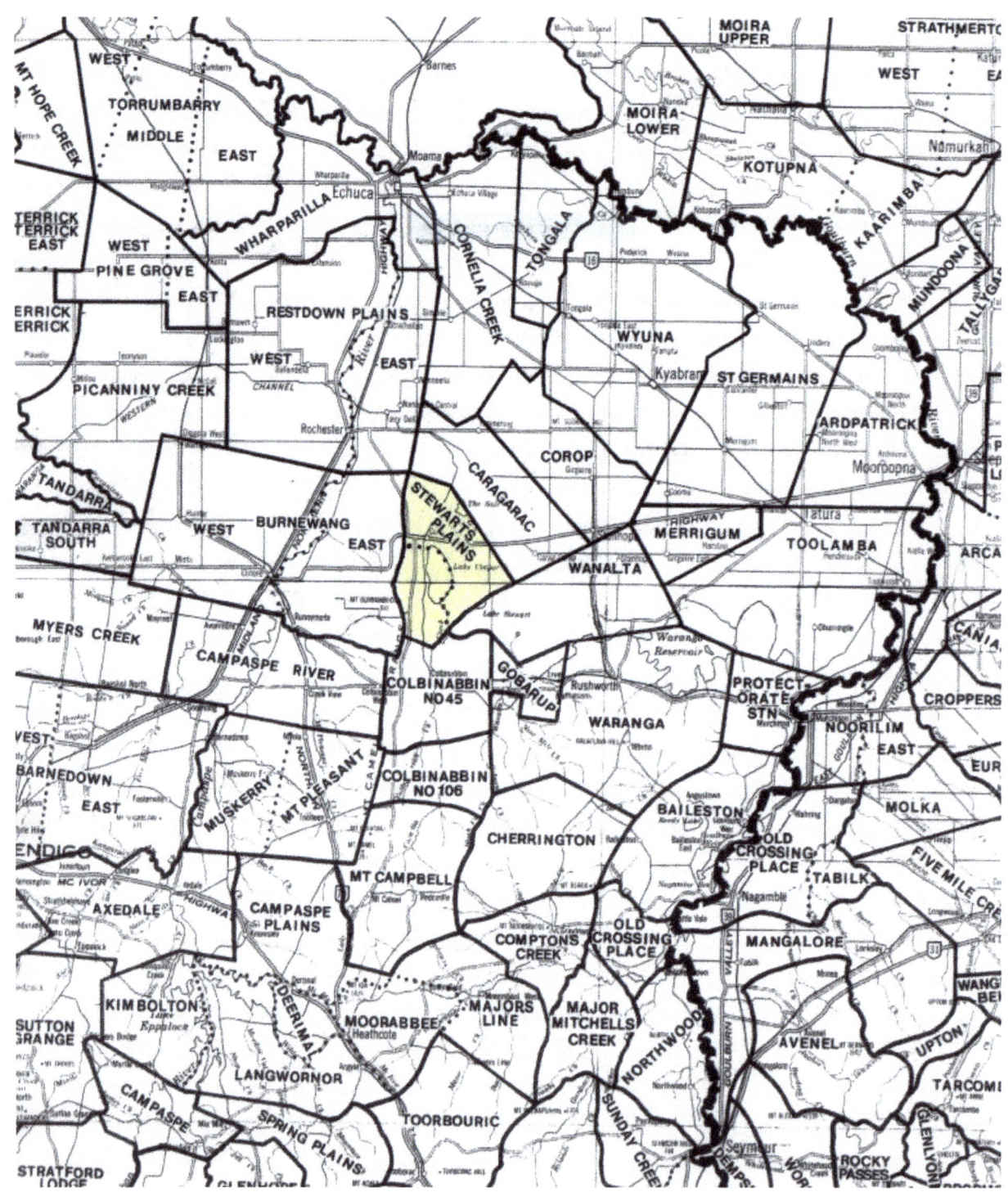

Squatting Runs Map 4 – Stewarts Plains

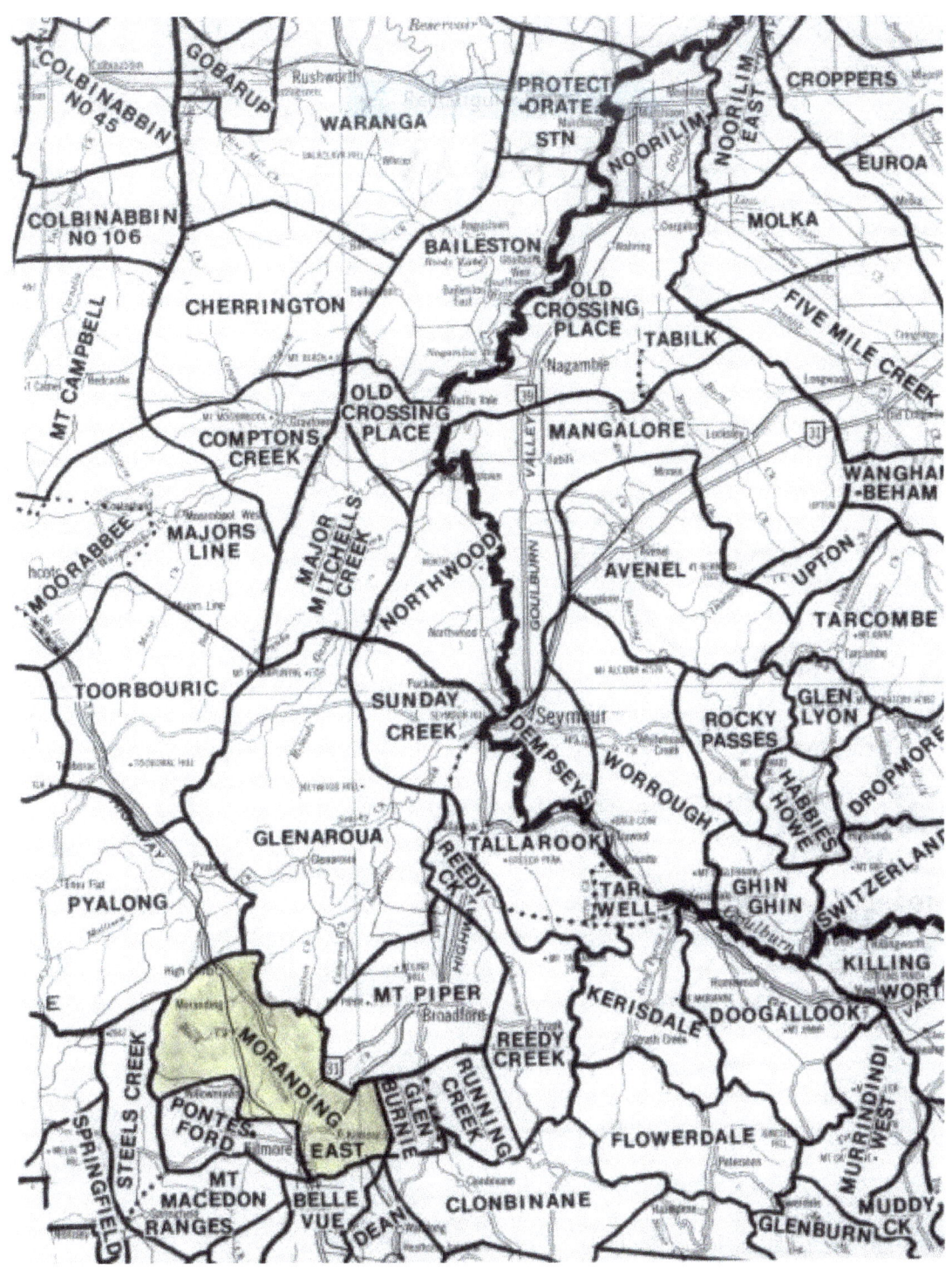

Squatting Runs Map 5(a) – Moranding (Small Scale)

Squatting Runs Map 5(b) – Moranding (Large Scale)

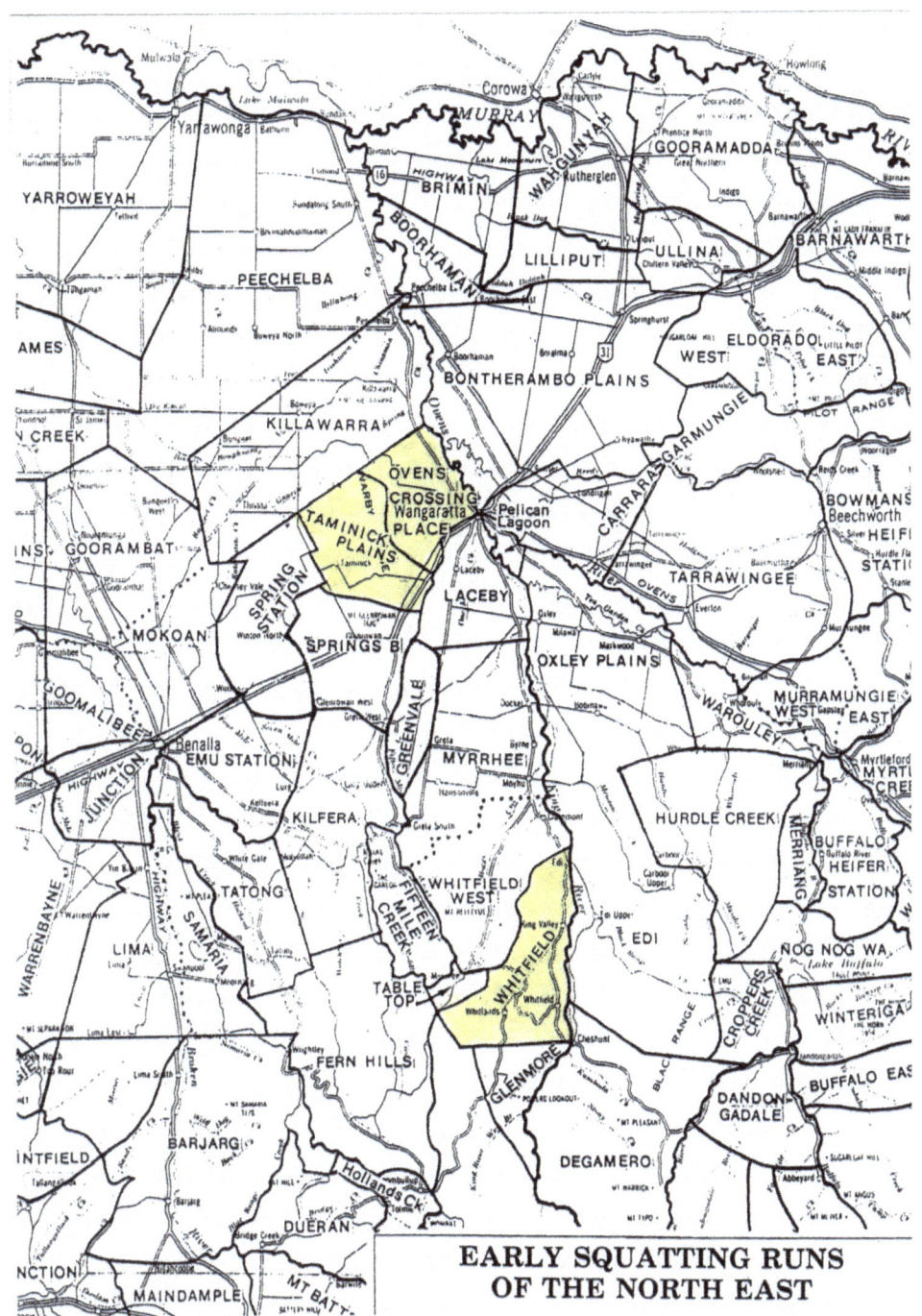

Squatting Runs Map 6 – Ovens Crossing Place and Whitfield

1851 Benalla Plan

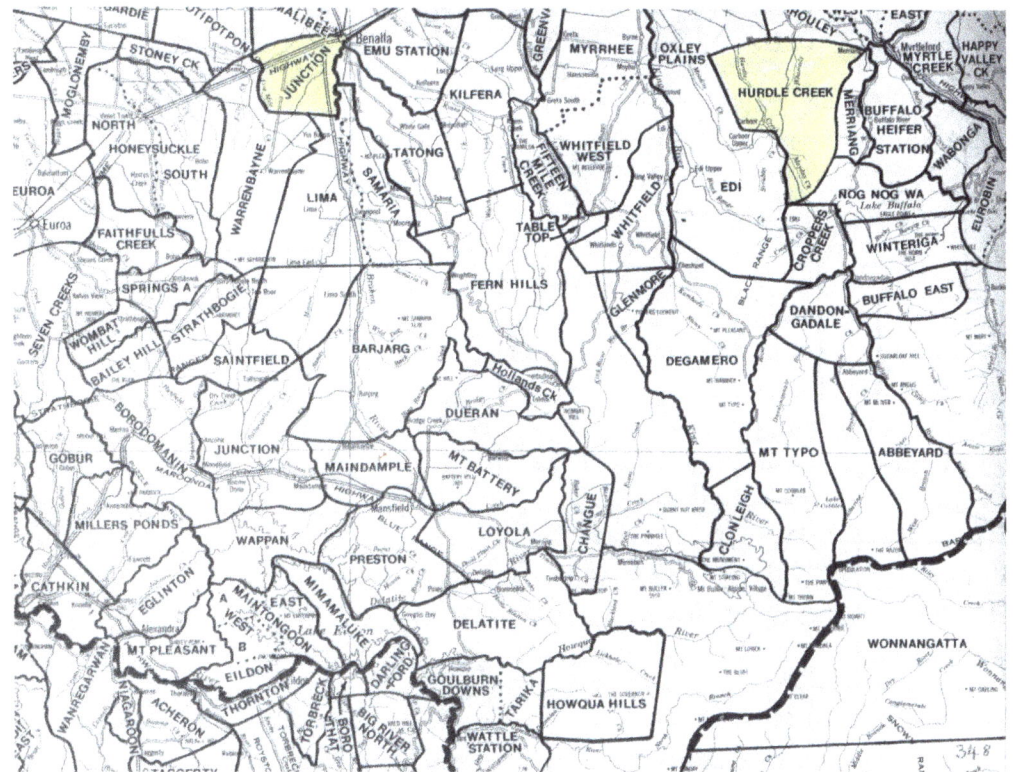

Squatting Runs Map 7 – Junction and Hurdle Creek

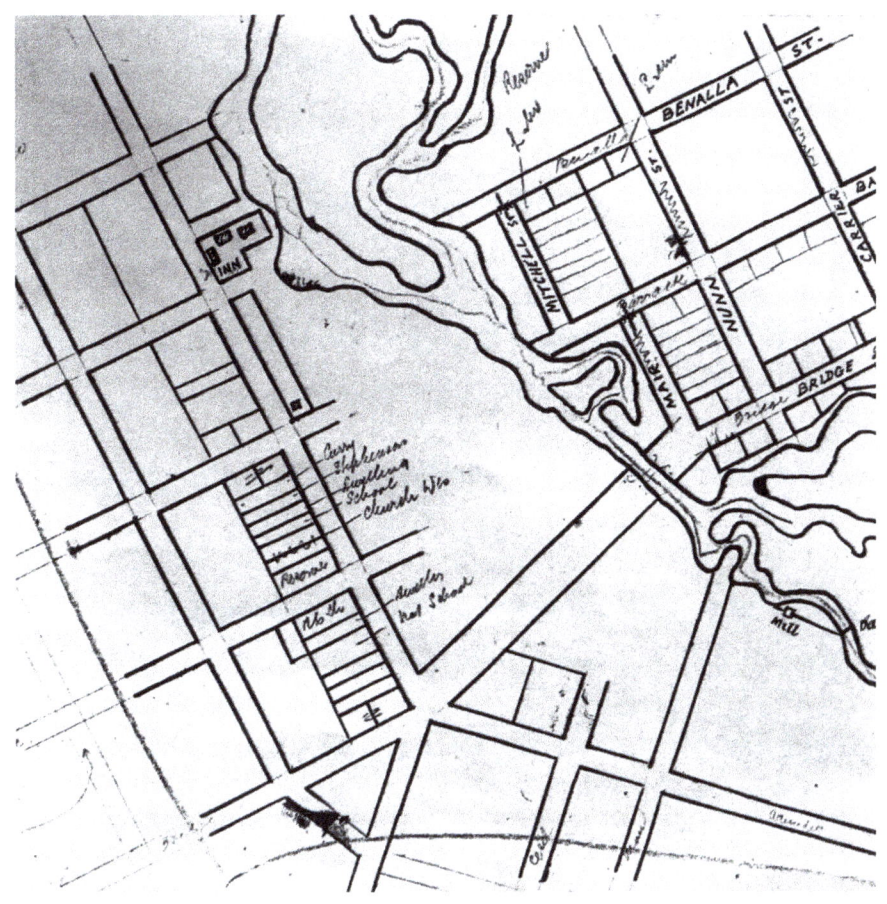

Edward Robertson's Benalla Plan

BIBLIOGRAPHY

Books

Anon.: *Benalla Past and Present: Illustrated History of the Town and District 1838 to 1929* (1929).

Anon.: *Mitchelton: An Adventure in History* (1974).

Anon.: *Worthy of Mention* (1992).

Atkinson, James: *An Account of the State of Agriculture and Grazing in New South Wales* (1826).

Bassett, Judy and Harman, Edna: *Wangaratta; Old Tales and Tours* (1982).

Bate, Weston: *A History of Brighton* (2nd ed., 1983).

Bateson, Charles: *The Convict Ships* (1959).

Benalla Past and Present – see Anon.: *Benalla Past and Present: Illustrated History of the Town and District 1838 to 1929* (1929.)

Billis, Ralph and Kenyon, Alfred: *Pastoral Pioneers of Port Phillip* (2nd ed., 1974).

Billis, Ralph and Kenyon, Alfred: *Pastures New: An Account of the Pastoral Occupation of Port Phillip* (1930).

Boyce, James: *1835: The Founding of Melbourne and the Conquest of Australia* (2011).

Boyes, Robert: *First Years at Port Phillip* (1935).

Bride, Thomas (ed.): *Letters from Victorian Pioneers* (Republished 1983).

Broome, Richard: *Aboriginal Victorians: A History Since 1800* (2005).

Bushby, John: *Saltbush Country: History of the Deniliquin District* (1980).

Byrne, J. C.: *Wanderings in the British Colonies from 1835 to 1847* (1848), Vol. 1.

Cannon, Michael: *Historical Records of Victoria* (1983), Vol. 2B – Aborigines and Protectors.

Cannon, Michael: *Life in the Country* (1973).

Christie, M. F.: *Aborigines in Colonial Victoria 1835-86* (1979).

Clark, Ian: *Goulburn River Aboriginal Protectorate* (2013).

Clarke, Susan and Argyle, Ian: *The Argyle Heritage* (2011).

Coulson, Helen: *Echuca – Moama: Murray River Neighbours* (2009).

Cox, Kenneth: *Angus McMillan: Pathfinder* (1973).

Cumpston, J. H. L.: *Thomas Mitchell: Surveyor General and Explorer* (1954).

Demarr, James: *Adventures in Australia Fifty Years Ago* (1893).

Dingle, Terry: *The Victorians: Settling* (1984).

Dodd, Stuart: *Looking Back at Willowmavin* (1984).

Dunlop, A. J.: *Benalla Cavalcade: A History of Benalla and District* (1973).

Eyre, Edward John: *Journals of Expeditions of Discovery into Central Australia, and Overland from Adelaide to King George's Sound, in the Years 1840-1* (1845), Vol. 2.

Eyre, Edward John (ed. Waterhouse, Jill): *Autobiographical Narrative of Residence and Exploration in Australia 1832-1839* (1984).

Ferguson, James: *Squatting: Romance and Reality* (2017).

Frost, Lenore (ed.): *The Fine Houses of Essendon and Flemington: 1846-1880* (2010).

Gammage, Bill: *Narrandera Shire* (1986).

Gormly, James: *Exploration and Settlement of Australia* (1921).

Hawdon, Joseph: *The Journal of a Journey from New South Wales to Adelaide* (Reprinted 1952).

Hearn, Judi: *Galleries of Pink Galahs: A History of the Shire of Murray 1838-1988* (1990).

Historical Records of Australia: Series 1, Vols. 19 and 21.

Holden, Colin: *Church in a Landscape* (2002).

Howitt, William: *Land, Labour and Gold or Two Years in Victoria* (1858), Vol. 1.

HRA – see *Historical Records of Australia*.

Ireland, William: *England's Topography: Or a New and Complete History of the County of Kent* (1829), Vol. 3.

Jennings, John: *Seymour's Wooden Wonder and Other Stories* (2010).

Jones, Graham: *On This Day in the North East* (1989).

King, C. J.: *An Outline of Closer Settlement in New South Wales* (1957), Part 1, The Sequence of Land Laws 1788-1956.

Knight, Heather: *Kilmore: Those That Came Before* (2007).

Macklin, Robert: *Hamilton Hume: Our Greatest Explorer* (2016).

Maher, James: *The Tales of a Century: Kilmore 1837-1937* (1938).

Martindale, Harold George: *New Crossing Place: The Story of Seymore and its Shire* (1958).

McGuire, Paul: *Inns of Australia* (1952).

Mc Laurin, Neil: *1838 Settlers: A History of the Family of James McLaurin and his Descendants* (2017).

Mitchell, Thomas: *Three Expeditions Into The Interior Of Eastern Australia* (1838), Vol. 2.

Montefiori, Simon Sebag: *The Word: A Family History* (2022).

Moore, Garry: *A Problematic Patriarch: Jonathan Harris* (2022).

Mossman, Samuel and Banister, Thomas: *Australia Visited and Revisited* (1853).

Murray, Peter: *As the Spirit Leads* (2013).

Nicholson, John: *The Incomparable Captain Cadell* (2004).

O'Callaghan, Bill: *The Wangaratta Story: Pre-Settlement -2009* (2009).

Packard, Brian: *Joseph Hawdon: The First Overlander* (1997).

Pastoral Pioneers – see Billis, Ralph and Kenyon, Alfred: *Pastoral Pioneers of Port Phillip* (2nd ed., 1974).

Pastures New – see Billis, Ralph and Kenyon, Alfred: *Pastures New: An Account of the Pastoral Occupation of Port Phillip* (1930).

Perry, Richard: *Contributions to an Amateur Magazine in Prose and Verse* (1857).

Perry, Thomas: *Australia's First Frontier: The Spread of Settlement in New South Wales 1788-1829* (1957).

Powell, Joseph: *The Making of Rural Australia* (1974).

Priestley, Susan: *Echuca: A History* (2009).

Priestley, Susan: *The Victorians: Making Their Mark* (1984).

Quick, John: *The History of Land Tenure in the Colony of Victoria* (1888).

Rushen, Elizabeth: *Colonial Duchesses: The Migration of Irish Women to New South Wales Before the Great Famine* (2014).

Rushen, Elizabeth and McIntyre, Perry: *Fair Game: Australia's First Immigrant Women* (2010).

Russell, Penny: *This Errant Lady: Jane Franklin's Overland Journey to Port Phillip and Sydney, 1839* (2002).

Spreadborough, Robert and Anderson, Hugh: *Victorian Squatters* (1983).

Strangio, Paul and Costar, Brian: *Victorian Premiers: 1856 – 2006* (2006).

Thornton-Kemsley, Colin: *Kentish Kemsleys and Their Descendants* (1980).

Turton, Keith: *Six and a Half Inches from Destiny: The First Hundred Years of the Melbourne – Wodonga Railway 1873-1973* (1973).

Whittaker, D. M.: *Wangaratta* (1963).

Wilson, G. J.: *Back to Whitfield: Whitfield Ramblings 1875-1975* (1975).

Worthy of Mention – see Anon.: *Worthy of Mention* (1992).

Articles

1849 Squatters' Directory of the Port Phillip District (https://tinyurl.com/yt6u7dsb).

About the Walter and Eliza Hall Institute (https://tinyurl.com/yy7cet8r).

Ancestry: *Letter from Edmund Lockyer to the Colonial Secretary dated 28 December 1842* (https://tinyurl.com/y7k5dqxp).

Andrews, Arthur: "The First Overland Mail and the Howlong Station on the Murray" in (1917) 5(19) *The Victorian Historical Magazine* 107.

Australian Cemeteries: *Wangaratta Cemetery Trust* (https://tinyurl.com/y3lzvul8).

Australian Shipping 1788-1969: *Vessels Arriving By Year* (https://tinyurl.com/yawma5ks).

Barwick, Diane: "Mapping the Clans: An Atlas of Victorian Clans 1835-1904" in *Aboriginal History* (1984), Vol. 8, Part 2.

Bassett, Judith: "The Faithfull Massacre at the Broken River 1838" in (2009) 13:24 *Journal of Australian Studies* 18.

Bean, Christine: *Gransden Family: From Tradesman to Poor House* (https://tinyurl.com/y7z2xkx4).

"Beechworth Mining District" in *Report of the Mining Surveyors and Registrars: Quarter Ending 31st March 1870* (https://tinyurl.com/k9zdnyb).

Beever, Margot: "Kerferd, George Briscoe (1831-1889)" in *Australian Dictionary of Biography* (https://tinyurl.com/mr2ewcz7).

Brighton Grammar School, Hall of Fame – Sir Stanley Argyle (https://tinyurl.com/3x34s4uy).

Brown, Richard: "Unlocking the Land" in *Looking at History* (https://tinyurl.com/lqrhu7v).

Browne, Geoff: "Stanley Argyle: The Incidental Premier" in Strangio, Paul and Costar, Brian: *The Victorian Premiers: 1856 – 2006* (2006).

City of Kingston: *Kingston Local History: Josiah Morris Holloway – Pioneering Land Developer* (https://tinyurl.com/3hdtj6sx).

Coates, Jenny: "1858 politics Wangaratta style" in *Conversations with Grandma* (https://tinyurl.com/yc5dmbvv).

Coates, Jenny: "George Clark and his unfortunate end" in *Conversations with Grandma* (https://tinyurl.com/y44gv9nd).

Coates, Jenny: "Sepia Saturday: a quartet of hotels" in *Conversations with Grandma* (https://tinyurl.com/bdehxjdp).

Coates, Jenny: "Sir Charles Hotham and the good citizens of Wangaratta" in *Conversations with Grandma* (https://tinyurl.com/bdf75euk).

Coates, Jenny: "Trove Tuesday – Wangaratta 1863 – Part 1" in *Conversations with Grandma* (https://tinyurl.com/3dtf456c).

Coates, Jenny: "Trove Tuesday – Wangaratta 1863 – Part 2" in *Conversations with Grandma* (https://tinyurl.com/59a52yru).

Coates, Jenny: "William Henry Clark and his hotels – a new chapter" in *Conversations with Grandma* (https://tinyurl.com/3b3wtmfb).

Convict Records- Kains Convict Ship (https://tinyurl.com/y514eusa).

Crockett, Roger: "The Early History of Bredhurst Manor" (https://tinyurl.com/jtgzunk).

Darley (https://tinyurl.com/bdf5bzsu).

Dicker, Canon Percy: "The Church in the North-East" in (Sept. 1949) 7(5) *The Witness* 2.

Dredge, Rhonda: "An Awful Silence Reigns: James Dredge at the Goulburn River" in (1988) 61 *The Latrobe Journal* 118.

Durrant, Jacqui: *Life on Spring Creek – Don't Mention the "C" Word* (2019) (https://tinyurl.com/mv278p2m).

Dutton, Geoffrey: "Eyre, Edward John (1813-1897)" in *Australian Dictionary of Biography* (https://tinyurl.com/y7wmntsn).

Early Mitchellstown – see Parris, Henry Speechly: "Early Mitchellstown and Nagambie" in (1950) 23(3) *The Victorian Historical Magazine* 126.

Echuca Historical Society: *Maiden's Punt* (https://tinyurl.com/mr4behtk).

Edwards, Reverend George: *History of Violet Town and the Anglican Church of St. Dunstan* (https://tinyurl.com/y8jkf4tx).

Edwards, W. H.: "Early Wangaratta" in (1920) 8(1) *The Victorian Historical Magazine* 38.

eGold: *A Nation's Heritage – Eaglehawk, VIC* (https://tinyurl.com/5n72rytc).

Engineering Heritage SA: *Nomination for Engineering Heritage Recognition – PS Mary Ann, Mannum Dock Museum* (https://tinyurl.com/yb7xgpza).

From Melbourne to the Murray – see Parris, Henry Speechly: "From Melbourne to the Murray: Extracts from the Diary of a Pioneer Naturalist, Dr. Edmund Charles Hobson" in (1950) 66 *Victorian Naturalist* 183.

Gibbney, H. G.: "Bonney, Charles (1813-1897) in *Australian Dictionary of Biography* (https://tinyurl.com/mr2yrv32).

Goss, Alan: "Hawdon, Joseph (1813-1871)" in *Australian Dictionary of Biography* (https://tinyurl.com/22rn658a).

Griffin, Carl J.: "Parish Farms and the poor law: a response to unemployment in southern England" in (2011) 59 *Agricultural History Review* 176.

Gustafson, Barry: "Employment in Benalla" in *The Early Years of Joseph Savage* (https://tinyurl.com/2rfct98t).

Gustafson, Barry: "Savage, Michael Joseph (Mick) (1872-1940)" in *Australian Dictionary of Biography* (https://tinyurl.com/39we39h4).

Health Direct: *Haemoptysis (coughing up blood)* (https://tinyurl.com/tjxdddsc).

Heritage Council of Victoria: *Holy Trinity Anglican Cathedral Close* (https://tinyurl.com/ksmmcrs).

Historic Mining Sites Assessment Project: *Eldorado Goldfield* (https://tinyurl.com/3buxfaas).

Historical Facts – Mornington Peninsula: *Bushrangers at Cape Schanck* (https://tinyurl.com/ya4jcj9u).

Kaye's Webpages – see *Kaye's Greta, Myrrhee and Winton Webpages* (https://tinyurl.com/2rzcmuc9).

King, Hazel: "Hall, Eliza Rowdon (1847-1916)" in *Australian Dictionary of Biography* (https://tinyurl.com/2s3uzm4s).

Lockyer Letter – see Ancestry: *Letter from Edmund Lockyer to the Colonial Secretary dated 28 December 1842*.

Mansfield Historical Society: *History of Mansfield* (https://tinyurl.com/ya8urd6l).

McCulloch, S. C.: "Gipps, Sir George (1791-1847)" in *Australian Dictionary of Biography* (https://tinyurl.com/2jurpx26).

McLaurin, James: "Memories of Early Australia" in McLaurin, Neil: *1838 Settlers: A History of the Family of James McLaurin and his Descendants* (2017).

Measuring Worth Foundation: *Measuring Worth* (https://tinyurl.com/bp9z77rt).

Mitchell, Jessie: *'Country Belonging to Me': Land and Labour on Aboriginal Missions and Protectorate Stations, 1830 – 1850* (https://tinyurl.com/pxv69bz7).

Morgan, Pat: *[AVNE] Clark Family – Wangaratta* (AUS-VIC-NE-LArchives) (https://tinyurl.com/hn537qa).

Murrindindi Shire Heritage Study: Vol. 1 – Thematic History Final (2011) (https://tinyurl.com/ydxfts9p).

National Portrait Gallery, Canberra: *Sir Stanley Argyle* (https://tinyurl.com/54muwavk).

New South Wales Convict Indents, 1788-1842: *Jonathan Harris* (https://tinyurl.com/y5jonf9h) and (https://tinyurl.com/y68vy9dc).

O'Brien, J. L.: "Laing, Charles (1809-1857)" in *Australian Dictionary of Biography* (https://tinyurl.com/y8gseb8z).

Parris, Harry Speechly: "Early Mitchellstown and Nagambie" in (1950) 23(3) *The Victorian Historical Magazine* 126.

Parris, Harry Speechly: "From Melbourne to the Murray: Extracts from the Diary of a Pioneer Naturalist, Dr. Edmund Charles Hobson" in (1950) 66 *Victorian Naturalist* 183.

Perry, T. M.: "Atkinson, James (1795-1835)" in *Australian Dictionary of Biography* (https://tinyurl.com/5n78rk27).

Pressreader: *Evolution of a River Crossing* (https://tinyurl.com/43w8xf7m).

"Reminiscences from Pioneers – Wangaratta Chronicle, Wednesday, April 29. 1929" in *Kaye's Greta, Myrrhee and Winton Webpages* (https://tinyurl.com/2rzcmuc9).

"Richard Clark's 1865 letter" in (2008) 12(1) *Snodland Historical Society Newsletter* 3 (https://tinyurl.com/j26229j).

Robertson, E. M.: "Robertson, Edward (1870-1969)" in *Australian Dictionary of Biography* (https://tinyurl.com/y9h8mdug).

Rootsweb:Wermore: *From Whence We Came For Family Ties To Gaele Arnott – Mary Sparrow* (https://tinyurl.com/3a7n8us3).

Rudolph, Ivan: *Eyre – Timeline and Data* (https://tinyurl.com/ybbxtrar).

Scott, Peter: "O'Brien, Henry (1793-1866)" in *Dictionary of Australian Biography* (https://tinyurl.com/2xy39tse).

Shaw, A. G. L.: "Argyle, Sir Stanley Seymour (1867-1940)" in *Australian Dictionary of Biography* (https://tinyurl.com/yf6ee7ej).

Shaw, A. G. L.: "Vandemonian Influences on Port Phillip Settlement" in (1989-90) 2(2) *Bulletin of the Centre for Tasmanian Historical Studies* 15.

Shaw, A. G. L.: "Victoria's First Governor" in (2003) 71 *The Latrobe Journal* 85.

Snodland Historical Society: *Genealogy, Snodland Parishioners, 1700-1799(c)* (https://tinyurl.com/yc3xemd7).

State Library of South Australia: SA Memory: *Did you know – Captain Sturt's Cannon* (https://tinyurl.com/5brftyvh).

Strathbogie Shire Heritage Study: Stage 2 (2013).

Victorian Heritage Database Report: *Saltwater River Crossing Site and Footscray Wharves Precinct* (https://tinyurl.com/ykkefpjb).

Victorian Heritage Database Report: *Rock House* (https://tinyurl.com/yacujut5).

Victorian Places: *Benalla* (https://tinyurl.com/ycwl4ml3).

Victorian Resources Online: Statewide: *Inland Pigface* (https://tinyurl.com/2zabmcbb).

Walker, James: *Account of the Present Situation of the Female Emigrants from Cork to New South Wales per the Ship Red Rover in the Year 1832* (CO 384/35).

"Wangaratta Dispatch and North-Eastern Advertiser, Wednesday, 26 June 1907 – Robert J. Mason" in *Kaye's Greta, Myrrhee and Winton Webpages* (https://tinyurl.com/2rzcmuc9).

Wikipedia: *Bandon, County Cork* (https://tinyurl.com/buk5jfb).

Wikipedia: *Bredhurst* (https://tinyurl.com/hwqzuck).

Wikipedia: *Brighton Grammar School* (https://tinyurl.com/2s4chn38).

Wikipedia: *Eastern Whipbird* (https://tinyurl.com/mr2ffpf4).

Wikipedia: *Hydrothorax* (https://tinyurl.com/ysx48cvf).

Wikipedia: *Jack Cade's Rebellion* (https://tinyurl.com/yyc46onf).

Wikipedia: *Michael Argyle (Judge)* (https://tinyurl.com/sbzcx57a).

Wikipedia: *Moama* (https://tinyurl.com/y8acwqtq).

Wikipedia: *Moody's Pub 1841* (https://tinyurl.com/mpbscjx5).

Wikipedia: *Stanley Argyle* (https://tinyurl.com/3kxausmj).

Wikipedia: *Tolmie, Victoria* (https://tinyurl.com/y7lrrv9t).

Wikipedia: *Yass, New South Wales* (https://tinyurl.com/yxg4qoka).

Woodward, Francis J.: "Franklin, Lady Jane (1791-1875)" in *Australian Dictionary of Biography* (https://tinyurl.com/4tz66t5p).

Genealogical Materials

Ancestry: *Approved Ticket of Exemption Location Transfer Application for Jonathan Harris, September 1831* (https://tinyurl.com/ybn6mmhr).

Ancestry: Australian Electoral Rolls for 1856 – William C. Sparrow (https://tinyurl.com/yaa72oak).

Ancestry: *England and Wales, Criminal Registers, 1791-1892 – Jonathan Harris* (https://tinyurl.com/yxolnu2c).

Ancestry: *Exemption from Government Labour for Jonathan Harris, 1832* (https://tinyurl.com/y6t2pwyh).

Ancestry: *Harris, Jonathan 1800-1891 & Baker, Elizabeth 1802-1836: Petition to Come to Colony* (Image 3 of 3) (https://tinyurl.com/be3se3fh).

Ancestry: *Harris, Jonathan – Trial Manuscript Notes* (https://tinyurl.com/y8aozndw).

Ancestry: *Jonathan Harris Family Tree – Elizabeth Harris* (https://tinyurl.com/y4dc6h3h).

Ancestry: *Parramatta Quarter Sessions Trial Register for 1842 – Jonathan Harris* (https://tinyurl.com/y835fbny).

Ancestry: *St. John's Church, Parramatta – Baptism Record for George Jarvis Harris* (https://tinyurl.com/y6c63h7t).

Ancestry: *United Kingdom, Prison Hulk Registers and Letter Books, 1802-1849, for Jonathan Harris* (https://tinyurl.com/y2jqssch).

Australian Surname Group: *Henry Thomas Williams* (https://tinyurl.com/yb9omy6e).

Bulleid Family History: *Bulleid News* (No. 37, 2 December 2009). (https://tinyurl.com/y9thkhkr).

East Malling Burials, 1570-1924: *Mary Jenkins 1823* (https://tinyurl.com/y3jb63ql).

Family Search: *England Births and Christenings, 1538 – 1975: John Clark* (1806) (https://tinyurl.com/yd2nsh8k).

Family Search: *England Births and Christenings, 1538 – 1975: Sarah (How) Clark* (1758) (https://tinyurl.com/2p83k3t3).

Family Search: *England Marriages, 1538 – 1975: John Clark and Elizabeth Jenkins* (1806) (https://tinyurl.com/54989ehu).

Family Search: *England Marriages, 1538 – 1975: William Clark and Sarah How* (1779) (https://tinyurl.com/3cvz2c5a).

Family Search: *Parish Registers and Poor Law Records for Mayfield: Jonathan Harris and Elizabeth Baker* (1821) (https://tinyurl.com/y3qdt88p).

King Family Tree: John Kemsley (https://tinyurl.com/ycyu7r6u).

King Family Tree: Robert Kemsley (1) (https://tinyurl.com/4knww5ep).

King Family Tree: Robert Kemsley (2) (https://tinyurl.com/2p83uvtj).

King Family Tree: Robert Kemsley (3) (https://tinyurl.com/bdz2n5h5).

King Family Tree: Thomas Kemsley (https://tinyurl.com/bdcn2npu).

King Family Tree: William Gregory Kemsley (https://tinyurl.com/6tem99x3).

Marr, Aitken, Watts Family Page: Adam Kemsley (https://tinyurl.com/bdf729w7).

Marr, Aitken, Watts Family Page: John Kemsley (1) (https://tinyurl.com/ycm5amxx).

Marr, Aitken, Watts Family Page: John Kemsley (2) (https://tinyurl.com/mu4xyctt).

Marr, Aitken, Watts Family Page: Robert Kemsley (1) (https://tinyurl.com/5497h578).

Marr, Aitken, Watts Family Page: Robert Kemsley (2) (https://tinyurl.com/2tp97yaj).

Marr, Aitken, Watts Family Page: Robert Kemsley (3) (https://tinyurl.com/2s4d24yy).

Marr, Aitken, Watts Family Page: Thomas Kemsley (https://tinyurl.com/yckts6yz).

Marr, Aitken, Watts Family Page: William Gregory Kemsley (https://tinyurl.com/ydtjr3yp).

Moore Considine Family Website (https://tinyurl.com/58ntx5sc).

New South Wales Births Register: *Jane S. Clark* (1840) (No. 2306/1840, V18402306 24A).

New South Wales Births Register: *Martha Clark* (1843) (No. 2877/1843, V18432877 27A).

New South Wales Births Register: *Rebecca Clark* (1844) (No. 3299/1844, V18443299 28A).

New South Wales Births Register: *Thomas John Clark* (1839) (No. 2305/1839, V18392305 25A).

New South Wales Deaths Register: *William Clark* (1871) (No. 2828/1872).

New South Wales Marriages Register: *James Maiden and Jane Davis* (1840) (Vol. 24B, No. 519).

New South Wales Marriages Register: *John Clark and Martha Davis* (1835) (Vol. 19, No. 1392).

New South Wales Marriages Register: *William Clark and Elizabeth Harris* (1839) (Vol. 23B, No. 420).

The Farrell Family (Section 4, Version 7a, January 2022) (https://tinyurl.com/ydes6374).

Victoria Births Register: *John Robert Clark* (1849) (No. 16234/1849).

Victoria Births Register: *Margaret Clark* (1848) (No. 15739/1848).

Victoria Births Register: *Mary Elizabeth Clark* (1849) (No. 16259/1849).
Victoria Births Register: *Sarah Jane Clark* (1845) (No. 14485/1845).
Victoria Deaths Register: *Amelia Elizabeth Clark* (1851) (No. 4953/1851).
Victoria Deaths Register: *Elizabeth Clark* (1873) (No. 11366/1873).
Victoria Deaths Register: *Elizabeth Clark* (1888) (No. 16158/1888).
Victoria Deaths Register: *George Clark* (1854) (No. 3603/1854).
Victoria Deaths Register: *John Clark* (1857) (No. 2568/1857).
Victoria Deaths Register: *John Robert Clark* (1934) (No. 15699/1934).
Victoria Deaths Register: *Lily Bull* (1851) (No. 465/1868).
Victoria Deaths Register: *Mary Ann Clark* (1851) (No. 28427/1851).
Victoria Deaths Register: *Richard Clark* (1869) (No. 514/1869).
Victoria Deaths Register: *Sarah Clark* (1868) (No. 6931/1868).
Victoria Deaths Register: *Sarah Clark* (1906) (No. 11848/1906).
Victoria Deaths Register: *Sarah Farrell* (1920) (No. 11837/1920).
Victoria Deaths Register: *Thomas Clark* (1879) (No. 3289/1879).
Victoria Marriages Register: *Edward Argyle and Mary Clark* (1852) (No. 5829/1852).
Victoria Marriages Register: *John George Baker and Sarah Ann Clark* (1864) (No. 1461/1864).
Victoria Marriages Register: *John Robert Clark and Sarah Hindes* (1884) (No. 2077/1884).
Victoria Marriages Register: *Michael Farrell and Sarah Jane Clark* (1866) (No. 1157/1866).
Victoria Marriages Register: *Richard Clark and Sarah Maddock* (1854) (No. 796/1854).
Victoria Marriages Register: *William McIntosh and Martha Clark* (1858) (No. 2162/1858).
Wesleyan Methodist Church, Melbourne, Port Phillip District, New South Wales: *Marriages 1841 – 1844: Richard Clark and Mary Sparrow* (No. 31) (https://tinyurl.com/y6ufvupa).
Willett Website – Family Tree (https://tinyurl.com/366jvy6f).
WikiTree: *Elizabeth (Harris) Clark (abt. 1823-1888)* (https://tinyurl.com/32bxvz7p).
WikiTree: *John Clark (abt. 1786-1848)* (https://tinyurl.com/y4atp97g).
WikiTree: *Richard Clark (1816-1869)* (https://tinyurl.com/2ybkgmtj).
WikiTree: *Sarah (How) Clark (1758)* (https://tinyurl.com/y8we8hny).
WikiTree: *Thomas Clark (abt. 1812-1879)* (https://tinyurl.com/y59u4tov).
WikiTree: *William Clark (abt. 1758-aft.1791)* (https://tinyurl.com/ybdw4434).

Legislation

An Act for Licensing Public-Houses, and for Regulating the Retail of Fermented and Spirituous Liquors in New South Wales 1833 (NSW) (3 Wm. 4, No. 8) (https://tinyurl.com/y9awn9hb).
An Act to Restrain the Unauthorised Occupation of Crown Lands 1836 (NSW) (7 Wm. 4, No. 4) (https://tinyurl.com/2zrntu8p).
An Act for Consolidating and Amending the Laws Relating to the Licensing of Public-Houses and for

Further Regulating the Sale and Consumption of Fermented and Spirituous Liquors in New South Wales 1838 (NSW) (2 Vic., No. 18) (https://tinyurl.com/ycpcouuz).

An Act Further to Restrain the Unauthorised Occupation of Crown Lands and to Provide the Means of Defraying the Expense of a Border Police 1839 (NSW) (2 Vic., No. 27) (https://tinyurl.com/yatb9lcj).

An Act for the Establishment of Municipal Institutions In Victoria 1854 (Vic) (18 Vict., No. 15) (https://tinyurl.com/58bf6m8s).

An Act to Amend the Law Relating to Divorce and Matrimonial Causes 1861 (Vic) (25 Vict., No. 125) (https://tinyurl.com/tyy3xvp5).

An Act to Enforce and Collect Duties on the Estates of Deceased Persons 1870 (Vic) (34 Vict., No. 338) (https://tinyurl.com/2yaf42r6).

Wangaratta Church of England Land Act 1930 (Vic) (21 Geo. 5, No. 3924) (https://tinyurl.com/2raccjxj).

John Thomas Clark v Martha McIntosh and Andrew Brown (Public Records Office of Victoria ("PROV"), *VPRS* 259/P1, Unit 68, Item 759).

National Bank of Australasia v Richard Clark (PROV, *VPRS* 267/P7, Unit 38, Item 1863/1074); (PROV, *VPRS* 267/P7, Unit 66, Item 1864/2537); (PROV, *VPRS* 267/P7, Unit 90, Item 1865/3054); (PROV, *VPRS* 267/P7, Unit 176, Item 1868/1224); and (PROV, *VPRS* 267/P/7, Unit 193, Item 1869/2652).

National Bank of Australasia v William Clark (PROV, VPRS 259/P1, Unit 111, Item 1151).

Government Gazettes

New South Wales Government Gazette (No. 364), Wednesday, 11 September 1833, p. 356.

New South Wales Government Gazette (No. 242), Wednesday, 5 October 1836, p. 745.

Supplement to the New South Wales Government Gazette (No. 87), Thursday, 7 October 1847, p. 341.

Port Phillip Government Gazette (No. 49), Tuesday, 3 December 1844, p. 219.

Port Phillip Government Gazette (No. 75), Wednesday, 11 June 1845, p. 339.

Port Phillip Government Gazette (No. 9), Wednesday, 3 March 1847, p. 74.

Supplement to the Port Phillip Government Gazette (No. 20), Thursday, 2 May 1849, p. 291.

Port Phillip Government Gazette (No. 49), Wednesday, 20 November 1850, p. 984.

Victoria Government Gazette (No. 121), Friday, 10 October 1862, p. 1952.

Victoria Government Gazette (No. 64), Friday, 19 June 1863, p. 1362.

Victoria Government Gazette (No. 70), Wednesday, 5 August 1964, p. 2245.

Court Reports

William Clark v Patrick Fennell, Supreme Court of New South Wales, in *Sydney Monitor*, Wednesday, 7 June 1837, p. 2; and *The Sydney Herald*, Thursday, 8 June 1837, p. 2.

R. v Bonjon in the *Port Phillip Patriot and Melbourne Advertiser*, Monday, 20 September 1841, p. 5.

R. v Walker: [1851] NSW SupCMB 52 (https://tinyurl.com/5h3haj59).

Jemima Kett v Arthur Smith (1900) (PROV, *VPRS* 7591/P2, Unit 3).

In re McInnes, deceased [1925] VLR 496.

Penfolds Wines Pty Ltd v Elliott (1946) 74 CLR 204.

Mabo v Queensland (No. 2) (1992) 175 CLR 1.

Other Government Records

Address of Loyalty to Lieutenant Governor Hotham (PROV, *VPRS* 1095/P0, Unit 7A, Bundle 3, No. 77.

Census of 1911: Population, 1836-1911, p. 219 (https://tinyurl.com/ybhqdqtl).

Convict Records: James Maiden (https://tinyurl.com/22cj4yzs).

Inquest Deposition Files – George Clark (PROV, *VPRS* 24/P0, Unit 20).

John Clark's Will (PROV, *VPRS* 7591/P0001, Unit 000005, Item 2/151).

John Clark's Will: Probate (PROV, *VPRS* 7591/P0001, Unit 5).

Labouchere, Henry: "Australian Aborigines: Copies of Extracts of Despatches Relative to the Massacre of Various Aborigines in Australia in the Year 1838" in *Australian Aborigines: Return to an Address of the Honourable House of Commons* (https://tinyurl.com/4r4ru4du).

Letter dated 4 June 1838 from Edward Deas Thomson to William Lonsdale (PROV, *VPRS* 4/P0000, Unit 4, Folder 122).

Letters of Administration of Richard Clark's Estate (PROV, *VPRS* 28/P1, Unit 20, Item 7/639).

Martha McIntyre's Will (PROV, *VPRS* 7591/P0001, Unit 28B).

Martha McIntyre's Will James Grassie's Renunciation of Probate (PROV, *VPRS* 28/P0000, Unit 73).

Museums of History New South Wales: State Archives Collection: Convicts Index 1791-1873: James Maiden (https://tinyurl.com/z897nx3n).

New South Wales – 1828 Census: Household Returns (AONSW; Series 1273, Reels 2506-2507 and 2551-2552).

New South Wales, Australia, Assisted Immigrant Passenger Lists, 1828-1896 – Martha Davis (https://tinyurl.com/ybga5zob).

New South Wales, Australia, Registers of Convicts Applications to Marry, 1826-1851 (1840) (https://tinyurl.com/ydg5mrq2).

New South Wales: Certificates of Freedom – James Maiden (https://tinyurl.com/y79uck90).

New South Wales Geographical Names Board Extract – Clarke's Creek (https://tinyurl.com/3jt2trtu).

New South Wales Legislative Council, *Report of Inquiry into the State of the Public Lands and the Operation of the Land Laws* (1883), p. 74.

Ownership of "Duck Ponds" (PROV, *VPRS* 267/P7, Unit 66, Item 1864/2537).

Parliament of Victoria; Re-Member (Former Members): *Reginald Ivon Argyle* (https://tinyurl.com/2p88fdek).

Sixth Report of the Commissioners of National Education for the Colony of Victoria for the Year 1858 (1859) (https://tinyurl.com/m8w5n9s).

Statistical Register of the State of Victoria for the Year 1914: Part V – Population, 1836-1911, p. 29 (https://tinyurl.com/ybhqdqtl).

Richard Clark's Estate: William Clark's Administration Bond (PROV, VPRS 28/P0, Unit 84, Item 7/639).

Thomas, William: *Quarterly Report to Superintendent Latrobe; March-May 1841* (PROV, VPRS 10, Unit 6, Item 1844/1761).

UK National Archives: *Service Records for Thomas Clark – Attestation Page* (RC 3368989-6729f21-4eda-49ac-b739-3b95b1c69435/WO 69_8_001.jpg).

UK National Archives: *Service Records for Thomas Clark – Description Page* (RC 3368989-6729f21-4eda-49ac-b739-3b95b1c69435/WO 69_8_002.jpg).

Victorian Legislative Council: *Occupants of Crown Lands, Victoria, 5th August 1852*.

Victorian Legislative Council: *Occupants of Crown Lands, Victoria, 13 September 1853*.

William Clark's Will (PROV, VPRS 28/P0, Unit 103).

William Clark's Will: First and Second Codicils (PROV, VPRS 28/P0, Unit 103).

William Clark's Will: Probate (PROV, VPRS 28/P2, Unit 2).

Newspapers and Journals

Australasian Chronicle (Sydney, New South Wales).

Albury Banner and Wodonga Express (Albury, New South Wales).

Bell's Life in Sydney and Sporting Review (Sydney, New South Wales).

Benalla Ensign and Farmer's and Squatter's Journal (Benalla, Victoria).

Benalla Standard (Benalla, Victoria).

Bendigo Advertiser (Bendigo, Victoria).

Brighton Gazette (Brighton, United Kingdom).

British Medical Journal (London, United Kingdom).

Catholic Press (Sydney, New South Wales).

Illustrated Australian News for Home Readers (Melbourne, Victoria).

Geelong Advertiser (Geelong, Victoria).

Kilmore Advertiser (Kilmore, Victoria).

Kilmore Free Press (Kilmore, Victoria).

Maitland Mercury and Hunter River General Advertiser (Maitland, New South Wales).

Melbourne Courier (Melbourne, Victoria).

Melbourne Daily News (Melbourne, Victoria).

Melbourne Weekly Courier (Melbourne, Victoria).

Moreton Bay Courier (Brisbane, Queensland).

North Eastern Despatch (Wangaratta, Victoria).

North Eastern Ensign (Benalla, Victoria).
Ovens and Murray Advertiser (Beechworth, Victoria).
Pastoral Times (South Deniliquin, New South Wales).
Port Phillip Courier (Melbourne, Victoria).
Port Phillip Gazette (Melbourne, Victoria).
Port Phillip Gazette and Settler's Journal (Melbourne, Victoria).
Port Phillip Herald (Melbourne, Victoria).
Port Phillip Patriot and Melbourne Advertiser (Melbourne, Victoria).
Port Phillip Patriot and Morning Advertiser (Melbourne, Victoria).
South Australian Register (Adelaide, South Australia).
Sussex Advertiser (Lewes, United Kingdom).
Sydney Gazette and New South Wales Advertiser (Sydney, New South Wales).
Sydney Herald (Sydney, New South Wales).
Sydney Monitor (Sydney, New South Wales).
Sydney Morning Herald (Sydney, New South Wales).
Tasmanian Colonist (Hobart, Tasmania).
The Advocate (Melbourne, Victoria).
The Age (Melbourne, Victoria).
The Argus (Melbourne, Victoria).
The Australasian (Melbourne, Victoria).
The Australian (Sydney, New South Wales).
The Chronicle (Wangaratta, Victoria).
Wangaratta Chronicle (Wangaratta, Victoria).
Wangaratta Despatch (Wangaratta, Victoria).
Yackandandah Times (Yackandandah, Victoria).

Miscellaneous Unpublished Documents

Baker, David: *One Hundred and Twenty-Four Years of P.M.G. Service at Benalla* (Copy manuscript held in the National Trust of Australia (Victoria) Files).

Bourke, John Conway: *Autobiographical Notes for Mr Wilson* (Royal Historical Society of Victoria, Box 38-f, MS 4117).

Bourke, John Conway: *John Conway Bourke's Diary* (Royal Historical Society of Victoria, Box 38-l, MS 4652).

Brooke, John: *Letters [Manuscript]* (https://tinyurl.com/2p93xyun).

Cole, Robert: *Index of Victorian Hotels – Country, A to Car.* (State Library of Victoria, manuscript, MS 7592).

Diaries and Letters of Lady Jane Franklin (Diary from 3 April to 20 April 1839) (National Library of Australia, MS 114 and Series A, File 2, Book 1).

Correspondence and Notes – see Robertson, Edward: *Correspondence and Notes compiled by Edward Robertson concerning the history of the Benalla district.*

Discovery and Settlement – see Robertson, Edward: *Discovery and Settlement of the Murray District of Port Phillip* (Part 2).

Dredge, James: *Brief notes of the aborigines of New South Wales* (Printed in 1845 by James Harrison in Geelong and included in a microfiche with *The Aborigines of Australia* by Joseph Orton: State Library of Victoria, LTMF 161).

Dredge, James: *Diaries, Notebook and Letterbook?, 1817-1845* (State Library of Victoria, MS 11625).

Dredge's Diaries – See Dredge, James: *Diaries, Notebook and Letterbook?, 1817-1845.*

Faithfull, John and Lewis, Jim: *From 16,000 to 5* (2003).

Family Transcript (Copy with the author).

Huddle, Lorraine: *Mitchell Shire Stage Two Heritage Study* (2006), Vol. 5.

Lorraine Key's manuscript (Copy with Lorraine Key).

"Max": *The Perils of a Pioneer: The Biography of John Bourke* (1902), Vol. 3 (Royal Historical Society of Victoria, Box 38-l, MS 000106).

McNeill, Ian: *In Search of our Colonial Heritage: A Story of John Jenkins and His Family* (An undated manuscript is in the possession of the Berrima and District Historical and Family History Society).

Robertson, Edward: *Correspondence and Notes compiled by Edward Robertson concerning the history of the Benalla district* (State Library of Victoria, manuscript, MSB 277-280A).

Robertson, Edward: *Discovery and Settlement of the Murray District of Port Phillip* (Part 2) (University of Melbourne Archives, manuscript, 1985.0068, Robertson, E 1855-1953).

Robertson, Edward: *Lease of the Black Swan Inn, 10 November 1853* (University of Melbourne Archives, manuscript, 1985.0068, Robertson, E 1855-1953, Box 2).

The Sydney Hotel – see Wangaratta Historical Society Files – Hotels: *The Sydney Hotel.*

Wangaratta Historical Society Files – Hotels: *The Sydney Hotel.*

Wesleyan Methodist Missionary Society, Australasia 1812-1889: *Letter from James Drudge to Jabez Bunting dated Saturday, 20 April 1839* (National Library of Australia, Box2, AJCP M125).

www.ingramcontent.com/pod-product-compliance
Lightning Source LLC
Chambersburg PA
CBHW061535010526
44107CB00066B/2877